Basic Fluid Mechanics and Hydraulic Machines

Basic Fluid Mechanics and Hydraulic Machines

Zoeb Husain
Principal
Hi-Point College of Engineering and Technology
Hyderabad.

Mohd. Zulkifly Abdullah
Associate Professor,
School of Mechanical Engineering
Deputy Dean, Academic
and Student Affairs
University Sains, Malaysia.

Zainal Alimuddin
Associate Professor,
School of Mechanical Engineering
University Sains, Malaysia

BSP BS Publications
4-4-309, Giriraj Lane, Sultan Bazar,
Hyderabad - 500 095 - A.P.
Phone : 040 - 23445688

Published by :

BS Publications

4-4-309, Giriraj Lane, Sultan Bazar,
Hyderabad - 500 095 - A.P.
Phone : 040 - 23445677, 23445688
e-mail : contactus@bspublications.net
www.bspublications.net

Printed at

Adithya Art Printers
Hyderabad.

Price : Rs.200.00

ISBN : 978-81-7800-147-0

Dedicated to

My wife Chand Sultana and sons Khursheed, Azhar, and Feroz Husain.
I can't forget my grand children Heena, Nida, Sara, Sofia, Sajjad.

-Zoeb Husain

Preface

In the planning of this textbook we have studied the syllabi of many Universities, including University Sains, Malaysia (USM), Penang. Basic Fluid Mechanics and Hydraulic Machines covers only essential topics, and is written in a simple easy-to-understand language by the engineering faculty. It will be helpful to the students of mechanical, electronics and electrical engineering degree courses. For the ease of references the book is divided into nine chapters – dimensional analysis, fluid flow, thermal and hydropower stations, fluid machinery, Pelton turbine, Francis and Kaplan turbines, turbo pumps, and positive displacement pumps. Both underground and surface hydropower plants are dealt with by giving examples of Tumut 1 and 2 power stations in Australia and JOR power station in Cameron Highlands, in Malaysia as regards their construction and working. The examples have been worked out based on specifications of power stations so as to make the subject real and interesting. The specific speeds have been calculated based on the parameters obtained from the turbine specifications and by checking the turbines selected.

Our years of experience in teaching this subject and technical visits made to hydropower stations and thermal power stations will surely benefit the students.

We have found the fluid mechanics in all multi-diciplinary manifestation to be the most stimulating of engineering areas. We hope that this text will communicate to the students our experience and inspire enthusiasm among the students of engineering disciplines.

Once again the authors would like to thank all the colleagues in India and overseas who have contributed to this book and for their support and comments. The authors are grateful to the staff of M/S BS Publications, K.S. Raju, Naresh, Sunil Dutt and Sandhya for their active support and co-operation in compiling the book.

-Authors

Acknowledgement

I am deeply indebted to Dr. Mohd. Vizarath Rasool Khan, chief promotor and founder of Shadan group of educational institutions for his motivation and encouragement for writing the book. I worked with him as Principal and Director of Hi-point College of Engineering and Technology and also as Professor of Mechanical Engineering in Shadan College of Engineering and Technology. Dr. Vizarath Rasool Khan is hard working, visionary, who is the son in law of late Mohd. Abdul Qayyum Khan, the founder of J.N. Polytechnic, from whom I commenced my teaching career.

I am also thankful Dr. Mohd. Zulkifly Abdullah and Dr. Zanial Alimuddin, Associate Professors, School of Mechanical Engineering, University Sains, Malaysia for their co-operation and co-authorship of this book.

-Zoeb Husain

Contents

CHAPTER - 3

Thermal and Hydropower Stations

CHAPTER - 4

Fluid Machinery

CHAPTER - 5

Pelton Turbine

CHAPTER - 6

Francis Turbine

CHAPTER - 7

Propeller and Kaplan Turbines

CHAPTER - 8

Turbo Pumps

Symbols

Symbol	Notation	Unit
a	Acceleration, area	m/s^2
A	Area	m^2
b	Width, breadth	m
B	Width, breadth	m
C	Veolocity of sound	m/s
C_v	Coefficient of velocity	–
C_α	Coefficient of discharge	–
d	Diameter	m
D	Diameter, depth	m
E	Euler's energy transfer	J/kg, m
E	Euler's head	m
F	Force	N
g	Gravitional acceleration	m/s^2
h	Head loss	m
l	Length	m
m	Mass, area ratio	kg, –
N	Rotational speed	rev/min
P	Pressure	Pa
P	Power	kW
Pa	Pascal	N/m^2
Q	Volume flow rate	m^3/s

Symbol	Notation	Unit
r	Radius	m
R	Radius	m
T	Temperature, Torque	Kelvin, N-m
u	Velocity, peripherical velocity of blade	m/s
v	Volume	m^3/s
V	Velocity	m/s
V_f	Velocity of flow	m/s
V_r	Relative velocity	m/s
V_X	Velocity component in the X-direction	m/s
V_Y	Velocity component in the Y-direction	m/s
V_W	Velocity of whirl	m/s
ω	Angular velocity	r/s
ρ	Density	Kg/m^3
γ	Specific weight	N/m^3
S	Specific gravity	–
μ	Dynamic viscocity	$N\text{-sec}/m^2$
ν	Kinamatic viscosity	m^2/sec
K	Ratio of two specific heat	–

CHAPTER - 1

Dimensions and Systems of Units

Wind Turbine.

1.1 Introduction

Fluid mechanics is concerned with the behaviour of liquids and gases at rest and in motion. The proper understanding of mechanics of fluids is important in many branches of engineering: in biomechanics the flow of blood is of interest; ocean currents require a knowledge of fluid mechanics; chemical processing of plants require a thorough knowledge of fluid mechanics; aeronautical engineers require knowledge of flow of air over the aircraft to reduce drag and increase lift; mechanical engineers require knowledge of fluid properties to design pumps, water turbines, gas turbines and rockets; civil engineers require fluid mechanics to study river currents and erosion; and environmentalists require knowledge of fluid properties for solving pollution problems of air and water to control flood, irrigation channels, etc.

There are specialised books on fluid mechanics for each of these areas and therefore this book will present only general properties of fluid flow.

1.2 Dimensions and Units

Before we study fluid mechanics let us discuss the dimensions and units that will be used in this book. There are four fundamental dimensions: length, mass, time and temperature. The dimensions of all other quantities can be expressed in terms of fundamental dimensions. For example, Force can be expressed in terms of fundamental dimensions of mass, length and time. Using Newton's second law, force can be expressed as

$$F = ma \qquad .....(1.1)$$

Written dimensionally

$$[F] = [m]\,[a] = \frac{M\,L}{T^2}, \qquad .....(1.2)$$

where M, L, and T are dimensions of mass, length and time respectively. There are various systems of measurement but we shall use the international system which is referred to as SI (System International) which is preferred and is used internationally except USA. Table 1.1 gives fundamental units and Table 1.2 derived units.

Table 1.1 Fundamental units.

Quantity	Dimensions	SI units
Length	L	Meter m
Mass	M	Kilogram Kg
Time	T	Seconds s
Temperature	T	Kelvin K

Table 1.2 Derived units.

Quantity	Dimensions	SI units
Area	L^2	m^2
Volume	L^3	m^3
Velocity	L/T	m/s
Density	M/L^3	Kg/m^3
Pressure	M/LT^2	N/m^2 (Pascal)
Work	ML^2/T^2	N.m
Power	ML^2/T^3	J/s (Watt)
Viscosity	M/LT	$N.s/m^2$
Flow rate	L^3/T	m^3/s

To relate weight to mass, we use

$$W = mg, \quad \text{.....(1.3)}$$

where 'g' is the local gravity. The standard value taken for 'g' is 9.80 m/s^2. In SI units weight is expressed in Newton's and never in kilograms.

1.3 Non-Dimensional Quantity

A non-dimensional quantity has no unit but only a number. The common dimensionless parameters in fluid mechanics and hydraulic machines are identified as follows.

Euler's number, $E_u = \dfrac{\Delta p}{\rho v^2}$

Reynold's number, $R_e = \dfrac{\rho l v}{\mu}$ .....(1.4)

Fronde number, $F_r = \dfrac{v}{\sqrt{l g}}$

Mach number, $M = \dfrac{v}{c}$

Weber number, $W_e = \dfrac{\rho l v^2}{\sigma}$

Strouhal number, $S_t = \dfrac{l \omega}{v}$

The physical significance of each parameter can be determined by observing that each dimensionless number can be written as the ratio of two forces. The forces can be expressed as

$$F_p = \text{pressure force} = \Delta p\, A \sim \Delta p\, l^2$$

$$F_l = \text{inertial force} = m\, v\, \frac{d\, v}{d\, s} \sim \rho\, l^3\, v\, \frac{v}{l} = \rho\, l^2\, v^2$$

$$F_\mu = \text{Viscous force} = \tau A = \mu . \frac{du}{dy}\, A \sim \mu\, \frac{v}{l}\, l^2 = \mu\, v\, l$$

$$F_g = \text{Gravity force} = mg \sim \rho l^3 g \qquad .....(1.5)$$

$$F_B = \text{Compressibility force} = BA \sim \rho\, \frac{d\, p}{d\, \rho}\, l^2 = \rho\, c^2\, l^2$$

$$F_\sigma = \text{Surface tension force} = \sigma\, l$$

$$F_\omega = \text{Centrifugal force} = m\, r\, \omega^2 \sim \rho\, l^3\, l\, \omega^2 = \rho\, l^4\, \omega^2$$

Thus we write

$$E_u = \frac{\text{Pressure force}}{\text{inertial force}} = \frac{\Delta p\, l^2}{\rho\, l^2\, v^2} = \frac{\Delta p}{\rho\, v^2}$$

$$R_e = \frac{\text{Inertial force}}{\text{Viscous force}} = \frac{\rho\, l^2\, v^2}{\mu\, l\, v} = \frac{\rho\, l\, v}{\mu}$$

$$F_r = \frac{\text{Interial force}}{\text{Gravity force}} = \frac{\rho\, l^2\, v^2}{\rho\, l^3\, g} = \frac{v^2}{g\, l} = \frac{v}{\sqrt{l\, g}}$$

$$M = \frac{\text{Inertial force}}{\text{Compressibility force}} = \frac{\rho\, l^2\, v^2}{\rho\, l^2\, c^2} = \frac{v^2}{c^2} = \frac{v}{c}$$

$$W_e = \frac{\text{Intertial force}}{\text{Surface tension force}} = \frac{\rho\, l^2 v^2}{\sigma\, l} = \frac{\delta\, l\, v^2}{\sigma}$$

$$S_t = \frac{\text{Centrifugal force}}{\text{Inertial force}} = \frac{\rho\, l^4\, \omega^2}{\rho\, l^2\, v^2} = \frac{l^2\, \omega^2}{v^2} = \frac{l\, \omega}{v} \qquad .....(1.6)$$

These dimensionless numbers will be helpful for particular flows of interest. For example, if viscous forces are important as in pipe flow, Reynold's number is a significant dimensionless parameter. Euler's number will be useful in flow of fluid in pumps where the pressure drop is significant. Mach number where compressibility is important in flows over aerofoils in aircraft. The dimensionless parameters are also useful in design of prototypes from the models and can save a lot of money and effort. For example, a model can be prepared in a laboratory and tested, and predictions can be made of the prototype for large machines with the help of suitable dimensionless parameters. This is usually done in making models of large hydraulic machines used in power stations or in construction of big dams by making suitable models in the laboratory.

1.4 Pressure Scales

In fluid mechanics the pressure results from a normal compressive force acting on an area. The pressure p is defined as force per unit area. In SI units the unit of measurement of pressure is Newtons per square meter (N/m^2) or Pascal (Pa). Since Pascal is small unit, the pressure is usually referred to in kilo Pascal (kPa) or even in Mega Pascal (M Pa). The standard atmospheric pressure at sea level is 101.3 kPa. The gauge pressure is the pressure recorded by the gauge or manometer. In engineering calculations absolute pressure is used and the conversion from gauge pressure to absolute pressure is carried out using the following equation.

Absolute pressure = gauge pressure + atmospheric pressure

$$P_a = P_g + P_{atm}$$

Zero gauge pressure is atmospheric pressure. Also, zero absolute pressure in ideal vacuum. Fig. 1.1 gives relation between gauge and absolute pressures.

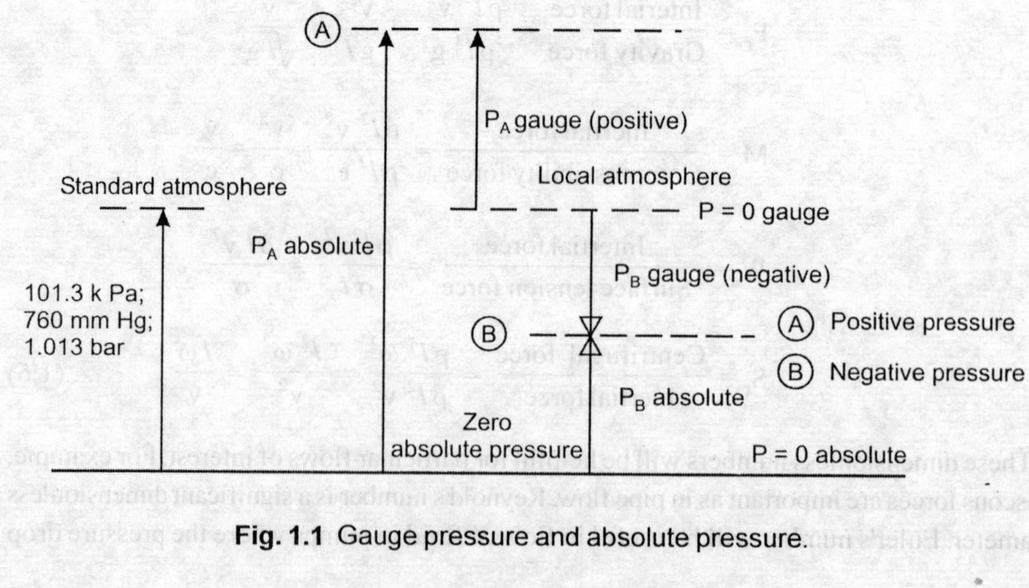

Fig. 1.1 Gauge pressure and absolute pressure.

The gauge pressure is negative whenever the absolute pressure is less than atmospheric pressure; it may be called vacuum. For negative pressures

$$P_{absolute} = P_{atm} - P_{gauge} \qquad .....(1.7)$$

1.5 Fluid Properties

The definition of a liquid is "A state of matter in which the molecules are relatively free to change their positions with respect to each other but restricted by cohesive forces, so as to maintain a relative fixed volume". A liquid occupies the shape of the vessel. In this section several of the more common fluid properties are presented.

1.5.1 Density and Specific Weight

Fluid density is defined as mass per unit volume. A fluid property directly related to density is specific weight or weight per unit volume.

$$\text{Density } \rho = \frac{\text{mass}}{\text{volume}}$$

$$\rho = \frac{m}{V} \qquad .....(1.8)$$

$$\text{Specific weight } \gamma = \frac{\text{weight}}{\text{volume}} = \frac{mg}{V}$$

thus

$$\gamma = \frac{mg}{V} = \frac{\rho V g}{V}$$

$$\gamma = \rho g \qquad ..... (1.9)$$

The specific gravity S is often used to determine the density of the liquid. It is defined as the ratio of the density of the liquid to that of water.

$$S = \frac{\text{density of liquid}}{\text{density of water}} = \frac{\rho}{\rho_{water}} \qquad .....(1.10)$$

The specific gravity of liquid is measured by hydrometer

Table 1.3 gives density, specific weight and specific gravity of water at standard conditions.

Table 1.3

	Density ρ Kg/m^3	Specific weight γ N/m^3	Specific gravity S
Water	1000	9800	1

1.5.2 Viscosity

Shear stresses are developed when the fluid is in motion; if the particles of the fluid move relative to each other, so that they have different velocities, causing the original shape of the fluid to become distorted. A fluid at rest has no shearing forces. Usually we are concerned with the flow past a solid boundary. The fluid in contact with the boundary sticks to it, and therefore will have the same velocity as the boundary. Considering successive layers parallel to the boundary as shown in Fig. 1.2, the velocity of the fluid varies from layer to layer in y-direction.

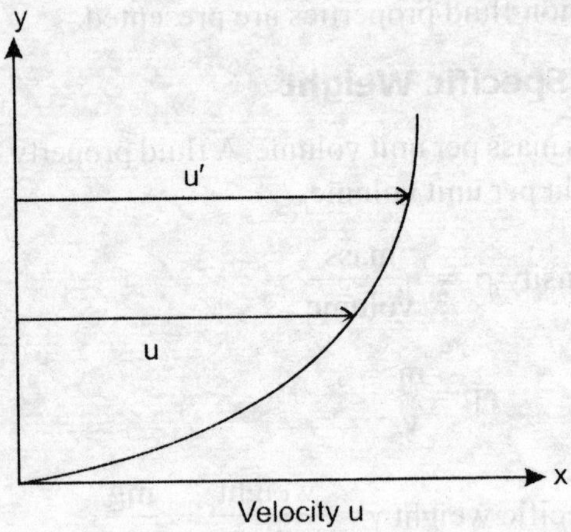

Fig. 1.2 Velocity profile.

For such a flow the shear stress τ in given by

$$\tau = \mu \left(\frac{du}{dy} \right) \qquad .....(1.11)$$

where τ is shear stress and u is the velocity in the X direction. The quantity du/dy is called velocity gradient and μ is called dynamic viscosity. The units of τ are N/m^2 or Pa and of μ are $N.s/m^2$. The kinematic viscosity ν is defined as ratio of dynamic viscosity to density

$$\nu = \frac{\mu}{\rho} \qquad .....(1.12)$$

The unit of ν is (m^2 s^{-1})

Viscosity is an extremely important fluid property in the study of fluid flows. A thick liquid like honey which has high viscosity will take long time to flow than water. Thus it controls the amount of fluid that can be transported in a pipe line during a specific period of time. It accounts for pressure and energy losses in pipes.

If the shear stress is directly proportional to velocity gradient as it was assumed in eq. (1.11), the fluid is said to be Newtonian. Common fluids such as water, air and oil are Newtonian. The other fluids which do not obey Newtonian law of viscosity are called Non-newtonian fluids. Milk, plastic, paints are non-Newtonian.

1.6 Surface Tension

Surface tension is a force which manifests itself only in liquids at an interface, usually a liquid-gas interface.

Surface tension has units of force per unit length, is N/m. The force due to surface tension is the surface tension multiplied by the length or the circumference in case of a bubble or droplet of water. A surface tension effect can be illustrated by analysing a free-body diagram of half a droplet as shown in Fig. 1.3.

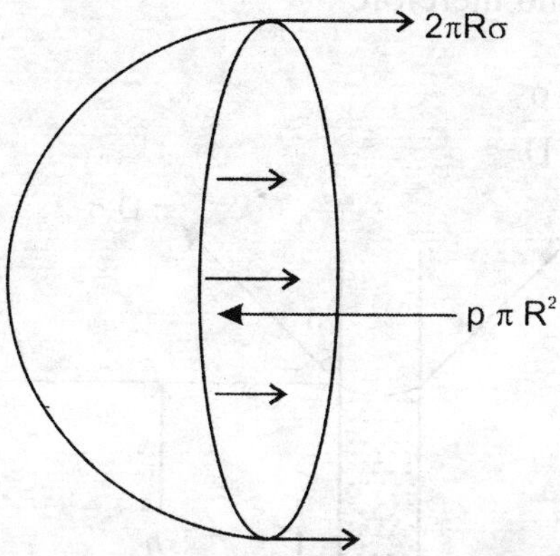

Fig. 1.3 Internal force in a droplet.

The pressure force exerted in the droplet is given by

$$F = p\,\pi\,R^2$$

The force due to surface tension is surface tension multiplied by the circumference and is

$$F = 2\pi\,R\,\sigma$$

The pressure force and tension force must balance each other

$$p\,\pi\,r^2 = 2\pi\,R\,\sigma$$

$$p = \frac{2\,\sigma}{R} \qquad .....(1.12)$$

1.7 Capillary Action

Fig. 1.4 shows the rise of liquid in a clean glass capillary tube due to surface tension. The liquid makes a contact angle β with the glass tube. For water and most of liquids this angle is zero whereas for mercury it is more than 90°. Such liquids have a capillary drop instead of rise. If h is capillary rise, D is the diameter of the tube, ρ the density of liquid and σ the surface tension then the capillary rise h can be determined from equating the vertical component of surface tension force and the weight of liquid column. Thus we have

$$\sigma \pi D \cos \beta = \gamma \frac{\pi}{4} D^2 h$$

$$h = \frac{4 \sigma \cos \beta}{\gamma D} \quad .....(1.13)$$

For water β = 0; cos β = 1 and therefore

$$h = \frac{4 \sigma}{\gamma D} \quad .....(1.14)$$

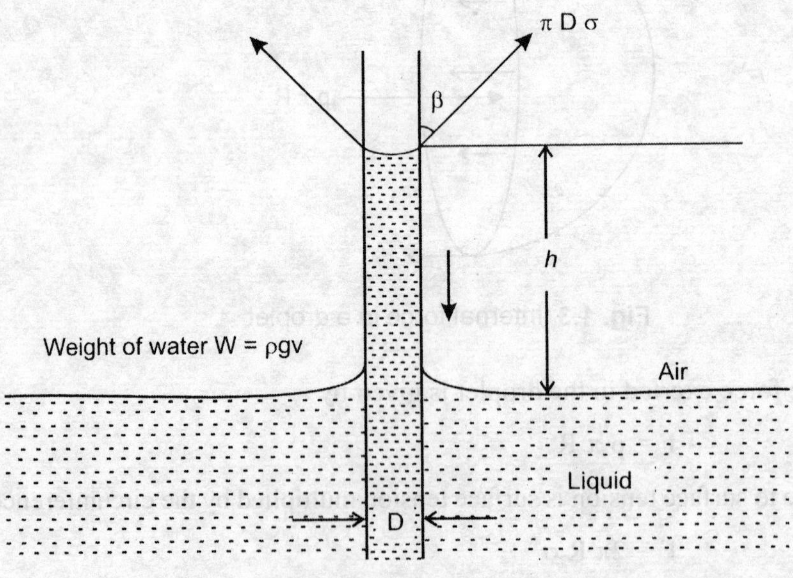

Fig. 1.4 Rise in capillary tube.

1.8 Compressibility and Mach Number

We discussed earlier deformation of fluids that results from shear stresses. Now we discuss deformation of fluids from pressure changes. As fluids are air or water, compress pressure increases resulting in increase in density. The coefficient of compressibility is defined as change in pressure (Δp) to relative change in density while the temperature remains constant.

$$\text{Coefficient of compressibility} = \frac{\Delta p}{\frac{\Delta \delta}{\rho}} = \rho \frac{\delta p}{\delta \rho}$$

To cause a 1% change in density for water a pressure of 21 M Pa is required. This is a very large pressure to cause such a small change in density and therefore water is considered incompressible whereas for gases density change is appreciable for change in pressure. The air is considered incompressible if the density variation is small, say, under 3%.

From knowledge of physics, the speed of sound (C) is related to changes in pressure and density of the fluid medium through the equation

$$C = \sqrt{\frac{dp}{d\rho}}$$

For gases undergoing an isentropic process

$$C = \sqrt{K\frac{P}{\rho}} \qquad \text{.....(1.15)}$$

and making use of ideal gas, and using characteristic equation it follows.

$$\frac{p}{\rho} = RT$$

and substituting this value in eq. 1.15, we get

$$C = \sqrt{KRT} \qquad \text{.....(1.16)}$$

The speed of sound is proportional to square root of the absolute local temperature.

For example, for air at 15 °C are T = 288 k, with K = 1.4 and R = 287 J/Kg, k and substituting these values in eq. 1.16.

$$C = \sqrt{1.4 \times 287 \times 288} = 340 \text{ m/s}$$

The ratio of velocity of the fluid to local velocity of sound is given by Mach number and is represented by M

$$M = \frac{V}{C} \qquad \text{.....(1.17)}$$

Based on this definition, compressible flow may be classified as subsonic M < 1, supersonic M > 1, transonic M = 1, and hypersonic M > 5. Air can be considered incompressible if M < 0.3 or air velocity around 100 m/s.

Solved Examples

E.1.1 A pressure gauge attached to a rigid tank measures a vacuum of 40 kPa inside the tank, which is situated at a site in Hinardi in the Himalyan range where the elevation is 6000 m. Determine the absolute pressure in the tank.

Solution

The vacuum is negative pressure i.e., – 40 kPa. From Table A.3 at an altitude of 6000 m: pressure is 47.2 kPa

$$P_a = P_{atom} - P_g = 47.2 - 40 = 7.2 \text{ kPa}$$

Note : Vacuum is always negative pressure.

E.1.2 A 2 mm diameter clean glass tube is inserted in water at 20 °C. Determine the height that the water will rise to capillary action in the tube. The constant angle for water can be taken as zero.

Solution

A free-body diagram of water is shown in Fig. 1.5. It shows that the upward surface tension force is equal and opposite to the weight of water.

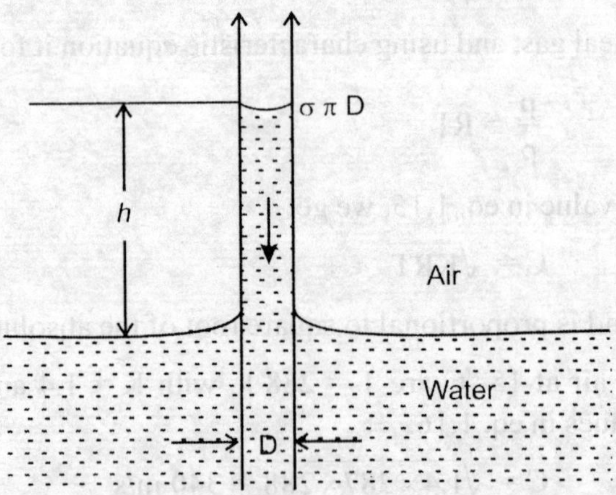

Fig. 1.5 Free body diagram of water.

$$\text{Weight of the water} = W = mg = \rho\ v.g = \rho g v = \gamma \frac{\pi}{4} D^2\ h$$

Surface tension force F = σ × length

Surface tension length = σπ D

From Table A.1

$$\sigma = 0.073 \text{ N/m}$$

Equating surface tension force to weight of water

$$\sigma \pi D = \gamma \frac{\pi}{4} D^2 h$$

$$h = \frac{4\sigma}{\gamma D} = \frac{4 \times 0.073}{9800 \times 2 \times 10^{-3}} = 14.89 \text{ mm}$$

E.1.3 An aircraft flies at a speed of 800 km/hr at an altitude of 10,000 m above sealevel. Determine Mach number assuming value of K = 1.4

Solution

From Table A.3

at $z = 10{,}000$ m, T = 223.3 k

The velocity of sound can be calculated by

$$C = \sqrt{KRT} = \sqrt{1.4 \times 287 \times 223} = 299.3 \text{ m/s}$$

Speed of aircraft $V = \dfrac{800 \times 1000}{3600} = 222.2$ m/s

$$M = \frac{V}{C} = \frac{222.3}{299.3} = 0.742$$

The aircraft is flying at subsonic speed whereas for M > 1 it will be flying at supersonic speed.

E.1.4 A Newtonian fluid having a viscosity of 0.38 N.s/m^2 and specific gravity of 0.91 flows through a 25 mm diameter pipe with a velocity of 1.6 m/s. Determine the value of Reynold's number in SI Units.

Solution

The fluid density is calculated from specific gravity

$$\rho = S \times \text{density of water} = 0.91 \times 1000 = 910 \text{ Kg/m}^3.$$

Reynold's number $Re = \dfrac{\rho D V}{\mu}$

Substituting proper values

$$Re = \frac{910 \times 25 \times 10^{-3} \times 2.6}{0.38}$$

$$Re = 155.6$$

If we use any other system of units the value of Re will not change.

E.1.5 A compressed air tank has a volume of 0.85 m^3. When the tank is filled with a gauge pressure of 3 bar, determine density of air and weight of air in the tank. Assume temperature of air 15 °C.

Solution

Absolute pressure in the tank in kPa

$$= 3 \times 101.3 + 101.3 = 403.9 \text{ kPa}$$

The density can be determined from the equation

$$\rho = \frac{p}{RT} = \frac{403.9 \times 10^3}{287 \times 288} = 4.88 \text{ Kg/m}^3$$

Weight of air $W = mg = \rho v g = \rho \times 0.85 \times 9.8$

$$= 4.88 \times 0.85 \times 9.8 = 40.7 \text{ Kg}$$

E. 1.6 Air is introduced through a nozzle into a tank of water to form a stream of bubbles. If the bubbles are intended to have a diameter of 2 mm, calculate by how much the pressure of air at the nozzle must exceed that of surrounding water. Assume $\sigma = 72.7 \times 10^{-3}$ N/m

Solution

Excess pressure $p = \dfrac{2\sigma}{R}$

where $R = 1 \times 10^{-3}$ m, $\sigma = 72.7 \times 10^{-3}$ N/m

Excess pressure $p = \dfrac{2 \times 72.7 \times 10^{-3}}{1 \times 10^{-3}}$

$$p = 145.4 \text{ N/m}^2$$

Again if R is very small, the value of ρ becomes very large. For small bubbles in the liquid, if this pressure is greater than pressure of vapour, the bubbles will collapse. In many engineering problems the magnitude of surface tension is small compared with other gravitational and viscous forces acting on the fluid and therefore it can be safely neglected.

E.1.7 Water is moving through a pipe. The velocity profile at some section is shown and is given mathematically as

$$V = \frac{\beta}{4\mu}\left(\frac{D^2}{4} - r^2\right)$$

where β = constant

r = radial distance from the centre line

V = velocity at any position r

What is the shear stress at the wall of the pipe from the water

What is the shear stress at position $r = D/4$

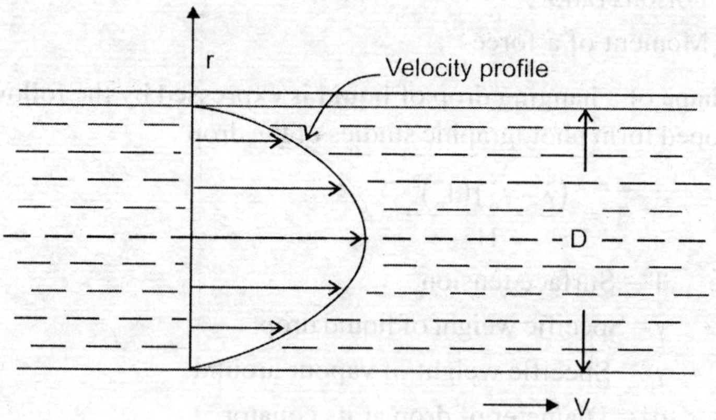

Fig. 1.6 Velocity profile.

Solution

Given $$V = \frac{\beta}{4\mu}\left(\frac{D^2}{4} - r^2\right)$$

Shear stress $$\tau = \mu\left(\frac{\delta V}{\delta r}\right)_{r=D/2} = \mu.\frac{\beta}{4.\mu}(-2r)$$

(a) $\therefore$ for $r = D/2$; $$\tau = -\frac{\beta D}{4}$$

(b) Also at position $r = D/4$; $$\tau = \frac{\beta}{4}\left(-2\frac{D}{4}\right)$$

$$\tau = \frac{-\beta D}{8}$$

Problems

P.1.1 What is the dimensional representation of

(a) Power

(b) Specific weight

(c) Energy

(d) Poisons ratio

(e) Moment of a force

P1.2 The shape of a hanging drop of liquid is expressed by the following formulation developed form photographic studies of the drop

$$T = \frac{(\gamma - \gamma_o)(d_e)^2}{H}$$

where T = Surface tension

γ = Specific weight of liquid drop

γ_o = Specific weight of vapour around

d_e = Diameter of drop at its equator

H = A function determined by experiment

For dimensionally homogeneous equation determine dimension of H.

P.1.3 Two parallel, wide, clean, glass plates separated at a distance d of 1 mm are placed in water. How far over the water rise due to capillary action away from the ends of the plates?

P.1.4 Calculate the density and specfic weight of water if 1 kg occupies 100 cm^3.

P.1.5 The velocity distribution in a 1.0 -cm diameters pipe is given by

$$\mu(r) = 16\left(1 - \frac{r^2}{r_0^2}\right) \text{ m/s},$$

where r_o is the pipe radius. Calculate the shearing stress at the centre line, at r = 0.25 cm, and at the wall if water at 20 °C is flowing.

P.1.6 A small 2-mm diameter bubble is formed by a stream at 20 °C water. Estimate the pressure inside the bubble.

P.1.7 Mercury makes an angle of contact of 130° when in contact with glass tube. What distance mercury depresres in a vertical, 2 mm glass tube σ = 0.5 N/m?

P.1.8 Calculate the speed of sound at 20 °C. (a) hydrogen (b) superheated steam (c) nitrogen.

Table A.1 Properties of Water.

Temperature t °C	Density ρ (Kg/m^3)	Viscosity μ ($N.S/m^2$)	Kinematic viscosity γ m^2/s	Surface tension σ N/m
0	999.9	1.792×10^{-3}	$1.79\,1 \times 10^{-6}$	0.076
10	999.7	1.308×10^{-3}	1.308×10^{-6}	0.074
20	999.2	1.005×10^{-3}	1.007×10^{-6}	0.073
30	996.7	0.801×10^{-3}	0.004×10^{-6}	0.071
40	992.2	0.656×10^{-3}	0.661×10^{-6}	0.070
50	998.1	0.549×10^{-3}	0.556×10^{-6}	0.068
60	983.2	0.469×10^{-3}	0.477×10^{-6}	0.066
70	977.8	0.406×10^{-3}	0.415×10^{-6}	0.065
80	971.8	0.357×10^{-3}	0.367×10^{-6}	0.063
90	965.3	0.317×10^{-3}	0.328×10^{-6}	0.061
100	958.4	0.284×10^{-3}	0.296×10^{-6}	0.059

Table A.2 Properties of air at atmospheric pressure.

Temperature t °C	Density ρ (Kg/m^3)	Viscosity μ (N.S/m^2)	Kinematic viscosity γ m^2/s	Velocity of sound C (m/s)
0	1.292	1.72×10^{-3}	1.33×10^{-6}	331
10	1.247	1.76×10^{-3}	1.42×10^{-6}	337
20	1.204	1.81×10^{-3}	1.51×10^{-6}	343
30	1.164	1.86×10^{-3}	1.60×10^{-6}	349
40	1.127	1.91×10^{-3}	1.69×10^{-6}	355
50	1.092	1.95×10^{-3}	1.79×10^{-6}	360
60	1.060	2.00×10^{-3}	1.89×10^{-6}	366
70	1.030	2.05×10^{-3}	1.99×10^{-6}	371
80	1.000	2.09×10^{-3}	2.09×10^{-6}	377
90	0.973	2.13×10^{-3}	2.19×10^{-6}	382
100	0.946	2.17×10^{-3}	2.30×10^{-6}	387

Table A.3 Properties of the standard atmosphere.

Altitude z (m)	Temperature t (K)	Pressure p (k Pa)	Density ρ (kg/m^3)
0	288.2	101.3	1.225
500	284.9	95.43	1.167
1 K	281.7	89.85	1.112
2 K	275.2	79.48	1.007
4 K	262.2	61.64	0.819
6 K	249.2	47.2	0.660
8 K	236.2	35.65	0.525
10 K	223.3	26.49	0.413
20 K	216.7	5.52	0.088
30 K	226.5	1.196	0.018
40 K	250.4	0.287	0.004

Note : K =1000 meters

Table A.4 Properties of common liquids at atmospheric pressure – approximately at 15-20 °C.

Liquid	Specific weight γ (N/m^3)	Density ρ (Kg/m^3)	Surface tension σ (N/m)
Alcohol-ethyl	7.44	789	0.022
Benzene	8.82	902	0.029
Gasoline	6.66	680	–
Glycerine	12346	1258	0.063
Kerosene	7933	809	0.025
SAE 10 oil	9016	917	0.036
SAE 30 oil	9016	917	0.035
Turpentine	8529	871	0.026
Water	9790	998	0.073

CHAPTER - 2

Fluid Flow

A large commercial air-cushion vehicle (ACV) built in 1969 by vosper thornycraft designed for 10 cars and 146 panengers, propelled by water screws.
Courtesy : Vosper Thorny Croft.

2.1 Introduction

Fluid mechanics deals with the behaviour of liquids and gases. The liquid is either at rest or in motion. Fluid at rest is *fluid statics*; examples such as water in a container or reservoir of water behind a dam. Fluid at rest has weight and exerts pressure. Fluid in motion is *fluid dynamics*. Examples are rivers, flow in pipes, flow in pumps and turbines. The fluids that are commonly studied are air and water. External flow is study of fluid flow over car, aeroplane, ships and rockets. Flow in pipes, impellers of pumps are referred to as internal flow. Compressible flow is when density does not remain constant with application of pressure. Incompressible flow is the density remains constant with application of pressure. Water is incompressible whereas air is compressible. Compressibility criteria is Mach number.

The chapter deals with the concept of momentum and Newton's second and third law of motion. With the knowledge of continuity equation and momentum equation, Bernoullis and Eulers equations are derived. With the help of second law of Newton force acting by a jet on stationary and moving plate is obtained. The impact of jet on vanes has direct application on hydraulic turbines.

2.2 Scope of Fluid Mechnanics

The dimensional analysis deals with the units of measurement in SI units both fundamental and derived units, and non-dimentional quatities.

The properties of fluids deal with measurement of mass, density, specific weight, specific gravity, compressibility of fluids, surface tension, capillary action.

The fluid statics deals with fluid pressure, fluid at rest, manometry, hydrostatic forces, buoyancy floation and stability.

The fluid kinematics deals with one, two and three-dimensional flows, steady and unsteady flows, Reynold's number, streamlines, streaklines and pathlines.

The internal flows deal with flow in pipes, pumps, laminar and turbulent flows in pipes, single and multipipe system, Moody chart, minor losses, velocity profiles for laminar and turbulent flows.

The external flow deals with flow over immersed bodies, lift and drag concepts, boundary layer laminar and turbulent, friction drag, pressure drag and drag coefficients.

The flow in turbomachines deals with energy considerations, angular momentum considerations, centrifugal pump and their characteristics, similarity laws, turbines, axial and rapid flow, impulse and reaction.

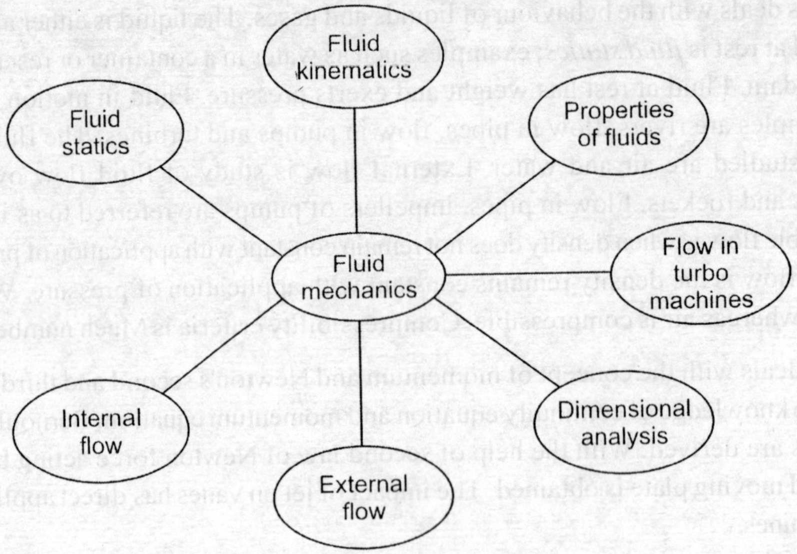

2.3 Laminar and Turbulent Flow

The transport of fluid is done in closed conduit commonly called a pipe usually of round cross-section. The flow in pipes is laminar or turbulent; Osborne Reynolds has done experiment in pipe flow. Laminar flow is one where the streamline moves in parallel lines and turbulent flow when streamlines cross each other and the flow is diffused. Example: Flow of highly viscous syrup onto a pan cake, flow of honey is laminar whereas splashing water is from a faucet into a sink below it or irregular gustiness of wind represents turbulent flow. Reynold's number is to distinguish the two types of flow.

Reynolds number for the pipe flow is given by

$$Re = \frac{\rho DV}{\mu}$$

where D diameter of pipe, ρ density, V velocity and μ viscosity of fluid.

If the flow is laminar Reynolds no. is less than 2100 and if the flow is turbulent Reynolds no. is more than 4000. The hydraulic losses depend on whether the flow is laminar or turbulent.

2.4 Momentum Equation for One-Dimensional Flow

The momentum of a particle of fluid is defined as the product of mass m and velocity V.

$$\text{Momentum} = mV$$

If there is a change in the velocity of the fluid there will be corresponding change in the momentum of the fluid. According to Newton's second law of motion, rate of change of momentum is proportional to the applied force.

In order to determine the rate of change of momentum, consider a control volume of the fluid ABCD as shown in Fig. 2.1.

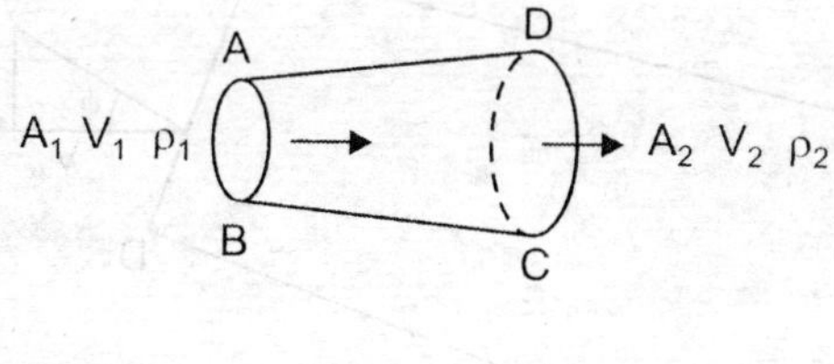

Fig. 2.1 Control volume for one-dimensional flow.

Assuming the flow to be steady and also assuming there is no storage within the control volume, we may write the continuity equation for mass flow rate

$$\dot{m} = \rho_2 A_2 V_2 = \rho_1 A_1 V_1 \quad .....(2.1)$$

Rate of momentum across the boundary CD is mass flow rate times the velocity

$$\rho_2 A_2 V_2 \cdot V_2$$

Rate of momentum across the boundary AB is mass flow rate times the velocity

$$\rho_1 A_1 V_1 \cdot V_1$$

Rate of change of momentum across the control volume ABCD

$$\rho_2 A_2 V_2 . V_2 - \rho_1 A_1 V_1 \cdot V_1$$

From the continuity of mass flow equation

$$\rho_1 A_1 V_1 \cdot (V_2 - V_1) = \dot{m} (V_2 - V_1)$$

Thus rate of change of momentum is

$$\therefore \quad \dot{m} (V_2 - V_1)$$

According to Newton's law it is caused by a force, such as

$$F = \dot{m} (V_2 - V_1) \quad .....(2.2)$$

Note: Here the velocities have been assumed to be in straight line. One must remember that this is the force acting on the fluid and according to Newton's third law of motion, force exerted by the fluid will be opposite to this force.

2.5 Momentum Equation for Two-Dimensional Flow

In section 2.4 flow is considered one-dimensional and velocities in a straight line, the incoming velocity V_1 and outgoing velocity V_2 are in the same direction. Fig. 2.2 shows a two-dimensional flow in which velocities are not in same direction and make angles θ and ϕ with X-axis.

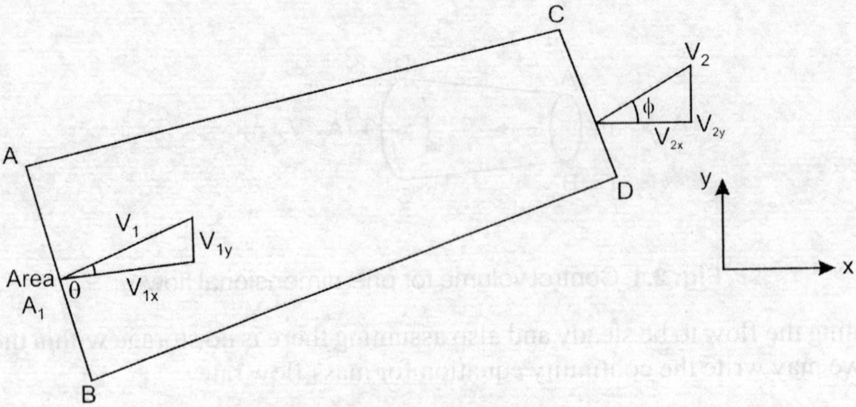

Fig. 2.2 A two-dimensional flow.

Resolving velocities V_1 and V_2 in x, y directions, the velocity components of V_1 in x, and y directions V_{1x}, V_{1y}, velocity component of V_2 are in x, y directions V_{2x}, V_{2y}. Similarly F_x and F_y are components of the force in x and y directions.

$$F_x = \text{Rate of change of momentum in x-direction}$$

$$F_x = \text{Mass flow rate} \times \text{change of velocity in x-direction}$$

$$F_x = \dot{m}\ (V_2 \cos\phi - V_2 \cos\theta) = \dot{m}\,(V_{2x} - V_{1x}) \qquad \text{.....(2.3)}$$

$$F_y = \dot{m}\ (V_2 \sin\phi - V_1 \sin\theta) = \dot{m}\,(V_{2y} - V_{1y}) \qquad \text{.....(2.4)}$$

Similarly the components can be combined to get the resultant force

$$F = \sqrt{F_x^2 \times F_y^2} \qquad \text{.....(2.5)}$$

***Note*:** The forces F_x and F_y are the components of the force F acting on the fluid and components of reaction force on a plate or vane are equal and opposite to F_x and F_y.

2.6 Jet Striking a Plate (3 cases)

(a) A jet of fluid striking the plate which is perpendicular (Fig. 2.3(a)),

(b) The plate is inclined to jet of fluid (Fig. 2.3(b)),

(c) The plate is moving in the direction of jet.

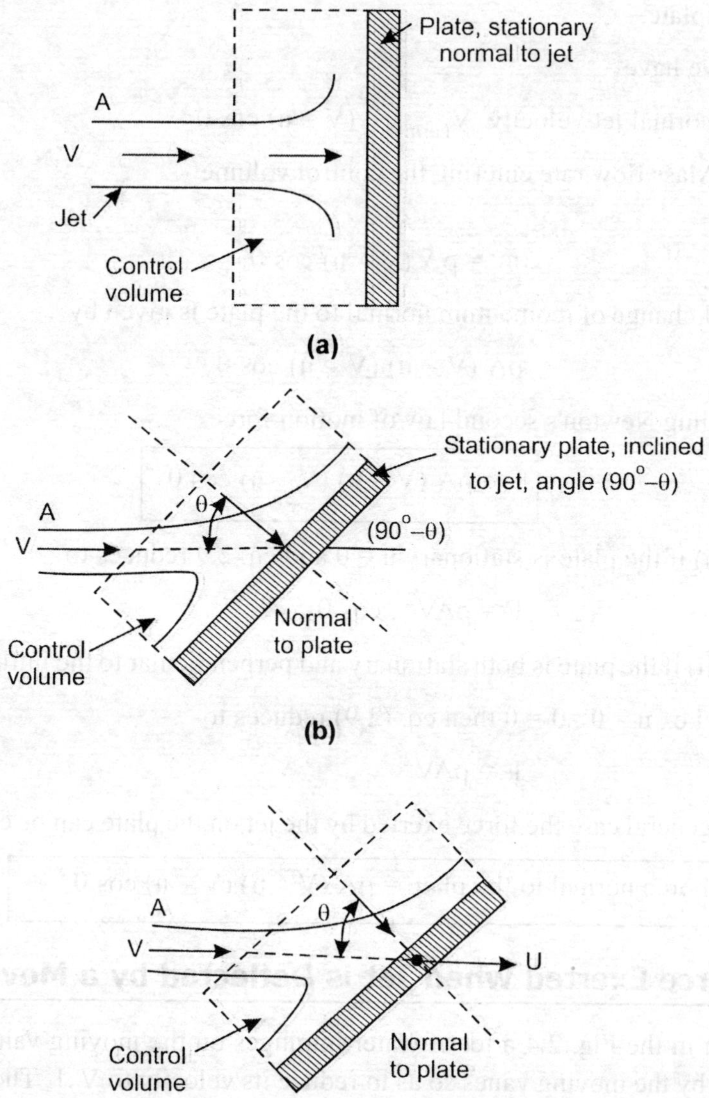

Fig. 2.3 Jet striking a plate.

A control volume enclosing the jet and the plate may be established. This control volume being fixed relative to the plate and is therefore moving with it. The components of velocities perpendicular to the plate are considered.

In cases where the plate is moving, the most helpful technique is to reduce the plate and associated volume to rest by superimposing on the system equal and opposite plate velocity. This reduces all cases illustrated in the Fig. 2.3(c) to a simple consideration of jet striking a stationary plate.

Thus we have

normal jet velocity $V_{normal} = (V - u) \cos \theta$ .....(2.6)

Mass flow rate entering the control volume

$$\dot{m} = \rho A (V - u) \cos \theta \quad .....(2.7)$$

Rate of change of momentum normal to the plate is given by

$$\rho A (V - u) (V - u) \cos \theta \quad .....(2.8)$$

According Newton's second law of motion force

$$\boxed{F = \rho A (V - u) (V - u) \cos \theta} \quad .....(2.9)$$

Case (i) if the plate is stationary u = 0 and eq. 2.9 reduces to

$$F = \rho A V^2 . \cos \theta \quad .....(2.10)$$

Case (ii) if the plate is both stationary and perpendicular to the initial jet direction

i.e., u = 0 ; θ = 0 then eq. (2.9) reduces to

$$F = \rho A V^2 \quad .....(2.11)$$

In the general case the force exerted by the jet on the plate can be expressed in the form

$$\boxed{\text{Force normal to the plate} = \rho A (V - u) (V - u) \cos \theta} \quad .....(2.12)$$

2.7 Force Exerted when Jet is Deflected by a Moving Vane

As shown in the Fig. 2.4 a jet of water impinges on the moving vanes V_1 at inlet and is deflected by the moving vanes so as to reduce its velocity to $V_2$1. The moving vanes have a velocity u in the x-direction. At inlet the absolute velocity V_1 makes an angle α_1 with the horizontal and adding vectorially the velocity u gives relative velocity V_{r1} making an angle β_1 with horizontal.

The fluid leaves the vane at relative velocity V_{r2} making an angle β_2 with the direction of vane. The velocity is tangential to the curvature of vanes at exit. The direction of the jet leaves the vane at absolute velocity V_2 at an angle α_2 with the horizontal.

The force in the direction of motion will be:

F_x = mass flow rate × change in velocity in the direction of motion of vane.

$$F_x = \dot{m}\,(V_{1x} - V_{2x})$$

The force at right angles to the direction of motion will be:

F_y = mass flow rate × change of velocity in direction perpendicular to direction of motion.

$$F_y = \dot{m}\,(V_{1y} - V_{2y})$$

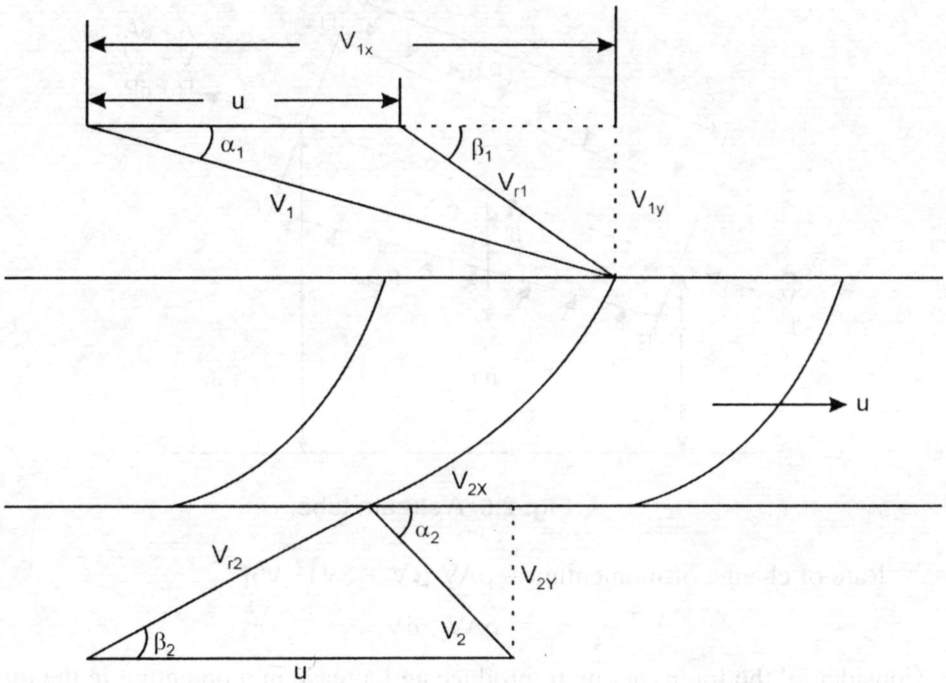

Fig. 2.4 Jet impingement on moving vane with velocity diagrams.

2.8 Euler's and Bernoullis Equations

It is possible to derive a relationship between velocity, pressure, elevation and density along a streamline.

A section of a stream tube surrounding the streamline, having a cross-sectional area over the section AB | CD separated by a distance δs is shown in Fig. 2.5.

At section AB, area is A, pressure p, velocity V and elevation z.

At section CD, the area is A + δA, Velocity v + δV, Pressure p + δp and elevation z + δz.

The surrounding liquid will exert pressure p_s from the sides of the element. The pressure will be normal to the tube in absence of shear stresses. The weight of the element mg will act downward vertically at an angle θ to the centre line.

Mass flow rate = ρAV

Momentum = mV

Rate of initial momentum = ρAV . V

Rate of final momentum = ρAV [(V + δV)]

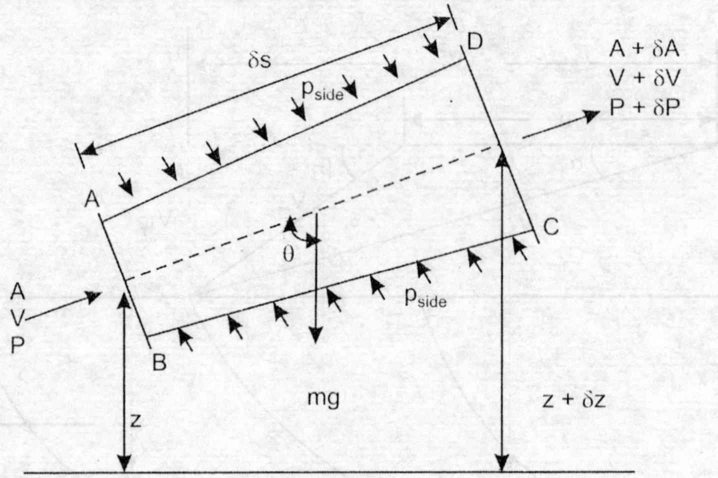

Fig. 2.5 A stream tube.

$$\text{Rate of change of momentum} = \rho AV\,[(V + \delta V) - V)]$$

$$= \rho AV\,.\,\delta V \qquad .....(2.13)$$

Consider all the forces acting to produce an increase in momentum in the direction of motion.

- Weight of the element = $mg = \rho g\,(A + \frac{\delta A}{2})\,\delta s$
- Force due to element in the direction opposing the motion

$$mg\cos\theta = \rho g\,(A + \frac{\delta A}{2})\,\delta s\cos\theta$$

$$\text{where } \cos\theta = \frac{\delta z}{\delta s}$$

- Force due to pressure p in the direction of motion = PA
- Force due to pressure $(P + \delta p)$ opposing the motion

$$= (P + \delta p)(A + \delta A)$$

- Force due to side pressure Ps in the direction of motion $P_s \delta A$.

(The value of Ps varies from p at AB, to $p + \delta p$ at CD and can be taken as

$p = k\,\delta p$ where k is a fraction.

- Force due to side pressure $(P + k\delta p)\,\delta A$

Resultant force in the direction of motion

$$= PA - (P + \delta p)(A + \delta A) - mg\cos\theta + p\delta A + k\,\delta p\,.\,\delta A$$

$$= PA - (P + \delta p)(A + \delta A) - \rho g\left(A + \frac{\delta A}{2}\right)\delta s\,\frac{\delta z}{\delta s} + p\delta A + k\,\delta p\,.\,\delta A$$

Neglecting products of small quantities,

Resultant force $= -A\delta p - \rho g\,A\,\delta z$ .....(2.14)

Applying Newton's second law of motion which states rate of change of momentum is equal to resultant force and equating eq. 2.13 and 2.14, we have

$$\rho AV\delta V = -A\,\delta p - \rho g\,A\,\delta z$$

Dividing by $\rho\,A\,\delta s$

$$\frac{1}{\rho}\frac{\delta p}{\delta s} + V\frac{\delta V}{\delta s} + g\frac{\delta z}{\delta s} = 0$$

or, in the limit as $\delta s \to 0$

$$\boxed{\frac{1}{\rho}\frac{dp}{ds} + V\frac{dV}{ds} + g\frac{dz}{ds} = 0} \quad .....(2.15)$$

This is known as Euler's equation in the differential form, the relation between pressure P, velocity V, density ρ and elevation z along a streamline flow.

For an incompressible fluid for which the density is constant, integration of equation along the streamline with respect to s, gives

$$\boxed{\frac{P}{\rho} + \frac{V^2}{2} + gz = \text{const}} \quad .....(2.16)$$

This is well-known Bernoullis equation

Dividing by 'g' in eq. 2.16, we get

$$\frac{P}{\rho g} + \frac{V^2}{2g} + z = \text{const}$$

or
$$\boxed{\frac{P}{\gamma} + \frac{V^2}{2g} + z = \text{const}} \quad \text{..... (2.17)}$$

The pressure P is the gauge pressure and unit of measurement in SI units is N/m^2, the specific weight γ is in N/m^3, therefore $\frac{P}{\gamma}$ is in meters. The, unit of $V^2/2g$ is $m^2/s^2 \times s^2/m$ in meters. The unit of elevation z is in meters. All the terms of Bernoulli equation is measured in meters. Therefore the const is total head in meters denoted by H along a streamline, but the constant may be different for different streamlines, eq. 2.17 is rewritten as

$$\frac{P}{\gamma} + \frac{V^2}{2g} \quad z = H \quad \text{.....(2.18)}$$

Note: the assumption made in deriving the Bernoullis equation

inviscid flow - steady flow

constant density - flow along a streamline

The Bernoullis equation cannot be used in following cases of fluid flow.

compressibility effect - unsteady flow

- rotational effect - viscous flow

2.9 Application of Bernoullis Equation

(a) Aerofoils (b) Automobile (c) Freejet

(d) Pump (e) Turbine (f) Venturimeter

Writing Bernoullis equation

$$\frac{P}{\gamma} + \frac{V^2}{2g} + z = \text{const}$$

In a differential form when there is no difference in elevation it is

$$\frac{dp}{\gamma} + \frac{Vdv}{g} = 0$$

$$\frac{dp}{\rho} = -V\,dV \quad \text{.....(2.19)}$$

The equation shows that where pressure is high, velocity is low and vice versa. A wind tunnel shown in Fig. 2.6 is very useful in studying models of aerofoils, motor cars, and ships. The models are tested in the test section of the wind tunnel.

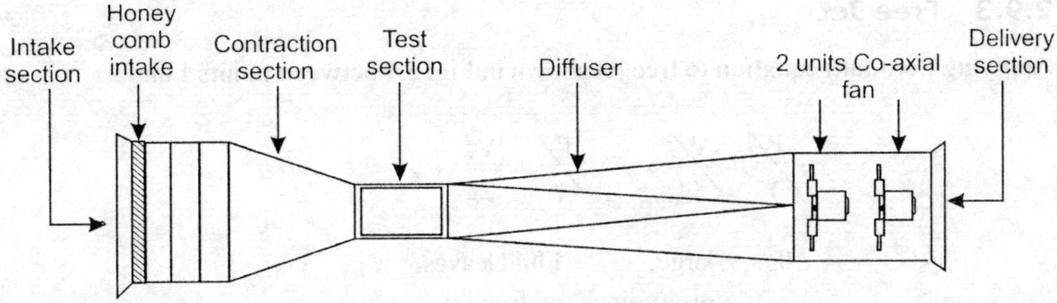

Fig. 2.6 Schematic diagram of the open circuit wind tunnel.

2.9.1 Air Foil

The pressure distribution test is carried out by wind tunnel for an airfoil shown in Fig. 2.7.

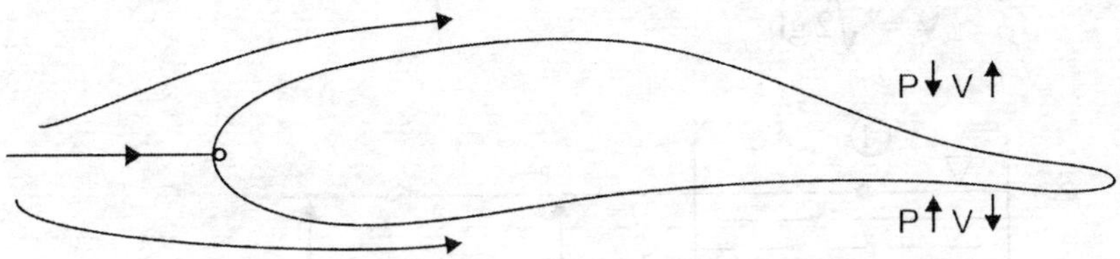

Fig. 2.7 Distribution of pressure over an airfoil.

2.9.2 Automobile

The distribution of pressure over a model of an automobile in wind tunnel is shown in Fig. 2.8.

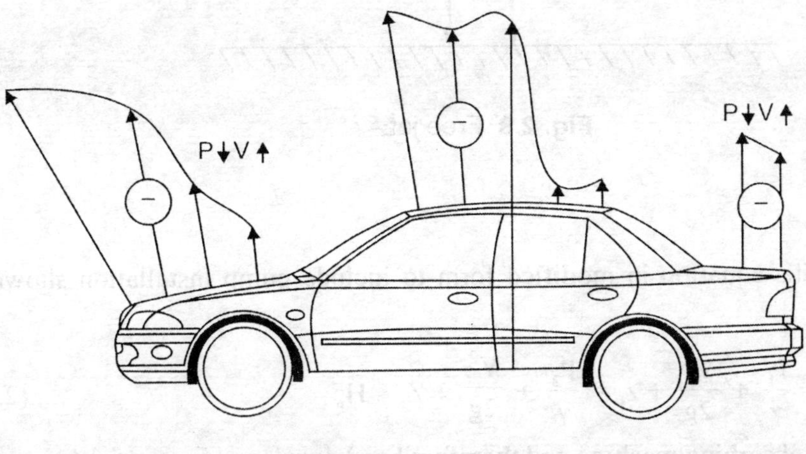

Fig. 2.8 Pressure distribution over the surface of the car by wind tunnel.

2.9.3 Free Jet

Applying Bernoulli equation to free jet shown in Fig. 2.9 between points 1 and 2.

$$\cancel{\frac{P_1}{\gamma}} + \cancel{\frac{V_1^2}{2g}} + z_1 = \cancel{\frac{P_2}{\gamma}} + \frac{V_2^2}{2g} + z_2$$

0   large reservoir $V_1 = 0$ Fluid leaves as free jet

$$\frac{V^2}{2g} = z_1 - z_2 = h$$

$$V = \sqrt{2\,gh} \qquad \text{.....(2.20)}$$

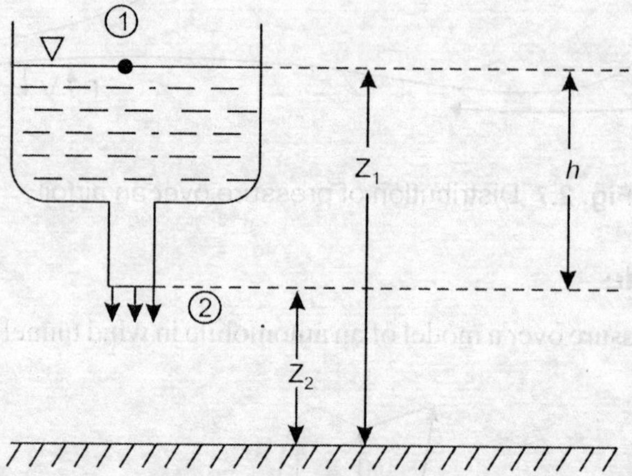

Fig. 2.9 Free jet.

2.9.4 Pump

Applying Bernoullis equation in modified form to include pump installation shown in Fig. 2.10.

$$\frac{P_1}{\gamma} + \frac{V_1^2}{2g} + z_1 = \frac{P_2}{\gamma} + \frac{V_2^2}{2g} + Z_2 - H_P \qquad \text{.....(2.21)}$$

Pump is power absorbing machine and therefore head developed is negative.

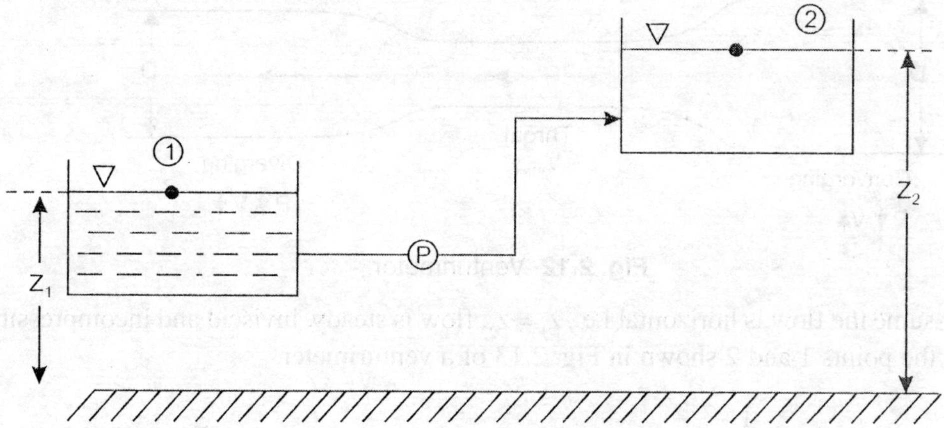

Fig. 2.10 Pump installation.

2.9.5 Turbine

Applying Bernoullis equation in modified form to turbine installation shown in Fig. 2.11.

$$\frac{P_1}{\gamma} + \frac{V_1^2}{2g} + z_1 = \frac{P_2}{\gamma} + \frac{V_2^2}{2g} + z_2 + H_T \qquad .....(2.22)$$

Turbine is power producing machine and therefore head developed is positive (H_T).

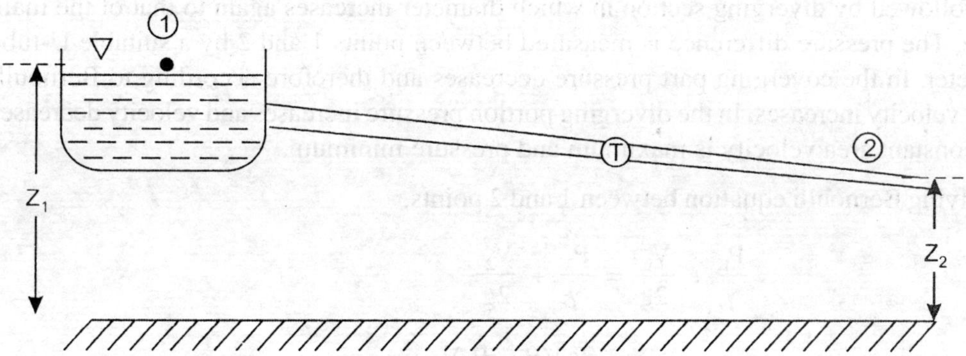

Fig. 2.11 Turbine installation.

2.9.6 Flow Measurement

Venturimeter

Bernoullis equation can be applied to measure flow rate in a pipe by venturimeter. The venturimeter has three important portions: a converging part, constant area (throat) and a diverging part as shown in the Fig. 2.12.

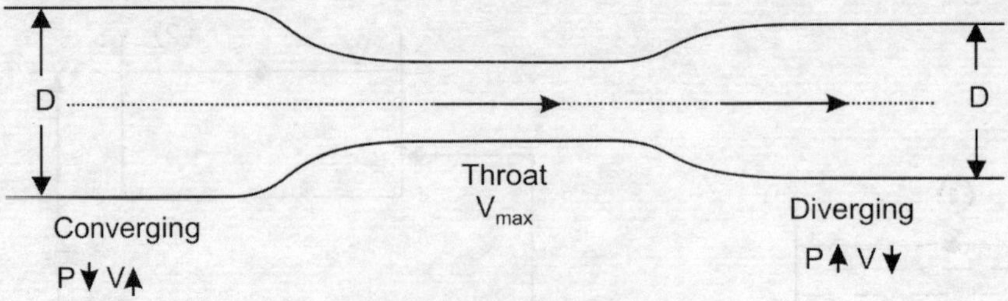

Fig. 2.12 Venturimeter.

We assume the flow is horizontal i.e., $z_1 = z_2$, flow is steady, inviscid and incompressible between the points 1 and 2 shown in Fig. 2.13 of a venturimeter.

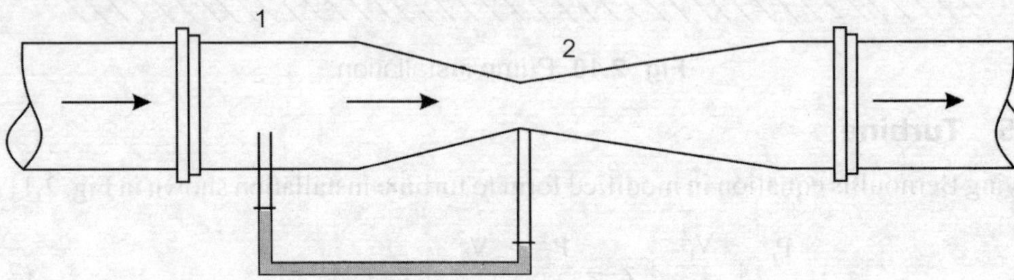

Fig. 2.13 Verturimeter.

It consists of a short converging conical tube leading to cylindrical portion called the throat, followed by diverging section in which diameter increases again to that of the main pipeline. The pressure difference is measured between points 1 and 2 by a suitable U-tube manometer. In the coverging part pressure decreases and therefore according to Bernoulli eq. 2.19 velocity increases. In the diverging portion pressure increases and velocity decreases and in constant area velocity is maximum and pressure minimum.

Applying Bernoulli equation between 1 and 2 points,

$$\frac{P_1}{\gamma} + \frac{V_1^2}{2g} = \frac{P_2}{\gamma} + \frac{V_2^2}{2g}$$

$$V_2^2 - V_1^2 = \frac{2g\,[(P_1 - P_2)]}{\rho g} \qquad .....(2.23)$$

For continuous flow $\quad a_1V_1 = a_2V_2$; or $V_2 = \frac{a_1}{a_2}\, V_1$

Substituting V_2 in eq. 2.23

$$V_1^2\left[\left(\frac{a_1}{a_2}\right)^2 - 1\right] = \frac{2g[(p_1 - p_2)]}{\rho g}$$

$$V_1 = \frac{a_2}{(a_1^2 - a_2^2)^{1/2}} \sqrt{\frac{2g(P_1 - P_2)}{\rho g}}$$

Volume flow rate $Q = a_1 V_1$

$$Q = \left[\frac{a_1 a_2}{(a_1^2 - a_2^2)^{1/2}}\right] \sqrt{2g\,H}$$

where $H = \dfrac{P_1 - P_2}{\rho g}$

If m = area ratio $= \dfrac{a_1}{a_2}$

$$Q = \frac{a_1}{\left(m^2 - 1\right)^{1/2}} \sqrt{2gH}$$

or

$$Q = a_2 \sqrt{\frac{2(P_1 - P_2)}{\rho\left[1 - \frac{a_2}{a_1}\right]^2}} \qquad .....(2.24)$$

In practice, some loss of energy occurs between points 1 and 2 and therefore actual discharge (Q_a) will be less than theoretical discharge (Q) and therefore a coefficient of discharge C_d is introduced

$$C_d = \frac{\text{Actual discharge}}{\text{Theoretical discharge}} = \frac{Q_a}{Q} \qquad .....(2.25)$$

The value of C_d is around 0.98. The venturimeters are commonly used in power plants and chemical industries to measure flow rate of fluids in pipes with fairly good accuracy. Thus for a given flow geometry (a_1 and a_2) the flow rate can be determined by measuring difference of pressures P_1 and P_2.

2.9.7 Measurement of Static and Stagnation Pressures

Bernoullis equation is re-written as

$$\frac{P_1}{\gamma} + \frac{V_1^2}{2g} + Z_1 = \frac{P_2}{\gamma} + \frac{V_2^2}{2g} + Z_2$$

The pressure P is called the static pressre and sum of two pressures $\left(\frac{P}{\gamma}+Z\right)$ is called the piezometric head, and sum of three terms $\left(\frac{P}{\gamma}+\frac{V^2}{2g}+Z\right)$ is total head. The sum of two terms $\left(P+\frac{\rho V^2}{2}\right)$ is called stagnation pressure and aften denoted by P_o.

$$P_o = P + \frac{\rho V^2}{2} \qquad .....(2.26)$$

Pizometric tube measures the static pressure shown in Fig. 2.14(a) and Fig. 2.14(b) measures total pressure and the difference of stagnation pressure and static pressure measured by pitot-static tube shown in Fig. 2.14(c).

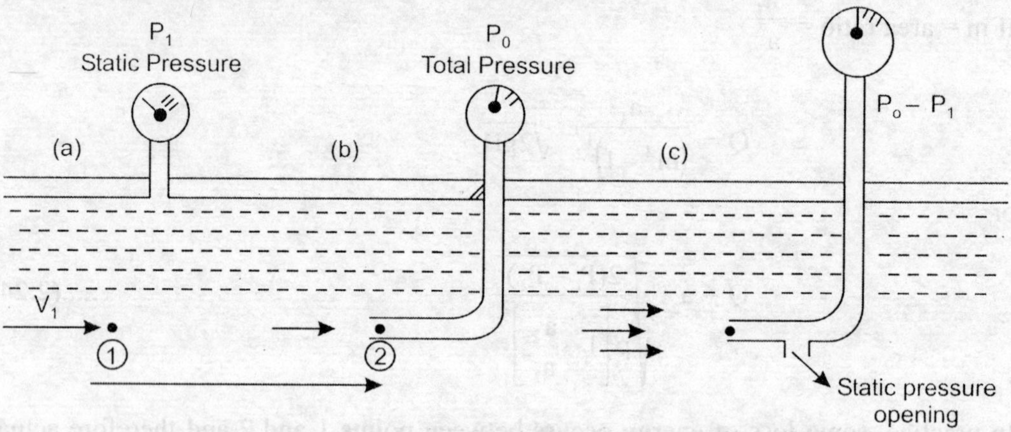

Fig. 2.14 Measurement of static pressure, total pressures.

Thus by using the readings of piezometer and pitot pressures separately or reading from pitot-static tube, velocity of the stream can be calculated assuming point 2 as stagnation point so that $V_2 = 0$, we have

$$\frac{P_1}{\gamma} + \frac{V_1^2}{2g} = \frac{P_2}{\gamma} + \frac{V_2^2}{2g}$$

$$\frac{P_1}{\rho g} + \frac{V_1^2}{2g} = \frac{P_o}{\rho g}$$

$$\frac{P_1}{\rho g} + \frac{V_1^2}{2g} = \frac{P_o}{\rho g}$$

$$\frac{V_1^2}{2g} = \frac{P_o - P_1}{\rho g}$$

$$V = \sqrt{\frac{2(P_o - P_1)}{\rho}} \qquad .....(2.27)$$

Solved Examples

E.2.1 A submarine moves through sea water of (specific gravity 1.03) at a depth of 50 m with velocity of 5 m/s as shown in Fig. 2.15. Determine the pressure at station point 2.

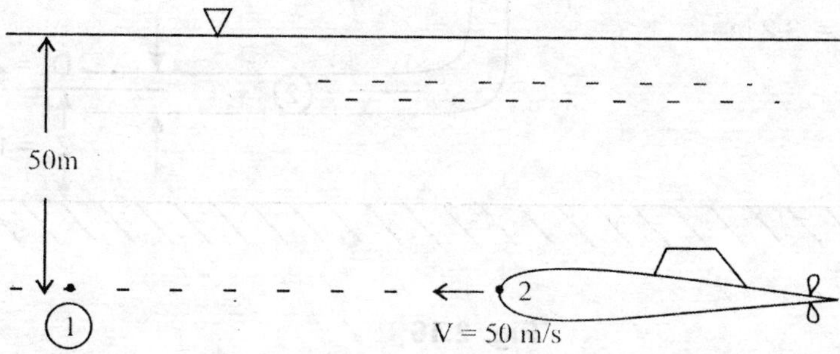

Fig. 2.15

Solution

Referring to Fig. 2.15, point 1 refers static pressure and point 2 stagnation pressure

Applying Bernoullis eq. 2.17 for 1 and 2.

$$\frac{P_1}{\gamma} + \frac{V_1^2}{2g} + z_1 = \frac{P_2}{\gamma} + \frac{V_2^2}{2g} + z_2$$

At stagnation point 2; $V_2 = 0$

$$\frac{P_2}{\gamma} = \frac{P_1}{\gamma} + \frac{V_1^2}{2g} = 50 + \frac{5^2}{2 \times 9.8} = 51.27$$

$$S = \frac{\rho_{sw}}{\rho_w} \quad \therefore r_{sw} = 1.03 \times 10^3 \text{ kg/m}^3$$

$$\frac{P_2}{\gamma} = 51.27; \quad P_2 = \rho_{sw} \times g \times 51.27$$

$$\therefore \quad P_2 = 1.03 \times 10^3 \times 9.8 \times 51.27 = 517.5 \text{ kPa}$$

E.2.2 Benzene flows in a pipe under condition shown in Fig. 2.16. Determine the pressure at point 2 if flow rate is 0.05 m³/s.

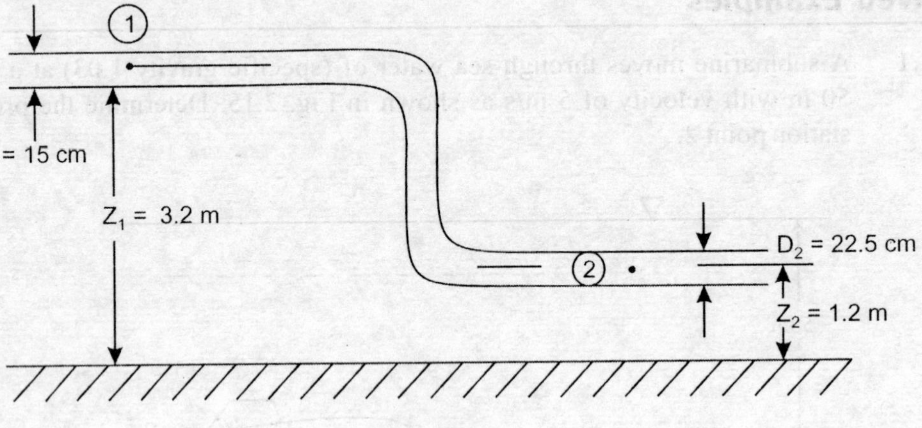

Fig. 2.16

Solution

The conditions at point 1 and 2 are

$P_1 = 4.4$ bar, $D_1 = 15$ cm, $Z_1 = 3.2$ m

$P_2 = ?$ $D_2 = 22.5$ cm, $Z_2 = 1.2$ m

Flow rate = 0.05 m³/s

Volume flow rate Q = 0.05 m³/s

$$a_1 = \frac{\pi}{4} D_1^2 = \frac{\pi}{4} \times 15^2 \times 10^{-4} = 176.6 \times 10^{-4} \text{ m}^2$$

$$a_2 = \frac{\pi}{4} D_2^2 = \frac{\pi}{4} \times 22.5^2 \times 10^{-4} = 397.4 \times 10^{-4} \text{ m}^2$$

$V_1 = Q/a_1 = 0.05/176.6 \times 10^{-4} = 2.83$ m/s

$V_2 = Q/a_2 = 0.05/397.4 \times 10^{-4} = 1.25$ m/s

From *Table A.4* (refer chapter 1) specific weight of Benzene = 8.82×10^3 kg/m³

Applying Bernoullis equation between 1 and 2

$$\frac{P_1}{\gamma} + \frac{V_1^2}{2g} + z_1 = \frac{P_2}{\gamma} + \frac{V_2^2}{2g} + z_2$$

Substituing proper values

$$\frac{4.4 \times 10^5}{8.82 \times 10^3} + \frac{2.83^2}{2 \times 9.8} + 3.2 = \frac{P_2}{\gamma} + \frac{1.26^2}{2 \times 9.8} + 1.2$$

$$\frac{P_2}{\gamma} = 49.8 + 0.4 + 3.2 - 0.08 - 1.2 = 52.12$$

$$P_2 = 8.82 \times 10^3 \times 52.12$$

$$P_2 = 459.6 \text{ kPa.}$$

E.2.3 A 50 mm diameter syphon drawing oil of sp. gravity 0.82 from a reservoir is shown in Fig. 2.17. The head loss from point 1 to 2 is 1.5 m and from point 2 to 3 is 2.4 m. Determine flow rate of oil from syphon and also the pressure at point 2.

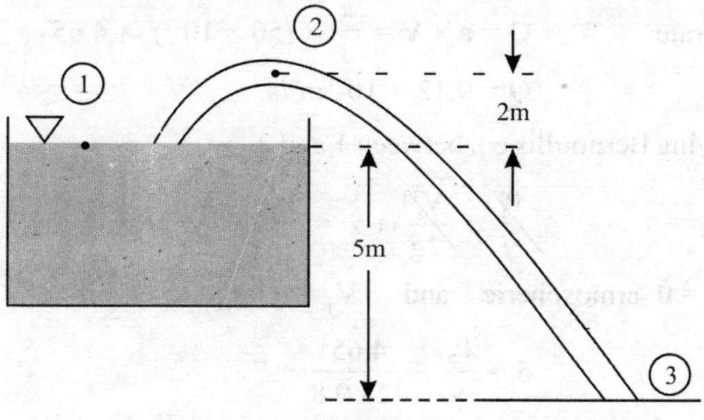

Fig. 2.17

Solution

Total head loss from 1 to 3 = 1.5 + 2.4 = 3.9 m

Fix the datum line at point 3

$$S = \frac{\rho_{oil}}{\rho_{water}}$$

$$\rho_{oil} = S \times \rho_{water} = 0.82 \times 10^3 = 820 \text{ kg/m}^3$$

Applying Bernoull is equation between 1 and 3

$$\cancel{\frac{P_1}{\gamma}} + \cancel{\frac{V_1^2}{2g}} + z_1 = \cancel{\frac{P_3}{\gamma}} + \frac{V_3^2}{2g} + z_3 + h_{loss}$$

The reservoir is considered large and therefore $V_1 = 0$

Also $P_1 = P_3$ = atmospheric pressure

Substituting properly,

$$0 + 0 + 5 = 0 + \frac{V_3^2}{2g} + 0 + 3.9$$

$$\frac{V_3^2}{2g} = 1.1 \qquad \therefore\ V_3 = \sqrt{2 \times 9.8 \times 1.1} = 4.65 \text{ m/s}$$

The velocity at exit is 4.65 m/s.

Diameter of the pipe = 50 mm is same ; $\therefore\ V_2 = V_3 = 4.65$ m/s

Flow rate $\qquad Q = a \times V = \frac{\pi}{4} \times (50 \times 10^{-3})^2 \times 4.65$

$\therefore \qquad Q = 9.12 \times 10^{-3}$ m³/s.

Applying Bernoullis eq. between 1 and 2

$$\frac{P_1}{\gamma} + \frac{V_1^2}{2g} + z_1 = \frac{P_2}{\gamma} + \frac{V_2^2}{2g} + z_2$$

as $p_1 = 0$ atmospheric and $V_1 = 0$ large reservoir

$$5 = \frac{P_2}{\gamma} + \frac{4.65^2}{2 \times 9.8} + 7$$

$$\frac{P_2}{\gamma} = 5 - 1.1 - 7 = -3.1$$

$\therefore \qquad P_2 = 820 \times 9.8 \times (-3.1)$

$P_2 = 24.9$ kPa (negative)

E.2.4 A person holds his hand out of an open car window while the car drives through still air at 90 km/hr. Under standard and atmospheric conditions what is the maximum pressure experienced by the person on the hand.

Solution

The maximum pressure is the stagnation pressure given by

$$P_o = \rho + \frac{\rho V^2}{2}$$

$$P_o = 101.3 \times 10^3 + 1.225 \times \left(\frac{90 \times 1000}{3600}\right)^2 \times \frac{1}{2}$$

$$P_o = 101300 + 382 = 101682 \text{ Pa}$$

The maximum pressure = 101.682 kPa

E.2.5 Blood of specific gravity 1 flows through an artery in the neck of a giraffe from its heart to the head. If the pressure at the beginning of the artery (outlet of the heart) is equal to 0.212 m of mercury, determine the pressure at the end of the artery when the head is:

(a) 2.4 m above the heart

(b) 1.8 m below the heart

Solution

Fig. 2.18 shows the position of heart 1 and neck 2 of the giraffe.

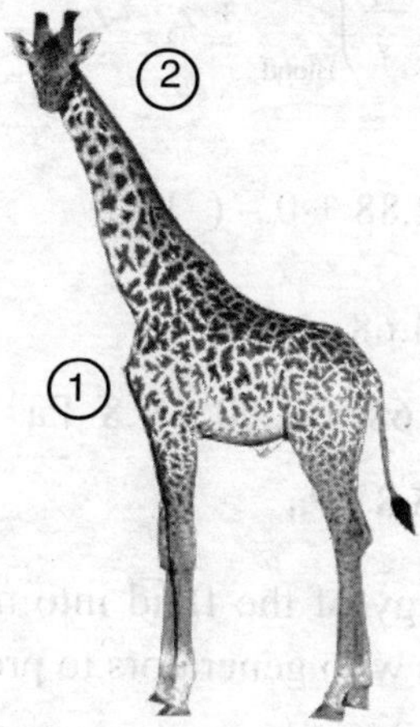

Fig. 2.18

(a) Applying Bernoullis equation between 1 and 2

$$\frac{P_1}{\gamma} + \cancel{\frac{V_1^2}{2g}} + Z_1 = \frac{P_2}{\gamma} + \cancel{\frac{V_2^2}{2g}} + Z_2$$

$$\therefore \quad \frac{P_2}{\gamma} = \left(\frac{P_1}{\gamma}\right)_{Hg} + Z_1 - Z_2$$

Equating pressure developed by column of mercury to column of blood, thus

$$P = \rho\, g\, h$$

$$\therefore \quad (\rho g\, h)_{Hg} = (\rho g\, h)_{Blood}$$

$$13.6 \times 1000 \times 0.212 = 1 \times 1000 \times h_{Blood}$$

$$h_{Blood} = 2.88 \text{ m}$$

$$\therefore \quad \frac{P_2}{\gamma} = \left(\frac{P_1}{\gamma}\right)_{Blood} + (z_1 - z_2)$$

$$\therefore \quad \frac{P_2}{\gamma} = 2.88 + 0 - 2.4 = 0.48$$

$$P_2 = 0.48 \times 1000 \times 9.8 = 4.7 \text{ kPa.}$$

(b) When the head is 1.8 m below the heart

$$\frac{P_2}{\gamma} = \left(\frac{P_1}{\gamma}\right)_{Blood} + z_1 - z_2$$

$$\frac{P_2}{\gamma} = 2.88 + 0 - (-1.8)$$

$$= 4.68$$

$$P_2 = 4.68 \times 1000 \times 9.8 \text{ Pa}$$

$$P_2 = 45.8 \text{ kPa.}$$

E.2.6 Turbines convert the energy of the fluid into mechanical energy. Turbines are often used in power plants with generators to produce electricity.

One such installation is shown in Fig. 2.19. A dam is constructed to store water and to produce required head. Water passes through the turbine and goes downstream. Determine power available to the turbine when the flow rate is 30 m³/s.

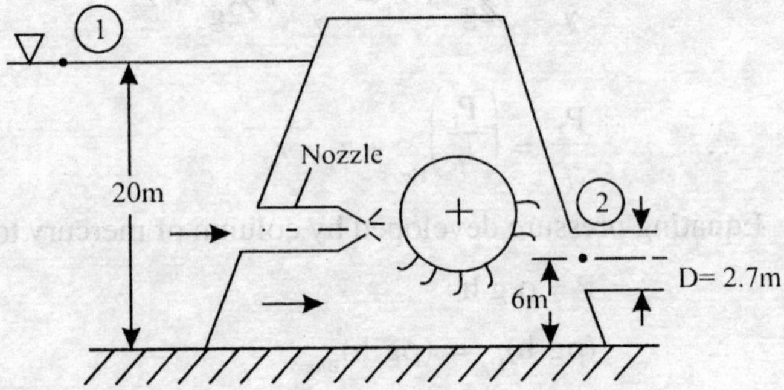

Fig. 2.19 Schematic of hydro power plant.

Solution

Area of exit pipe $a_2 = \frac{\pi}{4} D_2^2 = \frac{\pi}{4} \times 2.7^2 = 5.72 \text{ m}^2$

From equation of continuity $Q = a_2 V_2$

$\therefore \quad V_2 = Q/a_2 = 30/5.72 = 5.2 \text{ m/s}$

Applying Bernoullis equation in modified form at points 1 and 2

$$\frac{P_1}{\gamma} + \frac{V_1^2}{2g} + Z_1 = \frac{P_2}{\gamma} + \frac{V_2^2}{2g} + Z_2 + H_T$$

where

H_T = represents head developed by turbine

$P_1 = P_2$ = atmospheric pressure = 0

$V_1 = 0$ because of large reservoir.

Substituing proper values,

$$0 + 0 + 20 = 0 + \frac{5.2^2}{2 \times 9.8} + 6 + H_T$$

$$\therefore \quad H_T = 12.6 \text{ m}$$

Power developed by the turbine in KW

$$P = \gamma Q H_T = 9800 \times 30 \times 12.6 = 3704400 \text{ w}$$

$$P = 3704 \text{ kw}$$

E.2.7 A pitot-static tube is used to measure air velocity. If manometer connected to the instrument indicates a difference of head between tappings of 4 mm of water, calculate the air velocity assuming density of air 1.2 kg/m³.

Solution

A Pitot-static tube measures stagnation pressure and static pressure. The relation between difference of pressure and velocity is given by

$$V = \sqrt{\frac{2 \Delta P}{\rho_{air}}} \quad \text{also} \quad \Delta P = \gamma h = 9800 \times 4 \times 10^{-3} \text{ Pa}$$

Substituing proper values

$$V = \sqrt{\frac{2 \times 9800 \times 4 \times 10^{-3}}{1.2}}$$

$$V = 8.08 \text{ m/s}$$

E.2.8 The wind blows at a speed of 100 km/hr in a storm. Calculate the force acting on a 1 m × 2 m window which is facing the storm. The window is in a high-rise building. The wind speed is not affected by ground effects. Assume density of air as 1.2 kg/m³.

Solution

The pressure on the window facing the storm will be stagnation pressure as velocity of the wind is zero. Working with gauge pressures, the pressure upstream in the wind is zero.

$$\text{Velocity of the wind} = \frac{100 \times 1000}{3600} = 27.8 \text{ m/s}$$

Applying Bernoullis equation to calculate the pressure on the window

$$\frac{p_1}{\gamma} + \frac{V_1^2}{2g} + z_1 = \frac{P_2}{\gamma} + \frac{V_2^2}{2g} + z_2$$

where we have $z_1 = z_2$; $P_1 = 0$; $V_2 = 0$, and $P_2 = P_o$

$$\therefore \quad \frac{P_o}{\gamma} = \frac{V_1^2}{2g}; \qquad p_o = \frac{\rho V_1^2}{2}$$

Substituing proper values

$$P_o = \frac{1.2 \times (27.8)^2}{2} = 464 \text{ N/m}^2$$

$$\text{Force} = P_o.A = 464 \times 1 \times 2$$

$$F = 928 \text{ N}$$

E.2.9 The pressure head in an air pipe shown in Fig. 2.20 is measured with a piezometer as 16 mm of water. A pitot probe at the same location indicates 24 mm of water. The temperature is 20 °C. Calculate the Mach number and comment on compressibility of air.

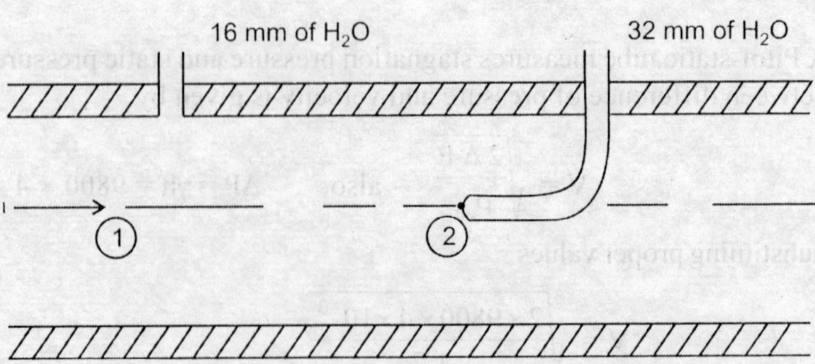

Fig. 2.20

Solution

Applying Bernoullis equation between two points 1 and 2 on the streamline, the point 1 refers to static pressure and point 2 is stagnation pressure, we can write.

$$\frac{P_1}{\gamma} + \frac{V_1^2}{2g} = \frac{P_o}{\gamma} \qquad \because V_1 = \sqrt{\frac{2(P_o - P_1)}{\rho}}$$

As air is considered ideal gas, and applying characteristic equation

$$P = \rho R T \quad \text{or} \quad \rho = \frac{P}{RT}$$

$$P = P_g + P_{atm} = 9800 \times 0.016 + 101000 = 101.156 \text{ k Pa}$$

$$\rho = \frac{101.156 \times 10^3}{287 \times (273 + 20)} = 1.2 \text{ kg/m}^3$$

$$\therefore \quad V = \sqrt{\frac{2}{\rho}(P_o - P)} = \sqrt{\frac{2(0.032 - 0.016)9800}{1.2}}$$

$$= 16.17 \text{ m/s}$$

$$\text{Velocity of sound } C = \sqrt{KRT} = \sqrt{1.4 \times 287 \times 293} = 343 \text{ m/s}$$

$$\text{Mach number } M = \frac{V}{C} = \frac{16.17}{343} = 0.047$$

The flow is incompressible as Mach number is less than 0.3.

E.2.10 A fire engine pump (shown in Fig. 2.21) delivers water to a nozzle at C located 30 m above the pump at the end of a 100 mm diameter delivery pipe. The pump draws water from a sump at A through a 150 mm diameter pipe. The pump is located at B at a height 2 m above the level of the sump. The velocity at the nozzle is 8.31 m/s and jet diameter 75 mm. Determine the flow rate from the nozzle and the power required to drive the pump.

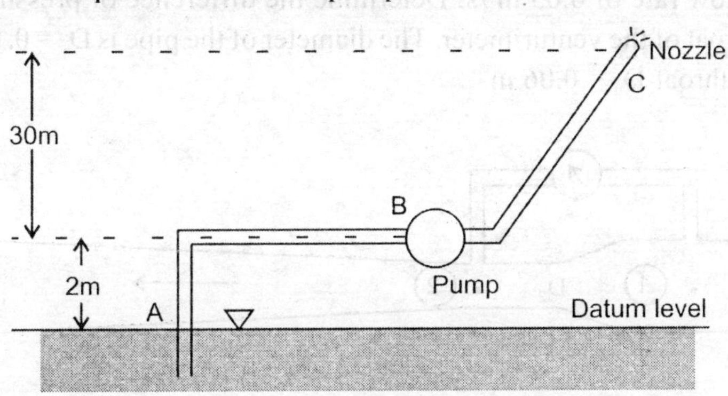

Fig. 2.21 Fire engine pump installation.

Solution

Applying equation of continuity $Q = a \times V$

$\therefore \quad Q$ = Velocity at C × area of the jet

$$Q = 8.31 \times \frac{\pi}{4} \times (75 \times 10^{-3})^2 = 0.0366 \text{ m}^3/\text{s}$$

Applying Bernoullis equation between points A and C

$$\frac{P_A}{\gamma} + \frac{V_A^2}{2g} + z_A = \frac{P_C}{\gamma} + \frac{V_C^2}{2g} + z_C - H_p$$

At the free surface of the sump, the pressure is atmospheric so that $P_A = 0$, the velocity V_A is also zero as the sump is considered very large and A can be taken as datum so that $Z_A = 0$ also P_C = atmospheric pressure = 0, the head developed by the pump is H_p, substituting proper values in the equation

$$\frac{P_A}{\gamma} + \frac{V_A^2}{2g} + z_A = \frac{P_C}{\gamma} + \frac{V_C^2}{2g} + z_C - H_p$$

$$0 + 0 + 0 = 0 + \frac{8.31^2}{2 \times 9.8} + 32 - H_p$$

$$H_p = 3.52 + 32 = 35.52 \text{ m}$$

Power required to drive the pump

$$P = \gamma Q H_p = 9800 \times 0.0366 \times 35.52 = 12.75 \text{ KW}$$

$$P = 12.75 \text{ KW}$$

E.2.11 Kerosene of sp.gravity 0.85 flows through a verturimeter as shown in Fig. 2.22 with flow rate of 0.05 m³/s. Determine the difference of pressure between inlet and throat of the venturimeter. The diameter of the pipe is $D_1 = 0.1$ m and diameter of the throat $D_2 = 0.06$ m.

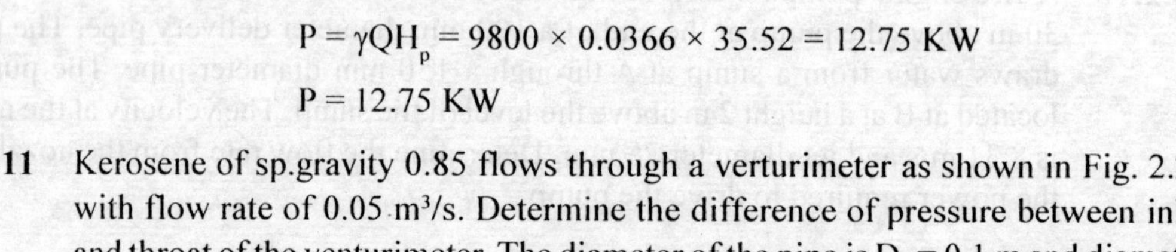

Fig. 2.22 Venturimeter.

Solution

The flow is considered inviscid steady and incompressible and the relation between flow rate and pressure difference is given by eq. 2.24

$$Q = a_2 \times \sqrt{\frac{2(P_1 - P_2)}{\rho(1-(a_2/a_1)^2}}$$

$$\therefore \qquad P_1 - P_2 = \frac{Q^2\rho\left[1-\left(\frac{a_2}{a_1}\right)^2\right]}{2a_2^2}$$

The density of kerosene ρ = specific gravity × density of water

$$= 0.85 \times 1000 = 850 \text{ kg/m}^3$$

Substituting proper values

$$\therefore \qquad P_1 - P_2 = \frac{(0.05)^2(850)\left[1-\left(\frac{0.06}{0.1}\right)^4\right]}{2\left[\left(\frac{\pi}{4}\right)(0.06)^2\right]^2} = 1.16 \times 10^5 \text{ N/m}^2$$

$$\therefore \qquad P_1 - P_2 = 116 \text{ kPa}$$

E.2.12 A jet of water 100 mm in diameter leaves a nozzle with a mean velocity of 36 m/s as shown in Fig. 2.23. It is deflected by a series of vanes moving with a velocity of 15 m/s in the direction at 30° to the direction of the jet so that it leaves the vane with an absolute velocity which is at right angles to the direction of the vane. Owing to friction the velocity of the fluid relative to the vanes at exit is equal to 0.85 of relative velocity at inlet.

Calculate

(a) inlet angle and outlet angle of the vane for no shock entry and exit.

(b) force exerted on the series of vanes in the direction of motion of vanes.

Solution

(a) With reference to the Fig. 2.23 given quantities are:

$V_1 = 36$ m/s; $\quad u = 15$ m/s; $\quad \alpha_1 = 30°$; $\quad \alpha_2 = 90°$

$V_{r2} = 0.85\ V_{r1}$; $\quad d = 100$ mm

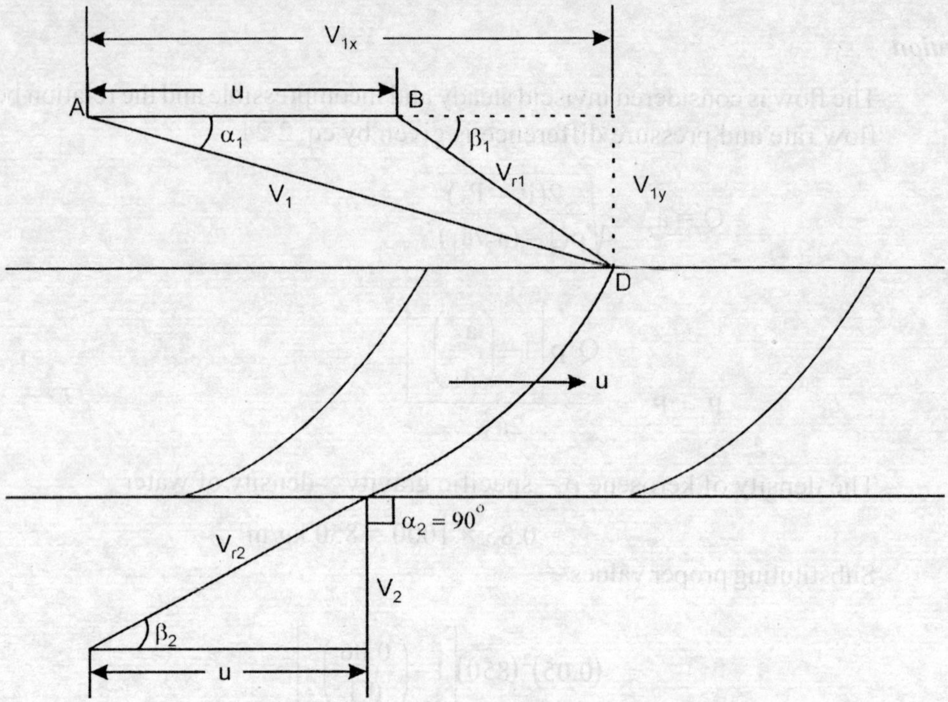

Fig. 2.23

To determine the inlet angle β_1, consider the inlet velocity triangle ABD. The velocity of the fluid relative to vane at inlet in V_{r1} must be tangential to the vane and make an angle β_1 with the direction of motion.

$$\tan \beta_1 = \frac{CD}{BC} = \frac{V_1 \sin \alpha_1}{(V_1 \cos \alpha_1 - u)}$$

Substituting $V_1 = 36$ m/s; $u = 15$ m/s and $\alpha_1 = 30^o$

$$\tan \beta_1 = \frac{36 \times 0.5}{(36 \times 0.866 - 15)} = 1.13 \quad \therefore \beta_1 = 48^o.$$

To determine outlet angle β_2, as V_2 has no component in the direction of motion, outlet angle β_2 in given by

$$\cos \beta_2 = \frac{u}{V_{r2}}, \text{ but } V_{r2} = 0.85\ V_{r1}$$

and from the inlet triangle

$$V_{r1} = \frac{CD}{\sin \beta_1} = \frac{V_1 \sin \alpha_1}{\sin \beta_1} = \frac{36 \times \sin 30}{\sin 48}$$

$$V_{r1} = 24.2 \text{ m/s}$$

$$V_{r2} = 0.85 \times V_{r1} = 0.85 \times 24.2 = 20.57$$

$$\cos \beta_2 = \frac{u}{V_{r2}} = \frac{15}{20.57} = 0.729$$

$$\therefore \quad \beta_2 = 43^o.$$

(b) Since the jet strikes series of vanes perhaps mounted on the periphery of a wheel so that each vane moves on its place is taken by the next in the series, the average length of the jet does not alter and whole flow from the nozzle of diameter d is deflected by the vanes.

Mass flow rate of the fluid from the nozzle

$$\dot{m} = \rho \times \frac{\pi}{4} d^2 \times V_1 = 1000 \times \frac{\pi}{4} (0.1)^2 \times 36 = 282.8 \text{ kg/s}$$

Velocity component of V_1 in direction of $X = V_1 \cos \alpha_1$

$$V_{1x} = 36 \times 0.866 = 31.17 \text{ m/s}$$

$$V_{2x} = V_2 \cos \alpha_2 = V_2 \cos 90^o = 0$$

Force on the direction of motion

$$F = \dot{m} (V_{1x} - V_{2x}) = 282.8 (31.17) = 8814 \text{ N}$$

$$F = 8814 \text{ N}$$

E.2.13 ***Example of a stationary deflector***

A deflector turns a sheet of water through an angle of 30° as shown in Fig. 2.24. What force is necessary to hold the deflector in place if mass flow rate is 32 kg/s?

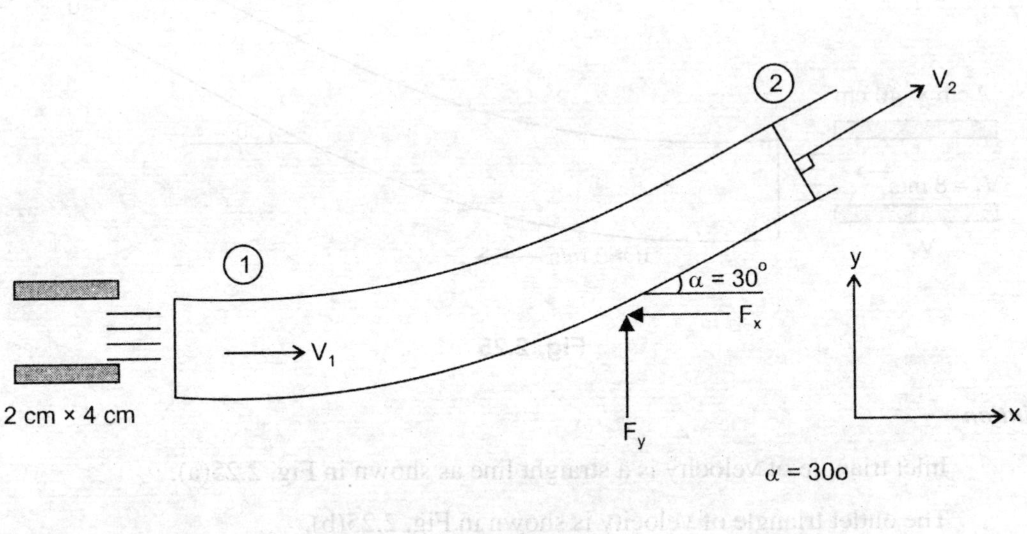

Fig. 2.24

Solution

Mass flow rate in = 32 kg/s

The velocity $V_1 = \dfrac{m}{\rho \times \text{area}} = \dfrac{32}{1000 \times 0.02 \times 0.04} = 40$ m/s

According to Bernoullis equation if there is no pressure drop in the deflector then velocity $V_1 = V_2$.

The force produced in the x-direction

$$F_x = \text{Mass flow rate} \times \text{change of velocity}$$

$$F_x = \dot{m}\,(V_1 - V_{2x}) = \dot{m}\,(V_1 - V_2 \cos\alpha) = 32\,(40 - 40 \times \cos 30)$$

$$= 32\,(40 - 34.6) = 172.8 \text{ N}$$

$$F_y = \dot{m}\,(V_1 - V_{2y}) = 32\,(40 - 40 \sin 30)$$

$$= 32\,(40 - 40 \times 0.5) = 640 \text{ N}$$

E.2.14 ***Example of a moving deflector***

A deflector shown in Fig. 2.25 moves to the right at 3 m/s while the nozzle remains stationary. Determine the force components needed to move the deflector. The jet velocity is 8 m/s. The nozzle area is 2 cm × 40 cm.

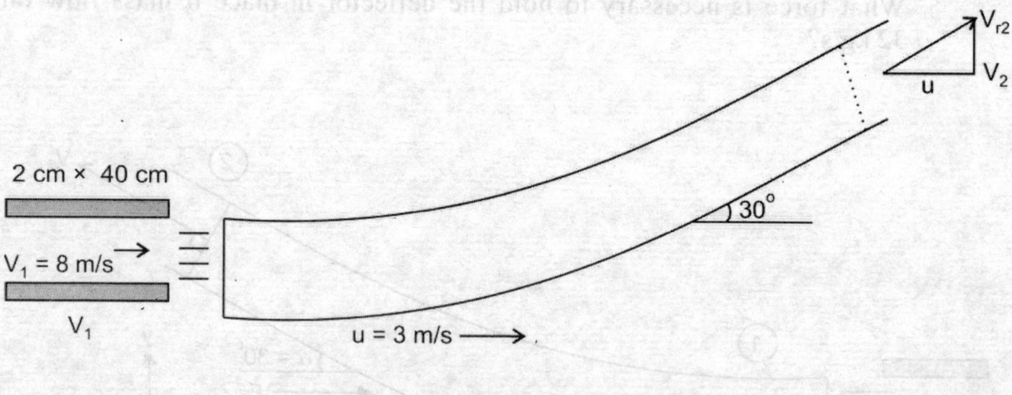

Fig. 2.25

Solution

Inlet triangle of velocity is a straight line as shown in Fig. 2.25(a).

The outlet triangle of velocity is shown in Fig. 2.25(b).

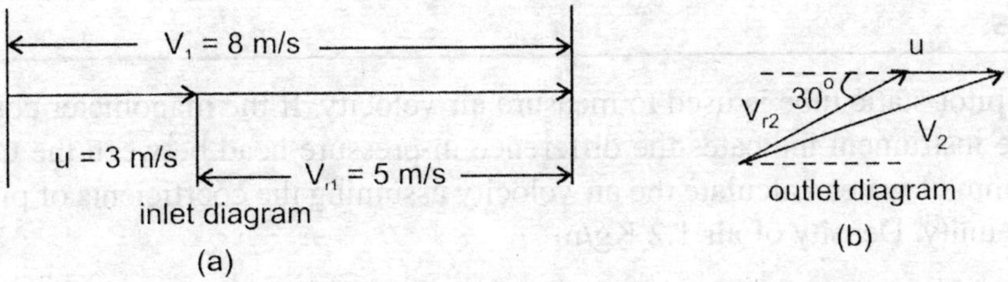

Fig. 2.25(a) & (b) Inlet and outlet velocity diagrams.

Bernoullis equation can be used to show that the velocity of the sheet $V_{r1} = V_{r2} =$ 5 m/s as observed from the deflector.

Mass flow rate is calculated on velocity $V_{r1} = 5$ m/s

$$\dot{m} = \rho A V_{r1} = 1000 \times 0.02 \times 0.4 \times 5 = 40 \text{ kg/s}$$

Force in the x-direction

$$F_y = \text{Mass flow rate} \times \text{change of velocity}$$

$$F_x = \dot{m}\ [(V_{r1x} - V_{r2x})]$$

$$= \dot{m}\ [(V_{r1x} - V_{r2} \cos 30^o)]$$

$$F_x = 40\ [5 - 5 \times 0.866] = 26.8 \text{ N}$$

$$F_y = [(V_{r1y} - V_{r2y})] \quad \text{as } V_{r1y} = 0$$

$$F_y = -\dot{m}\ V_{r2y} = -\dot{m}\ V_{r2y} \sin 30 = -40 \times 5 \times 0.5$$

$$= 100 \text{ N}$$

Problems

P.2.1 A pitot-static tube is used to measure air velocity. If the manometer connected to the instrument indicates the difference in pressure head between the tappings of 4 mm of water, calculate the air velocity assuming the coefficients of pitot tube to be unity. Density of air 1.2 Kg/m^3.

P.2.2 A nozzle is attached to a pipe as shown in Fig. 2.26. The inside diameter of the pipe is 100 mm while the nozzle jet diameter is 50 mm. If the pressure at inlet is 500 kPa, determine the jet velocity.

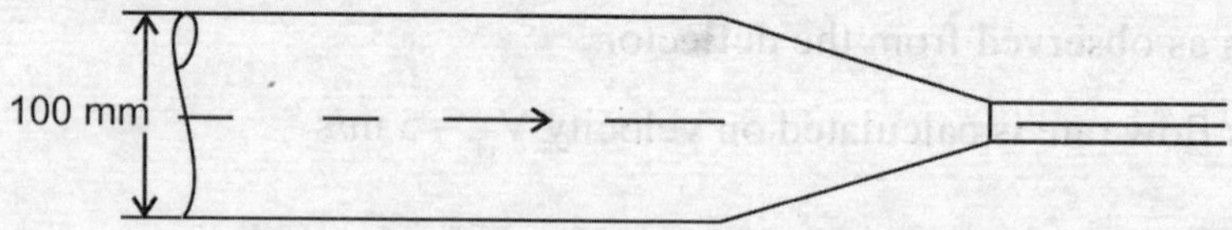

Fig. 2.26

P.2.3 Water flows from upper reservoir to lower reservoir while passing through a turbine as shown in Fig. 2.27. Determine the power generated by the turbine.

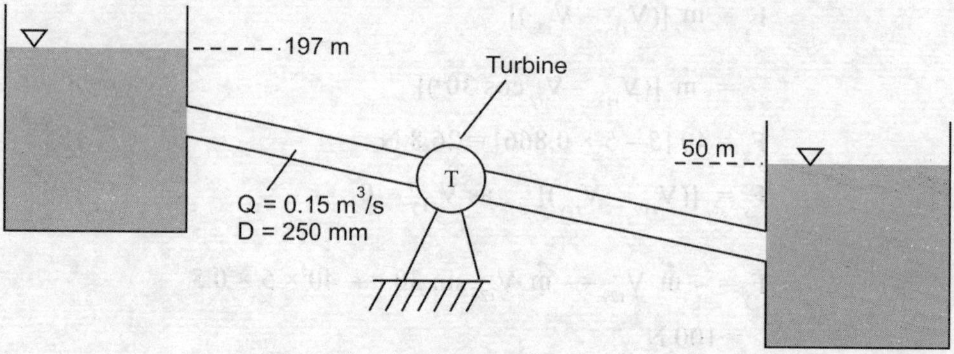

Fig. 2.27

P.2.4 A large artery in a person's body can be approximated by a tube of diameter 9 mm and length 0.35 m. Assume that the blood has a viscosity of approximately 4×10^{-3} and sp. gravity of 1.0 and that the pressure at the beginning of artery is equal to 120 mm of Hg. If the flow were steady (it is not in reality) with velocity equal to 0.2 m/s, determine Reynold's number and pressure at the end of the artery if it is oriented (a) horizontal (b) vertically up (flow upwards).

P.2.5 Glycerine of viscosity 0.9 N-s/m^2 and density 1260 kg/m^3 is pumped along a horizontal pipe 6.5 m long, of diameter 0.01 m at a flow rate of 1.8 *l*/min. Determine

Reynold's member and pressure drop using Hagen Poiseullie equation given below

$$\Delta p = \frac{128\, l\, \mu\, Q}{\pi\, d^4}$$

where

l = length of pipe in m

μ = viscosity in N-s/m^2

Q = flow rate in m^3/s

d = diameter of the pipe in m.

P.2.6 Water flows from a lake as shown in Fig. 2.28 at a rate of 0.112 m^3/s. Is the device inside the building a pump or a turbine? Explain and determine the power of the device. Neglect all minor losses and assume the friction factor f = 0.025 pipeline the hydraulic losses is calculated by the formula $h_f = f\frac{l V^2}{2gd}$, where f is friction factor, l is length of pipe, V the velocity and d the diameter of pipe.

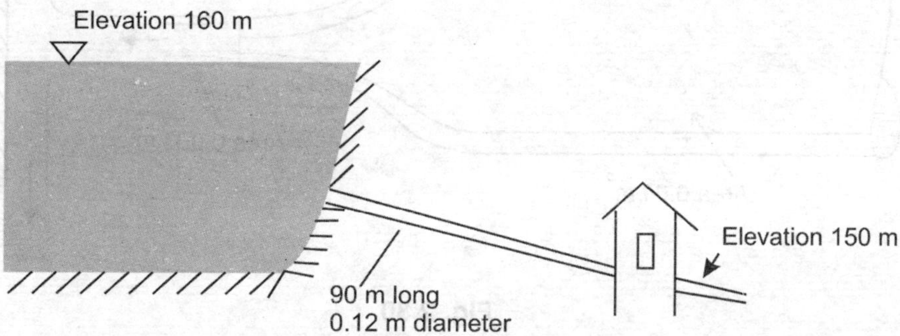

Fig. 2.28

P.2.7 A manometer positioned inside a cylinder is shown in the Fig. 2.29 and reads 4 cms of water. Estimate the velocity assuming inviscid flow. The temperature of air is 20 °C.

P.2.8 Air flows into the atmosphere from a nozzle and strikes a vertical plate as shown in Fig. 2.30. A horizontal force of 12N is required to hold the plate in place. Determine the reading on the pressure gauge. Assume the flow to be incompressible and frictionless.

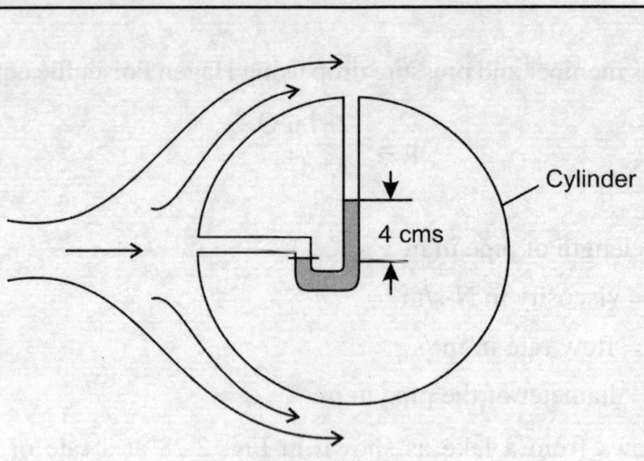

Fig. 2.29

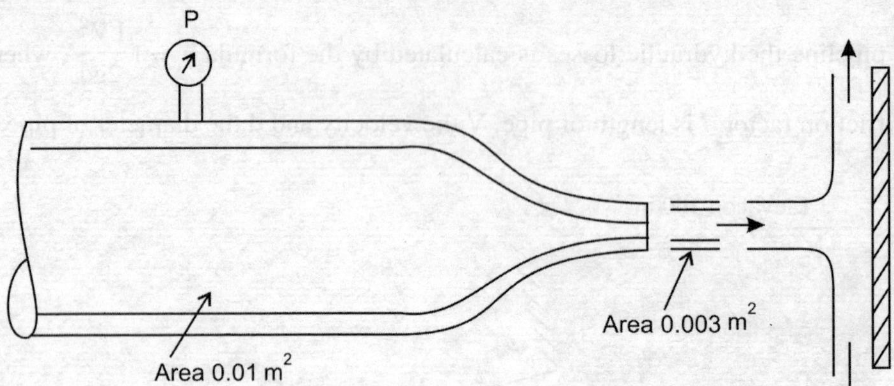

Fig. 2.30

P.2.9 For the flow shown in Fig. 2.31 estimate the pressure P_1 and velocity V_1, if $V_2 = 20$ m/s and H = 5 cm.

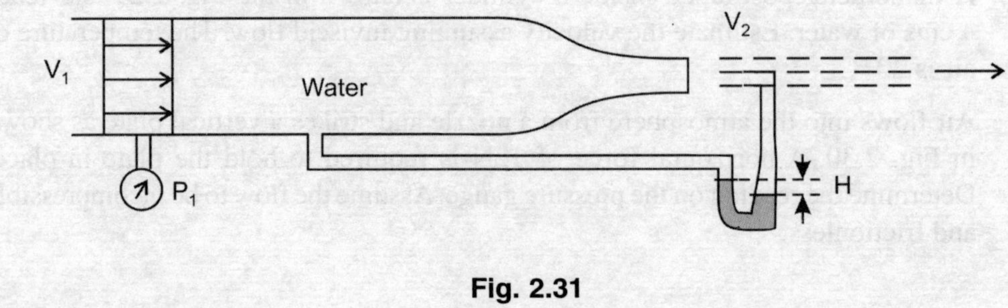

Fig. 2.31

P.2.10 A wind tunnel shown in Fig. 2.32 is designed to draw air from the atmosphere and produce a velocity of 100 m/s in the test section. The fan is located downstream of the test section. What pressure is to be expected in the test section if the atmospheric pressure and temperature 92 kPa and 20 °C.

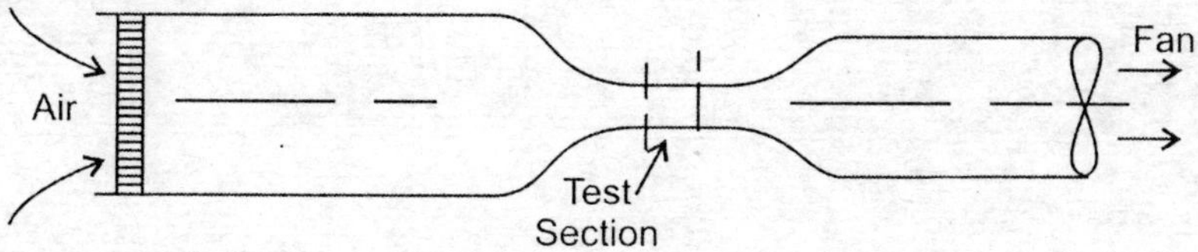

Fig. 2.32

P.2.11 A vacuum cleaner is capable of creating a vacuum of 2 kPa inside the hose. What maximum velocity would be expected in the hose?

CHAPTER - 3

Thermal and Hydropower Plants

Overall view of Two 640 MW each steam power station at Maastrich Netherlands built with Dutch company.

***Courtesy*: Black - Durr, Germany.**

3.1 Introduction

Electrical energy is the cleanest form of energy used in household appliances, street lighting, and in small and large industries. Energy is available in various forms and can be converted from one form to another. Electrical energy is produced in large power houses and is transmitted to users by cables. The more a country is developed the more the energy utilised by the people for good living. In fact the criteria for a developed nation is how much energy is being used by each person and that is the gauge of development of the country. If the energy needs are satisfied one can enjoy a comfortable life. Every effort is being made by engineers, research organisations and power plant producers to produce cheap electrical energy. In thermal power plants the fossil fuel generally used is coal, oil or gas. In hydro power plants the source is water. The countries which have large reserves of fossil fuel are in a better way to solve energy-related problems than countries which lack these reserves. The countries which have large oil reserves are Iran, Iraq, Saudi Arabia, Russia, USA and the countries which lack oil reserves are India, Japan, UK and some African nations. But the oil can be transported by pipelines from one country to another travelling some thousands of kilometers, or through pipelins under the sea, or by huge shipliners. Oil production is generally rated in barrels and each barrel is about 160 litres. Oil-producing countries produce several millions of barrel per day that is why oil is sometimes called 'Black Gold'. Crude oil is obtained by boring oil wells underground or under the sea bed. Coal is another source of fuel used in power plants. It is used in crushed or powder form (pulverised). Coal is obtained from coal mines, located several hundred meters below the surface of the earth. It has to be chemically treated before it can be used in power plants. Coal contains some percentage of ash about i.e., 3 to 10%. Ash removal is a big problem. Some varieties of coal found in India contain as much as 40% ash still being used as fuel. The coal-fired power plants has low thermal efficiency than oil-fired plants, as heating value of coal is generally 30-35 MJ/kg compared to oil which is about 45-48 MJ/kg. Moreover, oil is used in vapour form which mixes readily with the molecules of air giving high rate of combustion than coal. Gas is perhaps the ideal fuel to be used in thermal power plants. It is clean, efficient and available in gaseous state as air. So one can expect efficient combustion. The plants also have high thermal efficiency.

The cheapest way to produce electrical energy is by hydropower plants. First, water does not require any treatment as applied to fuels. It is abundant and free. The only criteria is water must have a fall from a height or create head, as it is called, and be available in large quantities for power generation. Dams are constructed across the river to store water. The water is conveyed to the turbines by penstock which convert hydraulic energy to mechanical energy. Electrical generators convert it to electrical energy. India has large number of hydropower stations which produce thousands of kilowatts. Another advantage of hydropower plants is water discharged from the turbine can be used for agriculture. Nuclear power plants and solar power plants also produce electrical energy.

A solar power plant is shown in Fig 3.1. The solar energy focussed with an array of heliostats on a central receiver at the top of the tower is transferred by liquid sodium as medium of heat transfer to a heat storage unit at the foot of the tower which is connected to steam generator. The high pressure super heated steam thus generated passes through a multi cylinder engine unit to drive a generator and produce electricity.

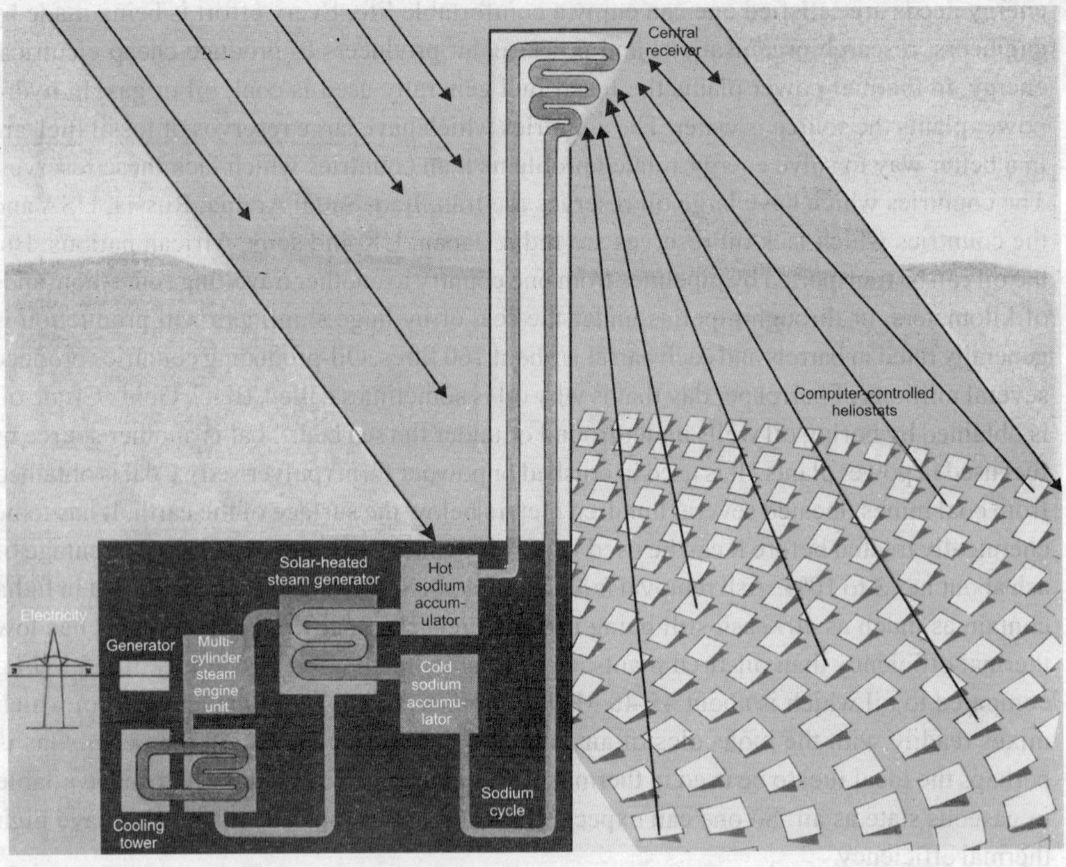

Fig 3.1 Solar energy power plant in Almenia, Spain.

Liquid sodium is heated to around 530 °C in the tube bundles. A heat exchanger transfers the solar thermal output to water/steam cycle for the steam power system. Liquid sodium has better heat transfer qualities than water. The 500 kw Almenia solar power plant has been supplying power to southern Spain grid system since 1981.

Steam power plant and gas turbine power plants are the two conventional ways to produce electricity on a large scale. The electricity can also be produced by diesel plants which work independently or in conjuction with steam and gas turbine power plants as peak units. Diesel power plants also work in hydropower plants as emergency units. Fossil fuels that are used in these power plants are depleting in the world and at one point of time will not be available. These are therefore non-renewable source of energy and cannot be depended upon the years to come. Mankind looks for other renewable sources such as solar energy. Technology as such is not economical and is still not available for solar energy to be utilised on large scale. Again bright sunlight is not available throughout the day at any place. Other renewable source of energy is wind mills. The energy produced by wind mills is intermittent and difficult to connect to main eletrical power grid.

So, where water is available for producing electric power it is perhaps the best renewable source of energy. Hydropower plants are clean, highly efficient and environmental friendly. They do not cause any pollution problems. They are also the source of tourist attraction.

3.2 Steam Turbine Power Plant

Steam turbine is the main component in power plants in both large and small units, and industrial steam systems. The steam turbine has been tailored for large fossil, nuclear, combined-cycle, geothermal, and small power facilitates and mechanical-drive service. The turbine island – including condensers, cooling systems, and cooling towers, instrumentation and control system, condensate/feed water pumps–make up water treatment systems, valves, pumps. Piping will continue to anchor the next generation of power plants. At present technology with high pressure superheat and reheat and expansion of steam in multi cylinders (high pressure medium and low pressure) on a single shaft steam turbine can produce more thant 1000 MW of power. Thus steam turbine has no match with other machines.

The basic thermo dynamic cycle of steam power plant is shown in Fig. 3.2.

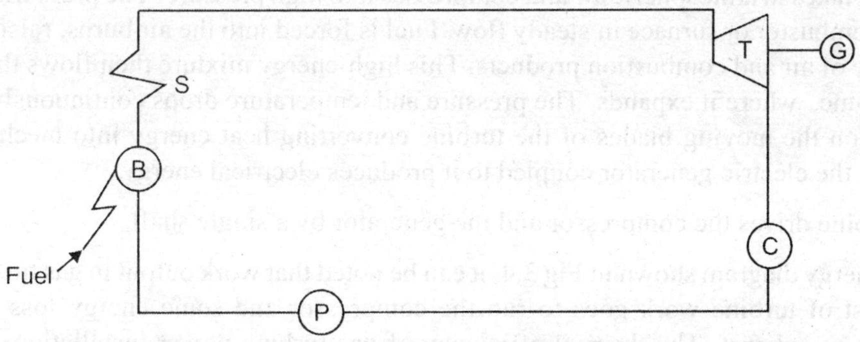

Fig 3.2 Schematic diagram of Steam Power Plant
B - Boiler, S - Super heater, T - Turbine, G - Generator, C - Condenser, P - Pump.

Fossil fuel is burnt in the furnace of the boiler and hot gases pass over the water tubes, heating the water inside the tubes. The water tubes are connected to the main boiler drum where high pressure, saturated steam is produced. The steam is then raised to a temperature higher than saturation temperature in the super heater. High pressure and high temperature super heated steam then enters the steam turbine. The steam expands in the turbine from a high pressure to low pressure area of the condensor. The heat energy is converted to mechanical energy to drive a generator to produce electricity. The exhaust steam from the turbine is condensed inside a condenser by circulating water of the condenser tubes. The condensate is sent back to the boiler by condensate pumps. The steam power plant needs a large quantity of water for producing power and much more water to cool the exhaust steam from the turbine. So it is imperative that steam plants are located near river, lake or sea.

The steam explands in the turbine from a very high pressure to a low pressure of the condenser (less than atmospheric) with a large enthalpy drop. A very large quantity of water has to be circulated in the condenser and that heated up by condensation of steam so circulating water is cooled in cooling tower–a visible sight for the power plant from outside. Power produced by the turbine is mass flow rate of steam multiplied by the enthalpy drop.

3.3 Gas Turbine Power Plant

Thousands of gas turbines are serving daily in prop-jet and jet engines for military and commercial aircraft with hundreds more found in rail, marine and automotive service as prime movers. Versatility of gas turbines is also demonstrated by its growing acceptance in a wide variety of stationery energy systems for processing, power generation and mechanical drives. Recent developments include adaptation of standard jet engines to base load generation and peaking services.

An open gas turbine cycle system employs a compressor, combustor, gas turbine and generator for producing electrical power. The schematic diagram is shown in Fig. 3.3. Rotating compressor takes in atmospheric air and compresses it to high pressure. The pressurised air goes into combustor or furnace in steady flow. Fuel is forced into the air burns, raising the temperature of air and combustion products. This high-energy mixture then flows through the gas turbine, where it expands. The pressure and temperature drops continuously as it does work on the moving blades of the turbine converting heat energy into mechanical energy, and the electric generator coupled to it produces electrical energy.

The turbine drives the compressor and the generator by a single shaft.

In the energy diagram shown in Fig 3.4, it can be noted that work output in gas turbine is less as most of turbine work goes to run the compressor and some energy loss to the atmosphere as exhaust. The thermal efficiency of gas turbine power installation is less compared to steam power plant.

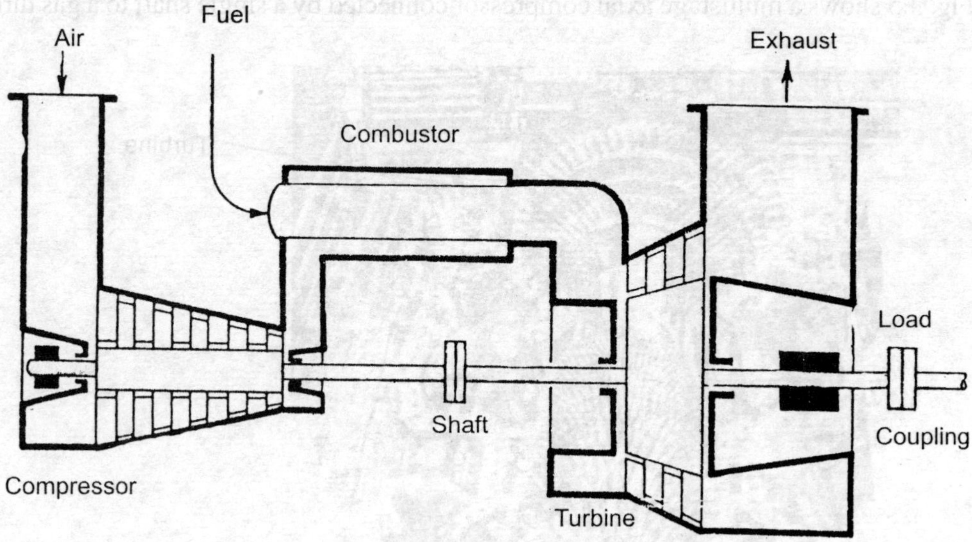

Fig 3.3 A schematic diagram of gas tubine power plant.

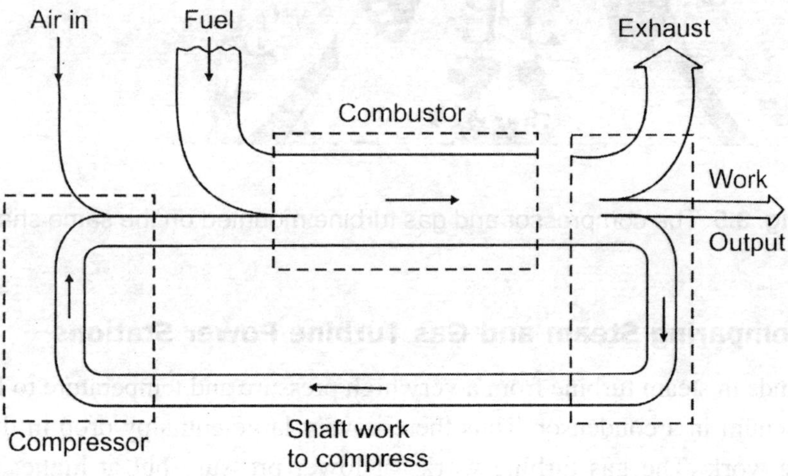

Fig. 3.4 Energy diagram of gas turbine power plant.

Fig. 3.5 shows a multistage axial compressor connected by a single shaft to a gas turbine.

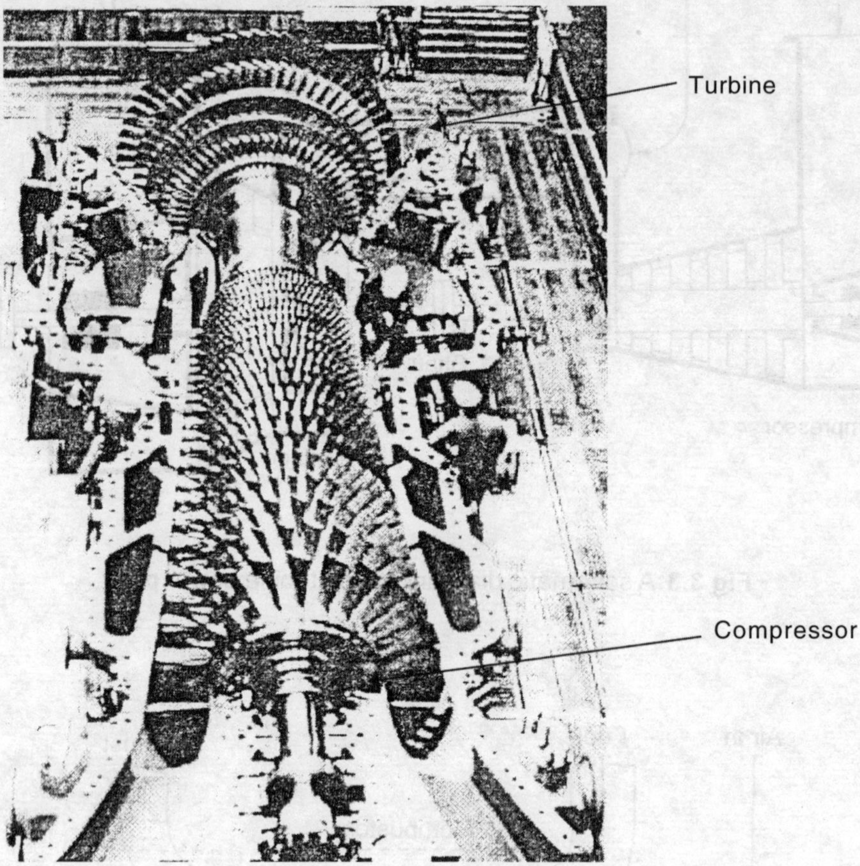

Fig. 3.5 The compressor and gas turbine mounted on the same shaft.

3.3.1 Comparing Steam and Gas Turbine Power Stations

Steam expands in steam turbine from a very high pressure and temperature to low pressure almost a vacuum in a condensor. Thus there is very large enthalpy drop in the turbine to produce the work. The gas turbine works at lower pressure but at higher temperature than steam turbine. The exhaust of gas turbine is atmospheric. Therefore the enthalpy drop in gas turbine is less and high temperature gas is exhausted into atmosphere which is energy loss. The overall efficiency of gas turbine power plant is almost half of steam power plant.

The steam turbine power plant requires lot of water whereas for gas turbine power plant water is not a criteria. It can be installed even in a desert. Time period is a factor in steam power plant for planning, installing and commissioning and it takes some years before it is ready for generating power.

The gas turbine power unit can be installed in a few days as compact units are available only to be connected to chimney. Steam power plant requires a lot of land for installing boiler, steam turbine, generator, and various other units such as condensing plant, heat recovery units. The gas turbine does not require so much land, and can easily be installed and can be connected to the grid in few minutes after the installation. With the present-day technology steam turbine can produce about 1000 MW on a single shaft, whereas gas turbines can produce 100-150 MW of power.

3.4 Combined Cycle Power Plants

Gas turbine can combine with steam power plants to form combined cycle plants as shown in Fig. 3.6. A high-efficiency steam turbine is combined thermodynamically to a low-efficiency gas turbine. The high temperature exhaust gas from the gas turbine is led into the heat recovery steam generator (HRSG) thus increasing the mass flow rate of gas circulation, decreasing the fuel of the steam unit, developing more power and thus increasing the

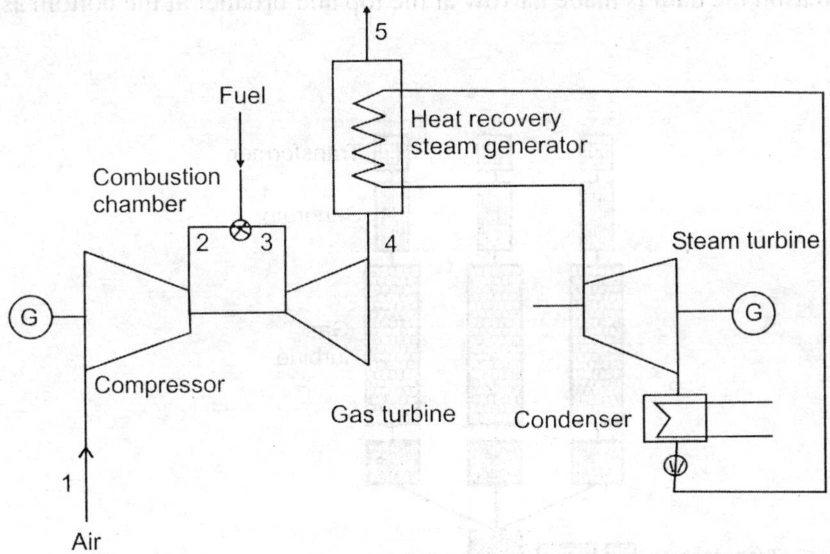

Fig. 3.6 A Schematic layout of combined cycle power plant.

efficiency. The combined cycle power plants have become very common in present times for their efficiency and better heat utilisation.

The arrangement of gas turbine and steam turbine at Lumut Power Plant is shown in Fig 3.7(a) & (b). The three gas turbines produce electric power by three electric generators. The exhaust gas is connected to three HRSGs. The steam produced by three HRSGs goes to a single steam turbine and electricity is produced by the generator. By this way steam turbine produces additional electric power by using exhaust gases with no additional fuel. Thus it raises the overall efficiency of the plant.

3.5 Hydropower Plants

In hydropower plants the potential energy of water is converted into mechanical energy in water turbine and then to electricity by electric generator. The potential energy is created by constructing a dam (Fig. 3.8) across the river. It is a cement concrete wall storing water as reservoir at upstream side of the dam. The water at head water - level which passes through the turbine and leaves downstream of the dam as tail water. The turbines work between head and tail water level. The forces acting on the dam are wind forces, pressure forces of water on the upstream side of the dam. The pressure is zero at top level and increases to a maximum at the bottom of the dam. The structure must withstand the pressure of water. Again the pressure of the silt deposits is zero at the top level and maximum at the bottom. For stability reason the dam is made narrow at the top and broader at the bottom as shown in Fig 3.8.

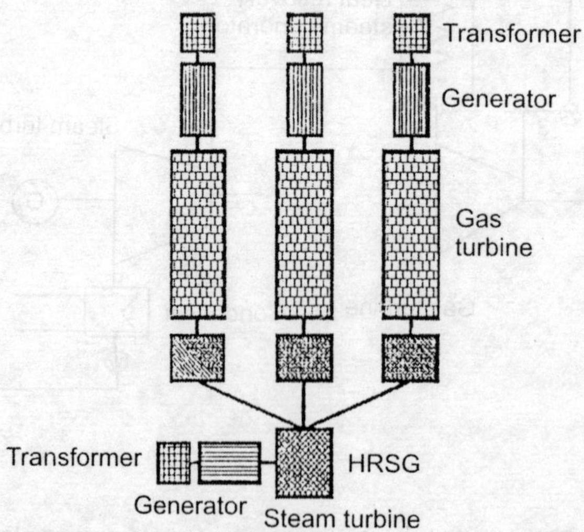

Fig. 3.7(a) Combined cycle power plant with gas turbine, HRSG, steam turbine.

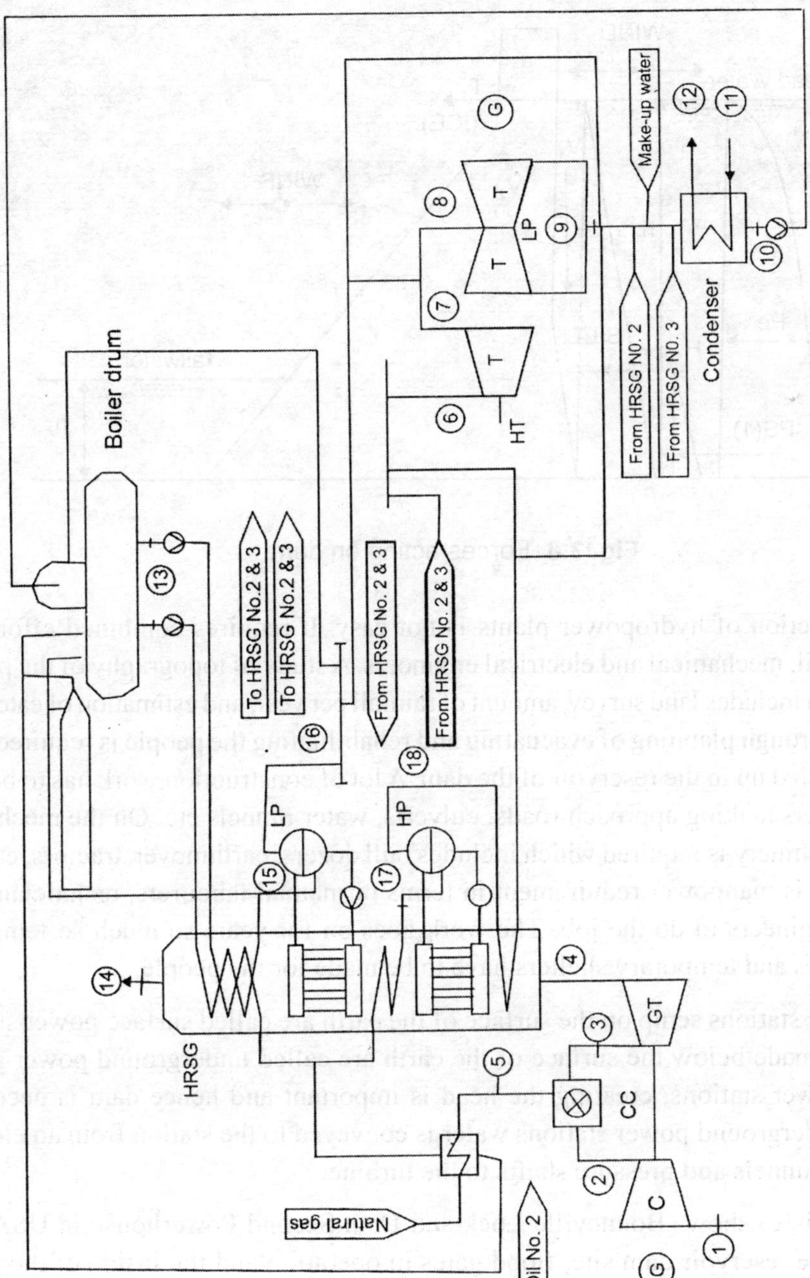

Fig. 3.7(b) Schematic layout of combined cycle power plant situated at Lumut Power Plant, Perak State in Malaysia.
Courtesy: National Power Electricity Board (Malaysia).

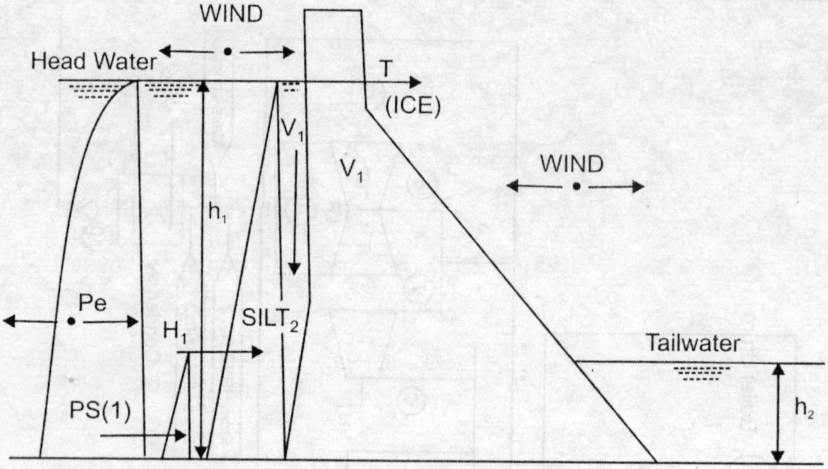

Fig. 3.8 Forces acting on dam.

The construction of hydropower plants is not easy. It requires combined efforts and expertise of civil, mechanical and electrical engineers. A study of topography of the place is important which includes land survey, amount of rainfall per year, and estimation of catchment area. Also a thorough planning of evacuating and rehabilitating the people is required when water will be filled up in the reservoir of the dam. A lot of construction work has to be done by civil engineers making approach roads, culverts, water tunnels etc. On the mechanical side, heavy machinery is required which includes bull dozers, earthmover, tractors, etc. The most important is manpower requirement in terms of manual labourers, technicians, and power plant engineers to do the job. The work goes on for years so much so temporary housing colonies and temporary shelters have to be made for the people.

Hydropower stations setup on the surface of the earth are called surface power stations whereas those made below the surface of the earth are called underground power plants. For surface power stations, creating the head is important and hence dam is necessary, whereas for underground power stations water is conveyed to the station from an elevated level by water tunnels and pressure shafts to the turbine.

Figs. 3.9(a, b, c) show Bonneville Lock and Dam Second Powerhouse in USA. The figures show the reservoir dam site, flood gates in operation and the inside of the power house with elevators, and escalators.The arrows indicate suggested flow of traffic. The hydropower plants are clean, neat and environment friendly. The dam site gives marvellous view of the reservoir and one hears only the humming sound of the generators in the power house.

Fig. 3.9(a) Benneville Lock and Dam Second Powerhouse.

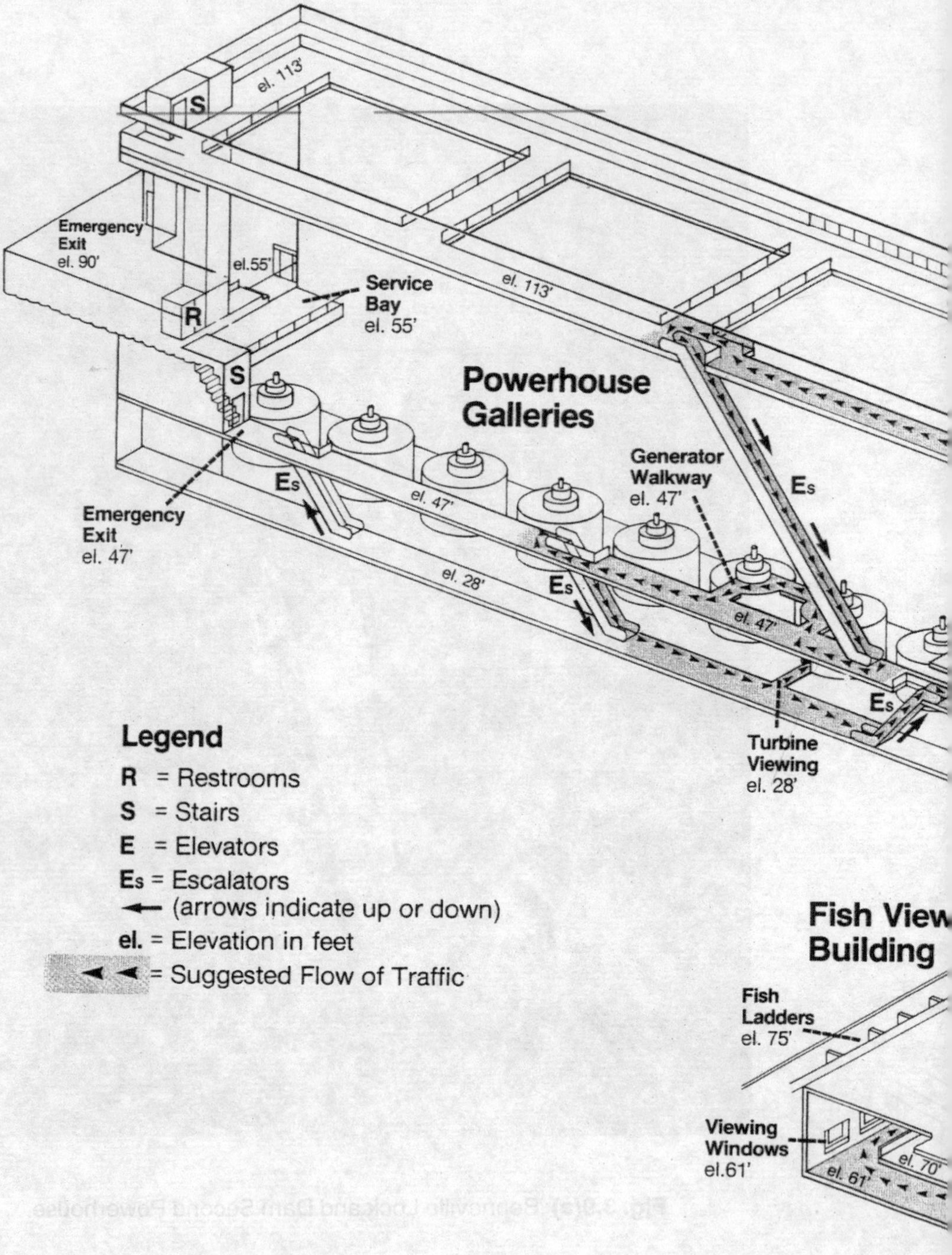

Fig. 3.9(b) Inside of the Po

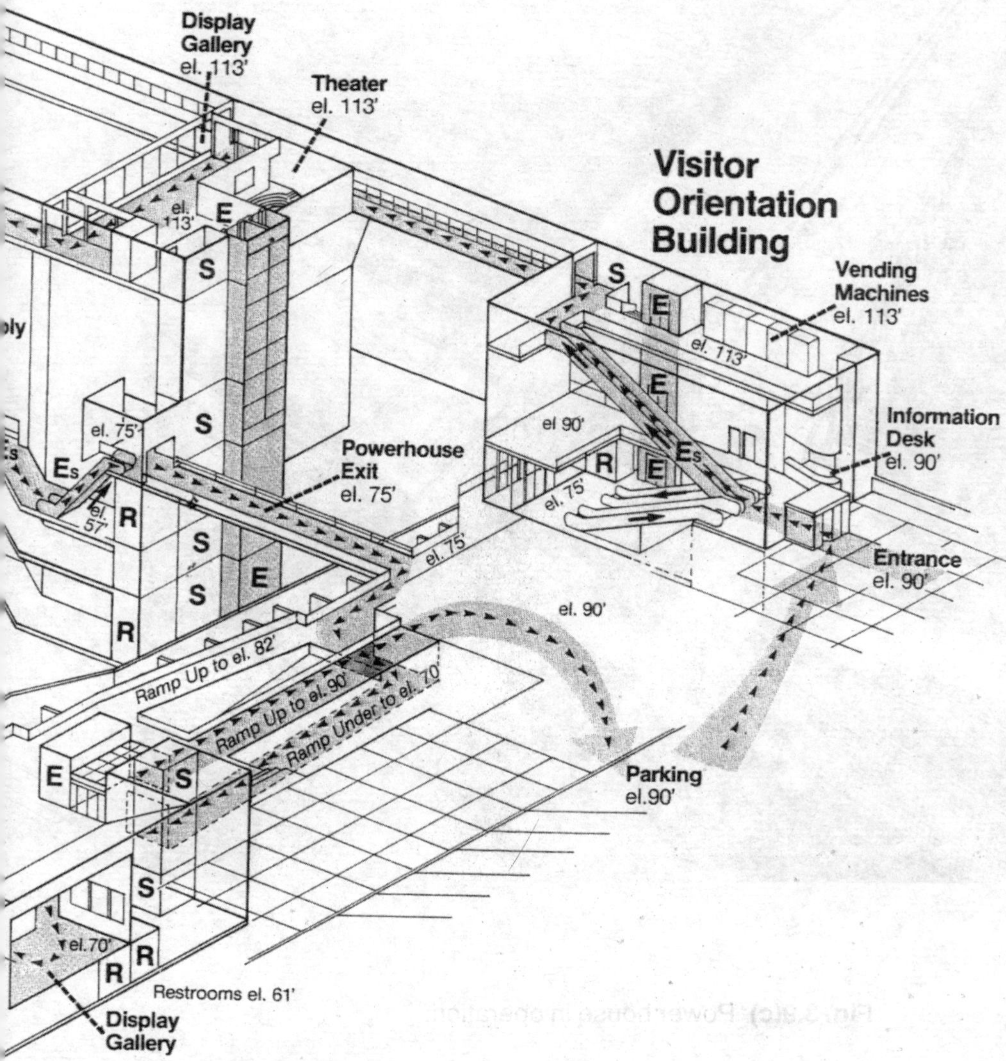

se with elevators and escalators.

Fig. 3.9(c) Power house in operation.

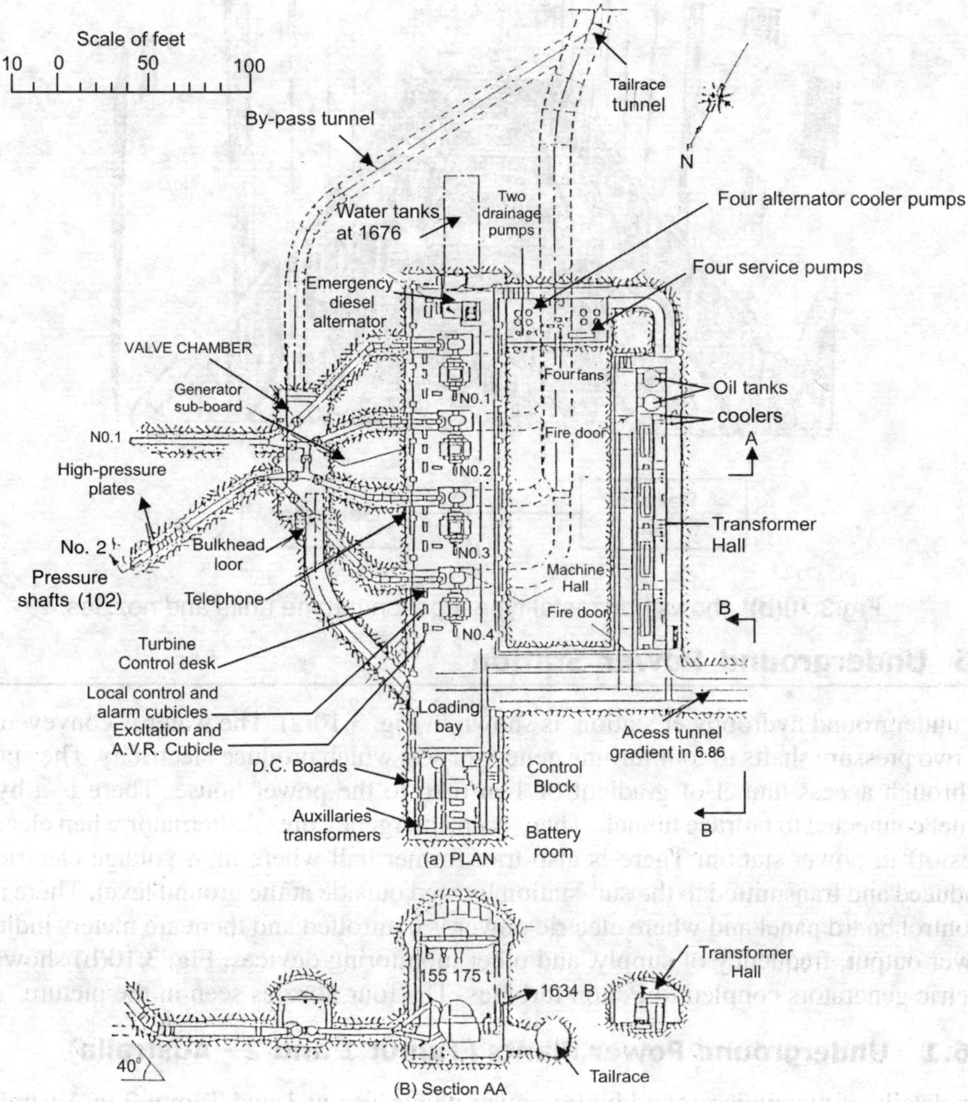

Fig. 3.10(a) Details of underground power station.

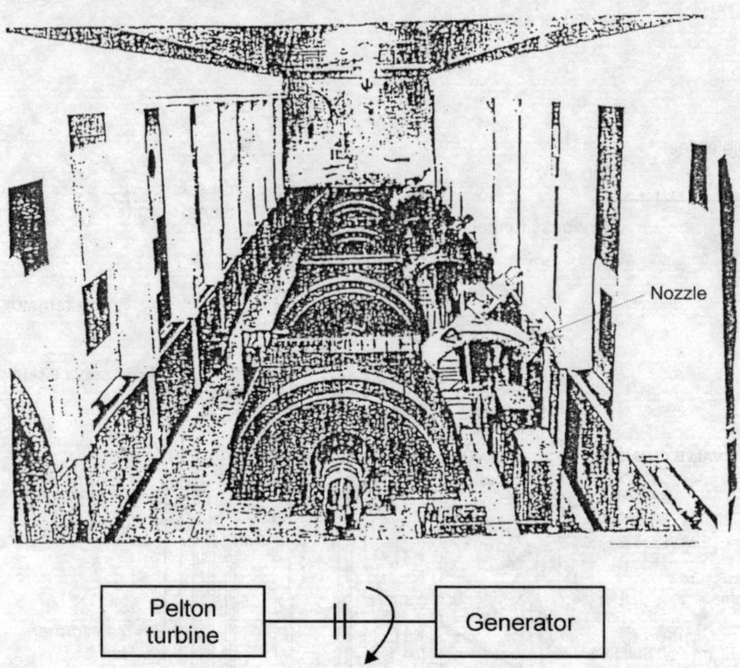

Fig 3.10(b) shows horizontal type 4 pelton turbine units and nozzles.

3.6 Underground Power Station

An underground hydropower station is shown in Fig. 3.10(a). The water is conveyed from the two pressure shafts to four turbine generator sets which produce electricity. The entrance is through access tunnel of gradient of 1 in 6.86 to the power house. There is a by-pass tunnel connected to tailrace tunnel. There is an emergency diesel alternator when electricity goes off in power station. There is also transformer hall where high voltage electricity is produced and transmitted to the sub-station located outside at the ground level. There is also a control board panel and where electric power is controlled and there are meters indicating power output, frequency of supply, and other monitoring devices. Fig. 3.10(b) shows four electric generators coupled to Pelton turbines. The four nozzles seen in the picture.

3.6.1 Underground Power Plants (Tumut 1 and 2 - Australia)

The details of two underground hydro power plants Tumut 1 and Tumut 2 in Australia are given. Also given are the details of Tooma-Tumut water tunnel. Fig. 3.11(a) gives the plan of the tunnel. The tunnel is about 14 km long with several intakes connected to tunnel Fig. 3.11(b) gives the profile of the tunnel and the elevation of the tunnel at different points and location of the intakes. Fig.3.11(c) gives the tunnel cross-section. The diameter of tunnel is 3.43 m with steel reinforcement and rock bolt supports to support the structure from landslide. There is also rail track for cleaning silt deposits which is very common in

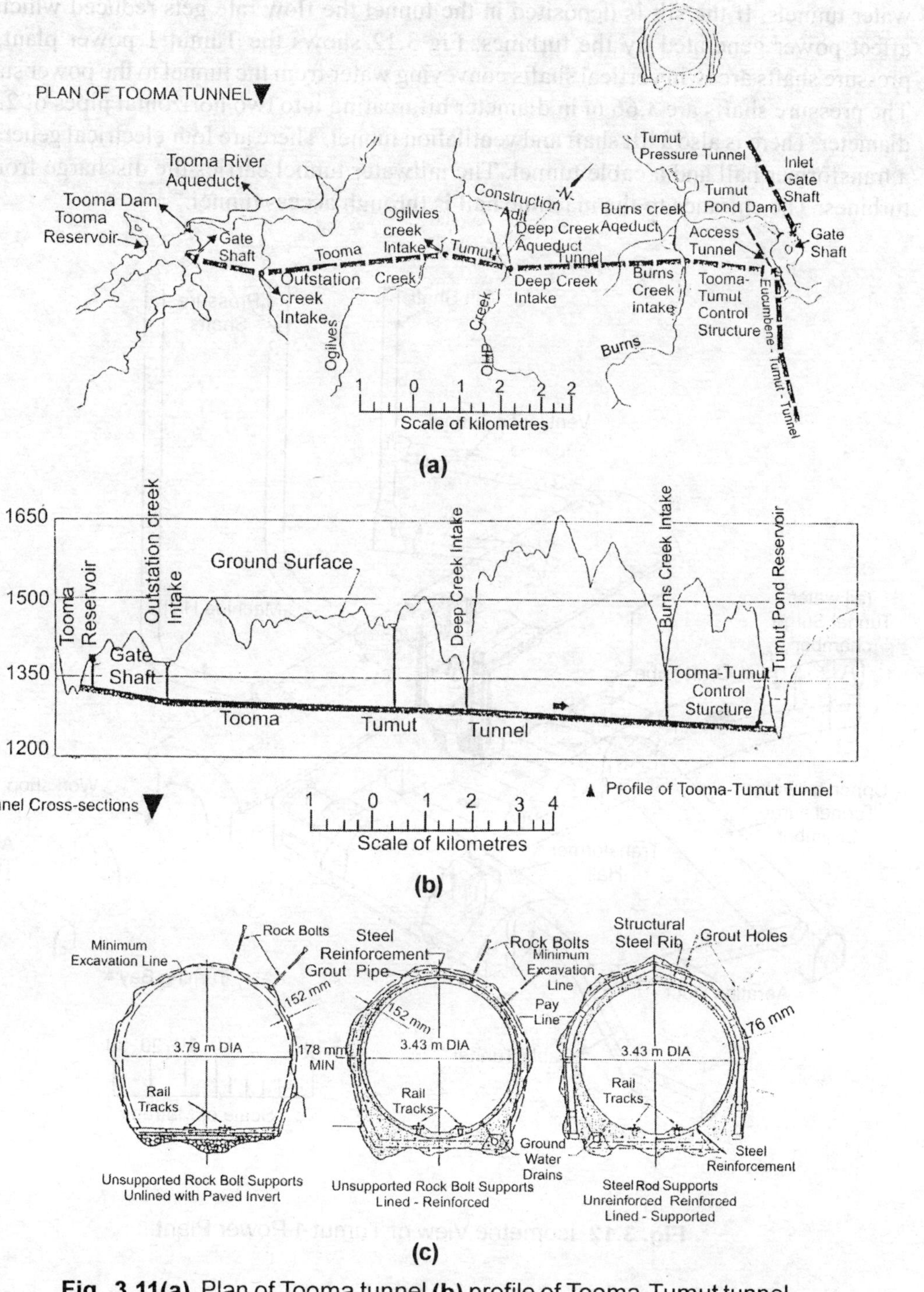

Fig. 3.11(a) Plan of Tooma tunnel **(b)** profile of Tooma-Tumut tunnel **(c)** Tunnel cross-section.

water tunnels. If the silt is deposited in the tunnel the flow rate gets reduced which will affect power generated by the turbines. Fig 3.12 shows the Tumut 1 power plant. The pressure shafts are twin vertical shafts conveying water from the tunnel to the power station. The pressure shafts are 3.66 m in diameter bifurcating into two horizontal pipes of 2.44 m diameter. There is also a lift shaft and ventilation tunnel. There are four electrical generators, a transformer hall and a cable tunnel. The tailwater tunnel carries the discharge from the turbines. The entrance to the machine hall is through access tunnel.

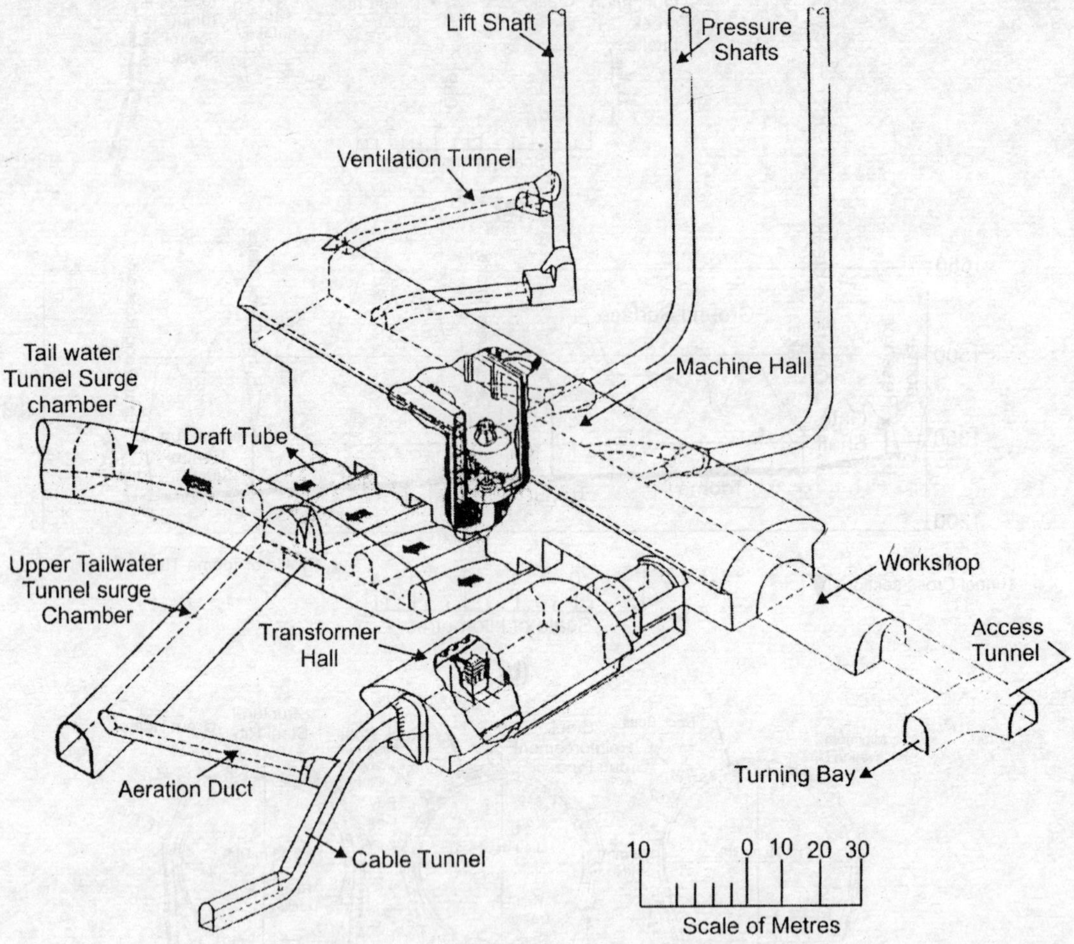

Fig. 3.12 Isometric View of Tumut 1 Power Plant.

Fig. 3.13 shows section through Tumut 2 power station. The water enters the turbine through main inlet valve. The turbine is vertical and electric generator is connected to the turbine by a vertical shaft with a coupling. There are 4 units with a total capacity of 280,000 kw. The discharge from the turbine is connected to the draft tube.

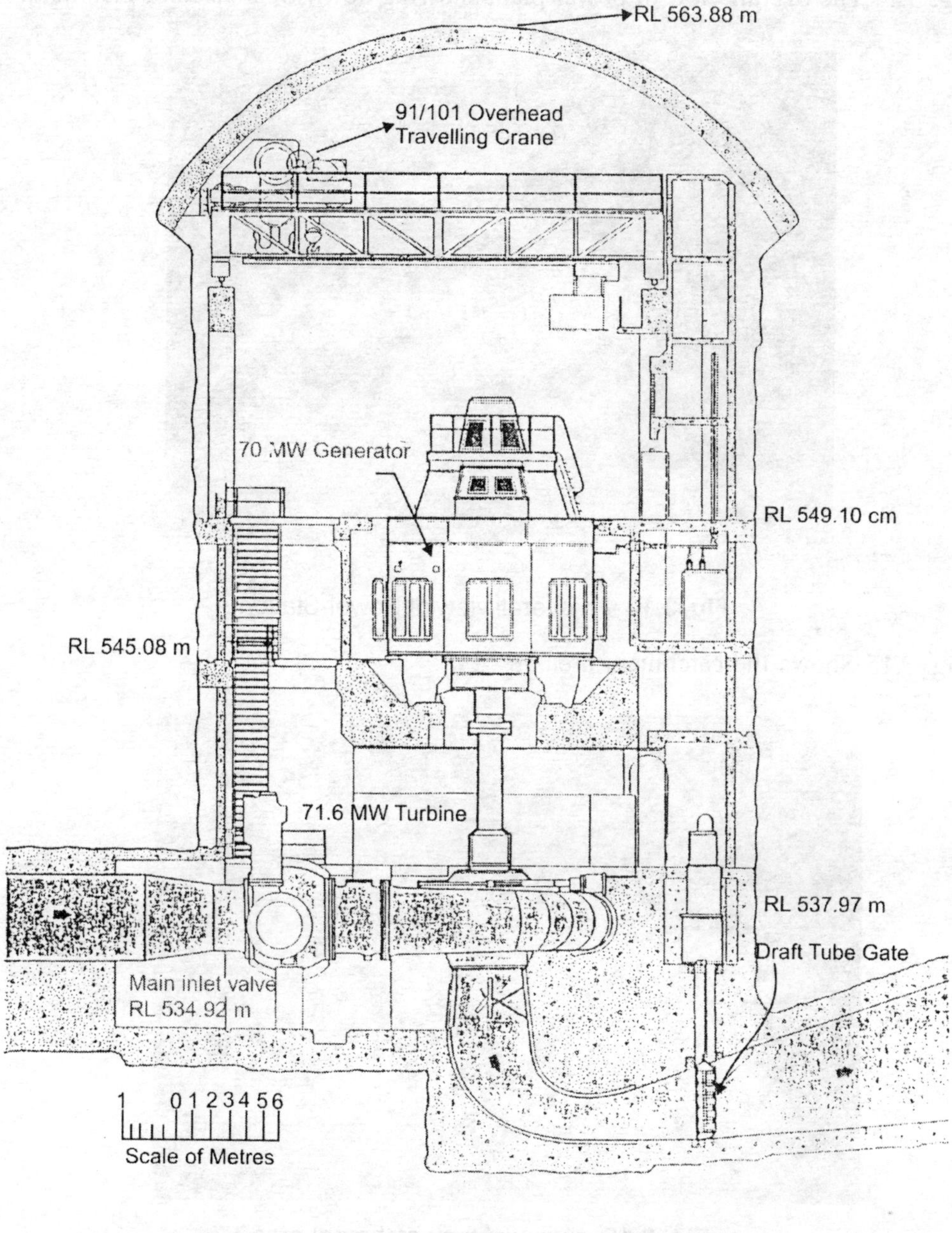

Fig. 3.13 Section through Tumut 2 power plant.

3.7 Surface Power Plant

The details of Temengor hydraulic power plant situated in Cameron Highlands, Perak State, Malaysia is shown in the following figures.

Fig. 3.14 The overall view of power plant showing downstream side of the plant.

Fig. 3.14 An overall view of Power Station.

Fig. 3.15 Shows the catchment area.

Fig. 3.15 A view of the catchment area.

Fig 3.16 Shows the gating system from where the water flows from the dam to 4 inlets.

Fig. 3.16 The gating system where water from the dam flows through 4 inlets.

Fig 3.17 Picture of one of the four inlets.

Fig. 3.17 Picture of one of the gates.

Fig 3.18 (a) (b): The spillway is used when the water rises above the maximum level or when it is flooding. The construction of power plant took $2\frac{1}{2}$ years. The installed capacity of power plant is 348 MW. There are 4 turbine units each of 90 MW capacity. The rated head is 101 m and speed of turbine is 214 rev/min.

Fig. 3.18(a) Spillway.

Fig. 3.18(b) Spillway.

3.7.1 Comparing Hydropower Plants with Thermal Power Plants

The cheapest way to produce electricity is by hydropower plants compared to thermal power plants. The capital cost is high and it takes long years of planning and construction. The maintenance cost is low. There is no pollution and the environment is clean. The hydropower plants are also useful for agriculture taking water of the tailrace. The overall efficiency is high as there are mainly hydraulic and mechanical losses. Life of the dam and hydro power plant is taken as 100 years whereas steam turbine plants have a life span ranging from 30 years to a maximum 50 years. The life of gas turbines is given in hours of working. The source in hydro power plants is water which is renewable source of energy whereas steam and gas turbines work on fossil fuels which are non-renewable source of energy. The generating capacity of the hydro power plants depends on reservoir capacity which depends on rainfall, whereas thermal power plants have no such problem.

The overall view of combined heat and power plant working on hard-coal fluid unit. The plant produces thermal output of 47 MW and electrical output of 19 MW (Fig. 3.19).

Fig. 3.19 The overall view of combined heat and power plant working on hard-coal fluid unit. The plant produces thermal output of 47 MW and electrical output of 19 MW.

KWU and the Japanese company Mitsubishi have each installed six gas turbine generator units at the R as Abq Fontas gas turbine power plant in Doha in the capital city of Sheikdom of Qater on the persian gulf. The exhaust from the gas turbines is used for desalination of sea water. The plant in capable of producing 630 MW electrical output and capable of producing 180,000 m^3 of drinking water (Fig. 3.20).

The overall view of Megalopolis coal-fired power plant with two 125 MW units and one 300 MW unit stands in the vicinity of a lignite field in Greece. The power plant is in operation since 1975. The lignite has a low heating value of 4000 KJ/Kg and has to be dressed in several stages. The power plant is justified because lignite reserves will last at least 50 years (Fig. 3.21).

After a construction period of 7 years the Graferenheinfild nuclear power plant near Schweinfurt supplied power to the grid system in Bavaria meeting about 20% of the energy demand(Fig. 3.22).

Fig. 3.20 Gas turbine power plant with disalination system.

Fig. 3.21 The overall view of Megalopolis coal-fired power plant with two 125 MW units and one 300 MW unit stands in the vicinity of a lignite field in Greece.

Fig. 3.22 A nuclear power plant.

CHAPTER - 4

Fluid Machinery

The 'Red Arrows' make their apperance in LIMA exhibition 1997, Malaysia.

4.1 Introduction

Fluid machines can be classified as:

- Positive displacement machines
- Rotodynamic machines.

In positive displacement machines fluid is drawn into a finite space bounded by mechanical parts, then sealed in it, and then forced out from space and the cycle is repeated. The flow is intermittent and depends on the dimensions of the space (chamber), and speed of the pump. Gear pumps, vane pumps are all positive displacement pumps.

In rotodynamic machines there is free passage between inlet and outlet of the machine without intermittent sealing taking place. In these machines there is a rotor which is able to rotate continuously and freely in the fluid. The transfer of energy is continuous which results in change of pressure or momentum of the fluid. Centrifugal blower, centrifugal pumps and hydraulic turbines are some examples of rotodynamic machines.

4.2 Classification of Fluid Machines

Fluid machines are dynamic fluid machines that add (for pump) or extract (for turbines) flow energy. The term pump is used when the working fluid is water or oil. The term compressor is used when the working fluid is air/gas. Fluid machines do a variety of jobs and are applied in hydro and thermal power stations, in aircraft as propulsive devices, in ships as propellers, in automobiles, and earth moving machinery.

Fluid machines serve in enormous array of applications in our daily lives, and they play an important role in modern world. The machines have a high power density (large power output per size of the machine) relatively few moving parts and high efficiency.

The two criteria, namely, the energy transfer and type of action, form the basis of classification of hydraulic machines, as shown in Fig. 4.1. From the chart it can be seen that pumps and compressors increase the energy of the fluid and may be positive displacement or rotodynamic. Fans are always rotodynamic. Turbine does work and is rotodynamic.

Further classification is based on flow and energy transfer. Fluid used as means of energy transfer.

(a) Classification based on the geometry of flow path:

- Radial flow;
- Axial flow;
- Mixed flow.

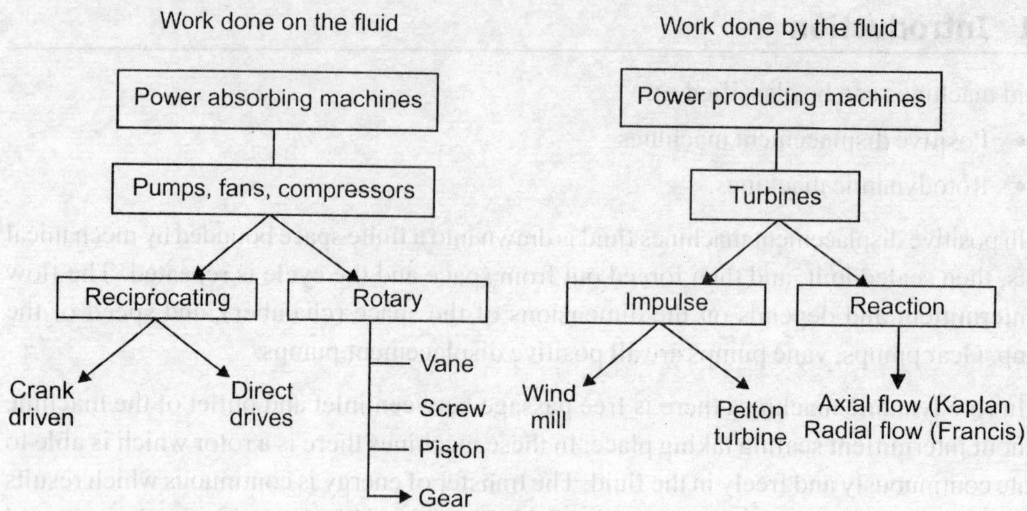

Fig. 4.1

In radial flow the flow path is essentially radial with significant changes in radius.

In axial flow machines the flow path is nearly parallel to the machine centre line and the path does not change.

In mixed flow it is partly axial and partly radial.

(b) Fluid machines can use any of the following forms of energy

- Heat energy (steam and gas turbines)
- Potential energy (hydraulic turbines)
- Kinetic energy (wind mills)

In power producing machines work is done by the fluid flow and in power absorbing machines work is done on the fluid to raise potential energy.

Fig 4.2(a) shows power producing machine.

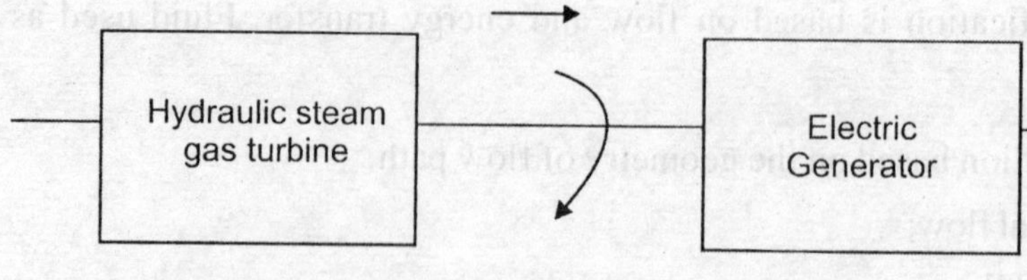

Fig. 4.2(a)

Fig 4.2(b) shows Power absorbing machine.

A pump is a turbo machine wherein the fluid is liquid and power is given by an electric motor to raise pressure of the fluid.

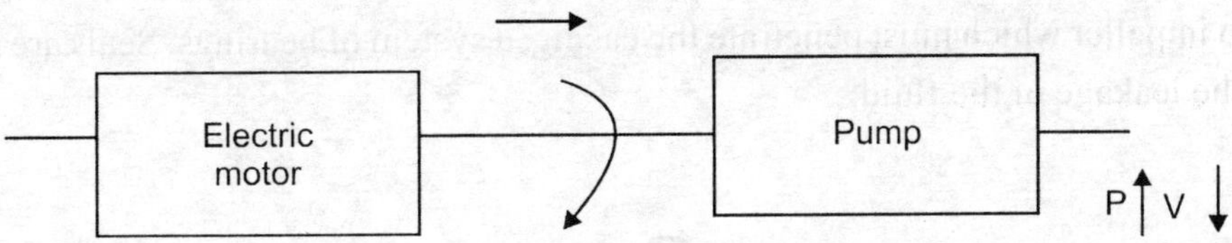

Fig. 4.2(b)

A compressor transmits power to a gas to raise pressure but with small increase in velocity (Fig. 4.2(c)).

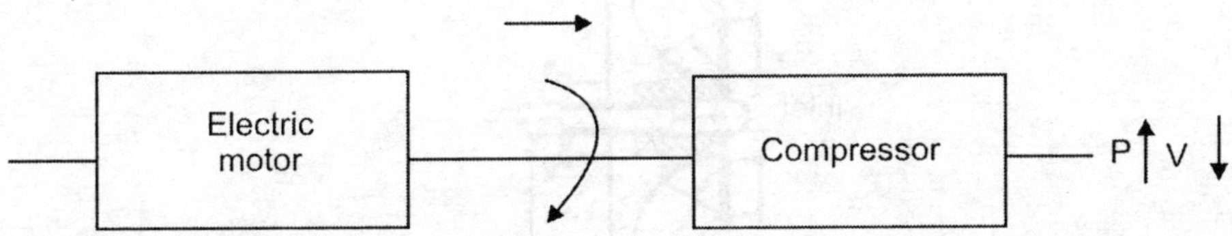

Fig. 4.2(c)

A fan imparts motion to gas with small change in pressure. (Fig. 4.2(d))

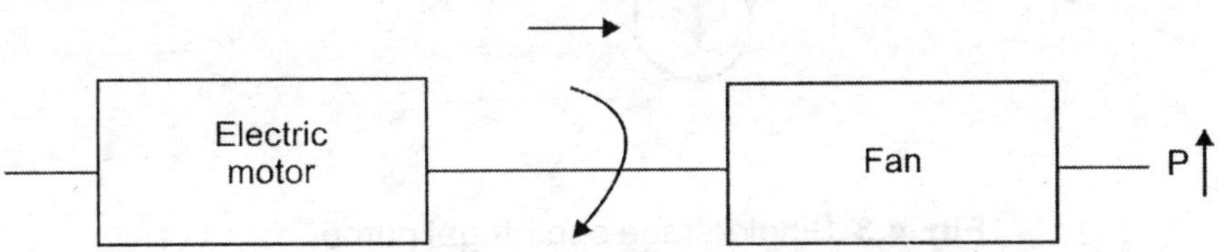

Fig. 4.2(d)

A fan blower increases the velocity of gas with small pressure Fig. 4.2(e). The steam and gas turbines, hydraulic machines come under first category, and pumps, fans, compressors come under second category. In power absorbing machines the driver is usually an electric motor but it can be also an I.C. engine or a gas turbine.

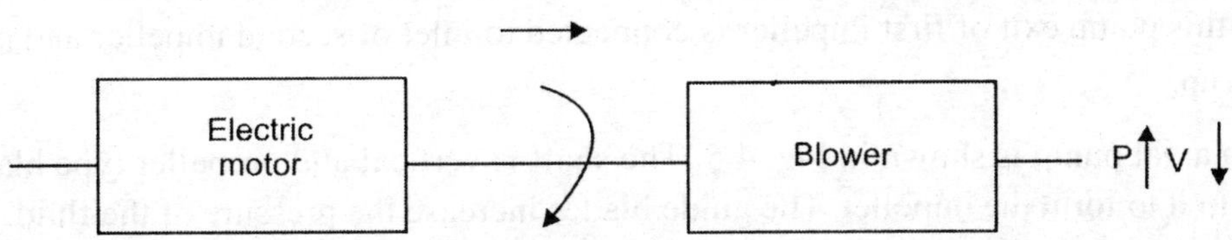

Fig. 4.2(e)

4.3 Pumps (Axial and Radial)

A single-stage centrifugal pump is shown in Fig 4.3. The rotating element is called the impeller which is contained within the pump housing or casing. The shaft transfers mechanical energy to impeller which must penetrate the casing, a system of bearings. Seals are required against the leakage of the fluid.

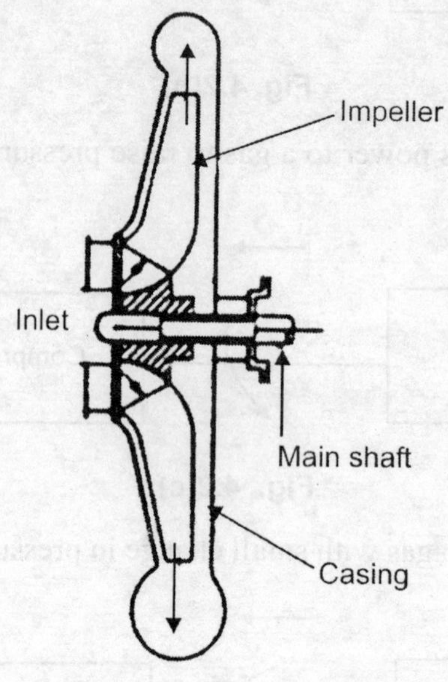

Fig. 4.3 Single-stage centrifugal pump.

Fluid enters the machine nearly in axial direction at inlet through the eye of the impeller and leaves the impeller radially out. Flow leaving the impeller is collected in a scroll or volute, which gradually increases in area as fluid moves out through exit. The impeller has vanes to convey the fluid. A multi-stage pump is shown in Fig 4.4.

In this pump exit of first impeller is connected to inlet of second impeller and pressure builds up.

An axial pump is shown in Fig. 4.5. The shaft is vertical and propeller type blades are fixed to it to form the impeller. The guide blades increase the pressure of the fluid.

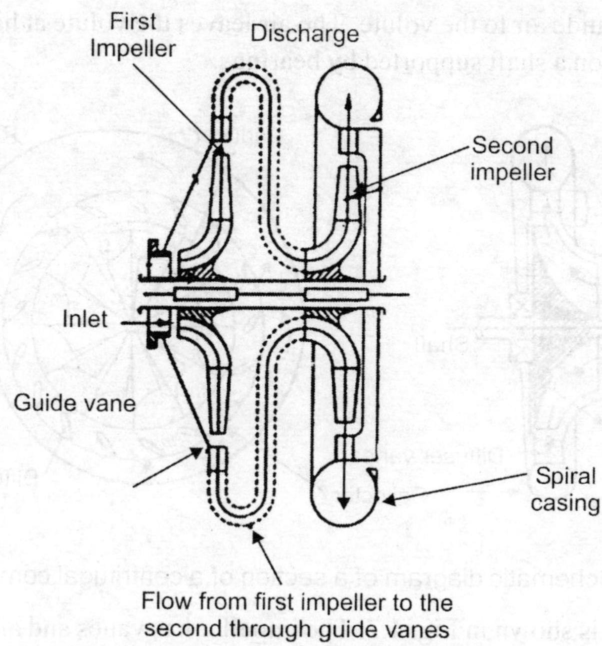

Fig. 4.4 Multi-stage centrifugal pump.

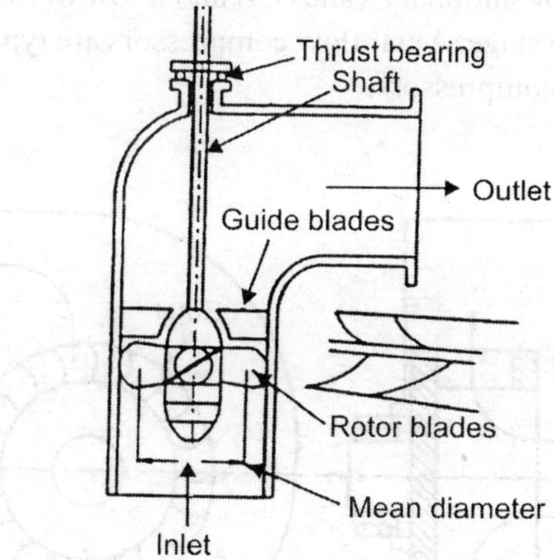

Fig 4.5 Schematic diagram of an axial flow pump.

4.4 Compressors (Axial and Radial)

A centrifugal compressor is shown in Fig. 4.6. Air enters the unit near axial through the eye of the impeller and flows radially outwards. There are diffuser vanes which increase the static pressure and guide air to the volute. The air leaves the volute at higher pressure. The impeller is mounted on a shaft supported by bearings.

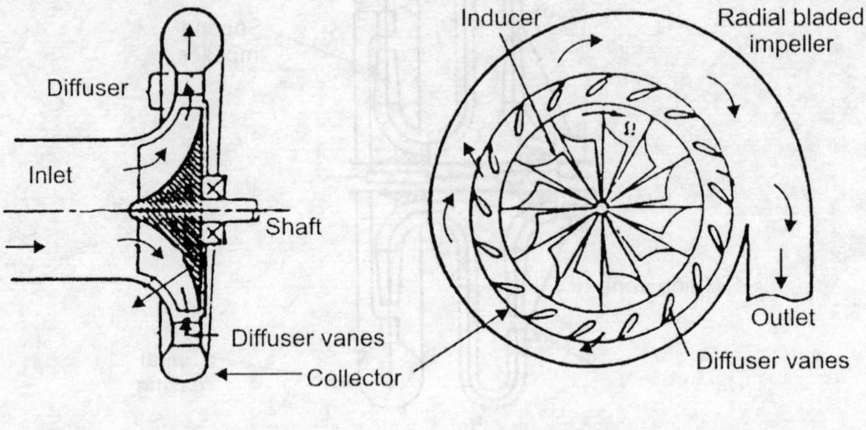

Fig 4.6 Schematic diagram of a section of a centrifugal compressor.

A typical blower is shown in Fig. 4.7. The impeller has vanes and air is discharged into volute which increases the pressure. An axial flow compressor is shown in Fig. 4.8. Flow enters nearly parallel to rotor axis and maintains nearly the same radius through the stage. A typical stage consists of a row of stationary vanes (S) and a row of rotating vanes (R) and pressure increases from stage to stage. Axial flow compressors are typically used in turbo-jet engines and are multi-stage compressors.

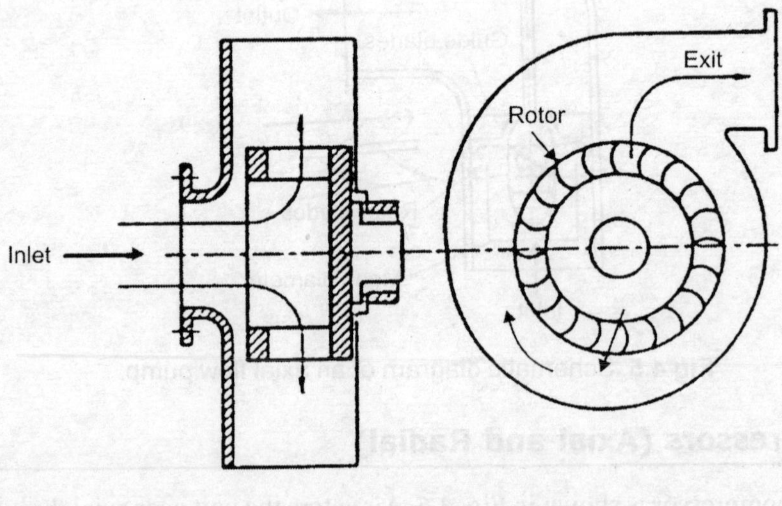

Fig 4.7 Centrifugal blower.

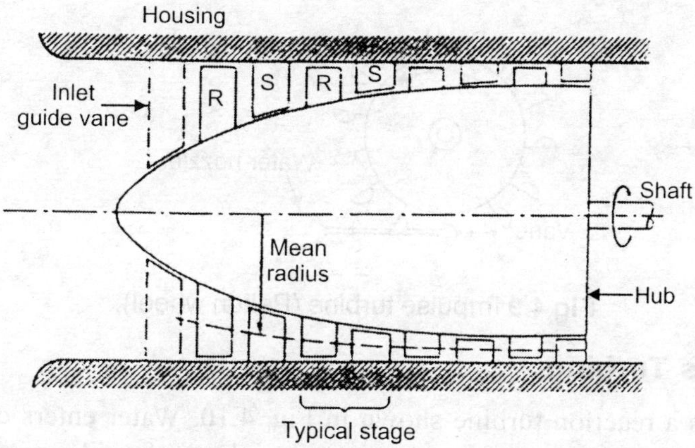

Fig 4.8 Schematic diagram of an axial flow compressor.

4.5 Turbines

Machines that extract energy from fluid stream are called turbines. They are classified as:

- Hydraulic turbines (Pelton, Francis, Kaplan)
- Steam turbines
- Gas turbines

In hydraulic turbines the working fluid is water and is incompressible. More general classification of hydraulic turbines are:

- impulse
- reaction

Impulse turbines are driven by one or two high velocity jets. Each jet is accelerated in a nozzle external to the turbine wheel known as turbine rotor. If friction and gravity are neglected the fluid pressure and relative velocity do not change as it passes over the blades/buckets.

4.5.1 Pelton Wheel

Pelton wheel is an impulse turbine. It is shown in Fig. 4.9. It is driven by a single jet which lies in the plane of runner. A high velocity jet prossesing kinetic energy strikes the bucket in succession. The water takes nearly 180° turn inside the buckets. The water falls into the tail race.

In reaction turbines part of the fluid pressure change takes place externally and part takes place within the runnet. External acceleration occurs in the guide vanes and flow is turned to enter the runner in proper direction. Additional acceleration of fluid relative to rotor occurs within the moving blades. So both relative velocity and pressure change over the runner. Reaction turbines run full of fluid.

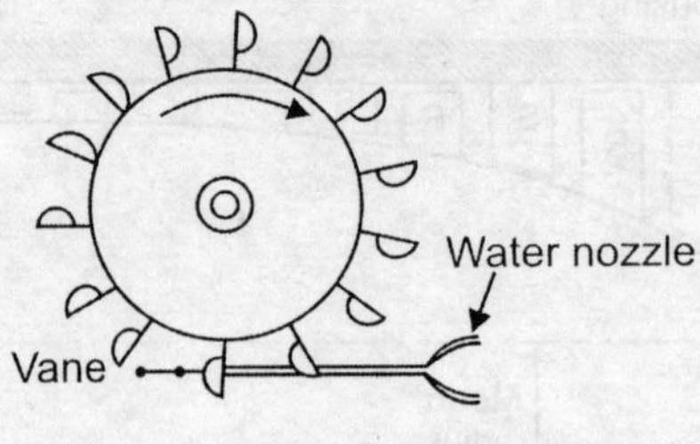

Fig 4.9 Impulse turbine (Pelton wheel).

4.5.2 Francis Turbine

Francis turbine is a reaction turbine shown in Fig. 4.10. Water enters circumferentially through turbine casing. It enters from the outer periphery of guide vanes and flows into runner. It flows down the rotor radially and leaves axially. Water leaving the runner flows through a diffuser known as draft tube before entering the tail race.

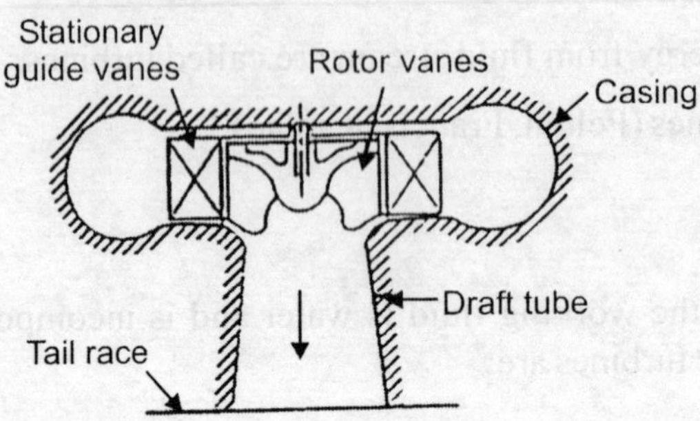

Fig 4.10 Reaction turbine (Francis).

4.5.3 Kaplan Turbine

Kaplan turbine is a reaction turbine shown in Fig. 4.11. The water from the spiral casing enters guide blades similar to Francis. The Kaplan turbine consists of an axial flow runner with 4 to 6 blades of an airfoil section. In this turbine both guide vanes and moving beades are adjustable and therefore high efficiency can be obtained.

4.5.4 Steam Turbines

In steam turbines expansion of high pressure and temperature is expanded in fixed and moving blades of a turbine. Steam is produced in high pressure boiler and after expansion steam condensed in condenser.

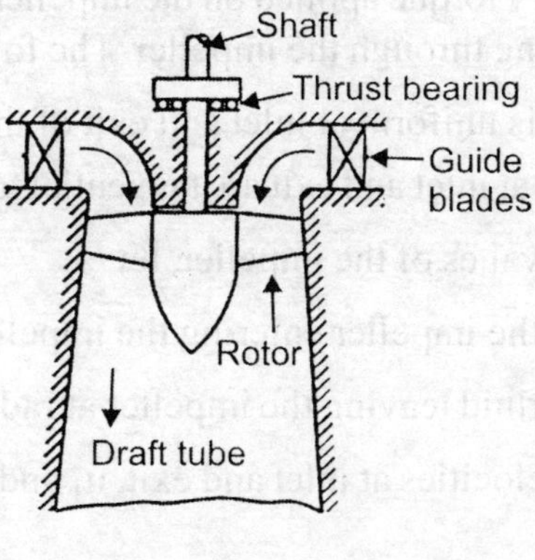

Fig 4.11 Reaction turbine (Kaplan).

4.5.5 Gas Turbine

In gas turbine expansion of high pressure and temperature of gas is expanded in fixed and moving blades of turbine. The exhaust gases after expansion go into the atmosphere.

4.6 Euler's Theory Applied to Turbo Machines

Euler's Theory : The fluid flow through an impeller of a centrifugal pump is shown in Fig. 4.12.

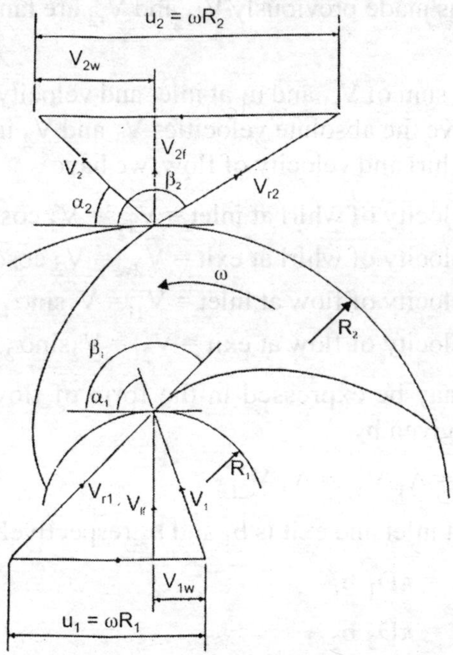

Fig 4.12 Velocity diagrams for pump impeller.

According to Euler's theory torque applied on the impeller is the rate of change of angular momentum of the fluid passing through the impeller. The following assumptions are made.

- The velocity of water is uniform at inlet and exit of the impeller.
- The relative velocities at inlet and exit are tangential to inlet and exit tips of the vanes.

Fig 4.12 shows only two vanes of the impeller, let

V_1 - absolute velocity of the impeller entering the impeller at radius R_1

V_2 - absolute velocity of fluid leaving the impeller at radium R_2

V_{r1} and V_{r2} are relative velocities at inlet and exit, u_1 and u_2 tangential velocities at inlet and exit.

α_1 and α_2 inlet and exit angles of V_1 and V_2

β_1 and β_2 vane tip angles at inlet and exit.

The angles are measured from the forward directed tangents so that both angles β_1 and β_2 are greater than 90°. The angular velocity ω is connected to tangential velocities u_1 and u_2.

$$u_1 = \omega R_1 \quad .....(4.1)$$

$$u_2 = \omega R_2 \quad .....(4.2)$$

According to assumptions made previously V_{r1} and V_{r2} are tangents to the vane tips at inlet and exit.

The velocity V_1 is vector sum of V_{r1} and u_1 at inlet and velocity V_2 is vector sum of V_{r2} and u_2 at exit of vane. Resolve the absolute velocities V_1 and V_2 into tangential and radial components as velocity of whirl and velocity of flow, we have

$$\text{Velocity of whirl at inlet} = V_{1w} = V_1 \cos\alpha_1$$

$$\text{Velocity of whirl at exit} = V_{2w} = V_2 \cos\alpha_2$$

$$\text{Velocity of flow at inlet} = V_{1f} = V_1 \sin\alpha_1$$

$$\text{Velocity of flow at exit} = V_{2f} = V_2 \sin\alpha_2$$

The volume flow rate may be expressed in the form of flow component and flow area A either at inlet or exit given by

$$Q = A_1 V_{1f} = A_2 V_{2f} \quad .....(4.3)$$

If the width of impeller at inlet and exit is b_1 and b_2 respectively, we have

$$A_1 = \pi D_1 b_1 \quad .....(4.4)$$

$$A_2 = \pi D_2 b_2 \quad .....(4.5)$$

where D_1 and D_2 are impeller diameters at inlet and exit

The flow rate Q is then given by

$$Q = \pi D_1 b_1 V_{1f} = \pi D_2 b_2 V_{2f}$$

Also mass flow rate is given by

$$\dot{m} = \rho Q,$$

where ρ is density of fluid

Rate of angular momentum $\overset{o}{M_1}$ of impeller being the product of mean flow rate $\dot{m}$, whirl componant V_{w1} and radius R_1.

$$\overset{o}{M_1} = \dot{m}\ V_{1w} R_1 \qquad .....(4.7)$$

$$\overset{o}{M_2} = \dot{m}\ V_{2w} R_2$$

Rate of change of angular moment is equal to applied torque

$$T = \dot{m} V_{2w} R_2 - \dot{m} V_{1w} R_1 \qquad .....(4.8)$$

The power input to drive this torque is given by

$$P = T.\omega$$

$$P = \dot{m}\,\omega(V_{2w}\ R_2 - V_{1w} R_1)$$

$$P = \dot{m}\ (u_2 V_{2w} - u_1 V_{1w}) \qquad .....(4.9)$$

4.6.1 Euler's Head

If the whole of mechanical power is converted into hydraulic power then total head H would be given by the relation

$$P = \gamma QH \qquad .....(4.10)$$

where Q is flow rate and γ sp. weight of the fluid.

Equating eqs. (4.9) (4.10) we get,

$$\boxed{H = \frac{(u_2 V_{2w} - u_1 V_{1w})}{g}}$$

or

$$\boxed{E = \frac{(u_2 V_{2w} - u_1 V_{1w})}{g}} \qquad .....(4.11)$$

This is called Euler's head of the pump. The head available is actually less than Euler's head. If the water enters the impeller without whirl such that $V_{1w} = 0$ then Euler's equation is written as

$$E = \frac{u_2 V_{2w}}{g} \quad .....(4.12)$$

4.6.2 Euler's Equation in the Kinetic Form

It is useful to express Euler's head in terms of their absolute velocities rather than their components. From the velocity triangles of Fig 4.12, we have

$$V_{1w} = V_1 \cos\alpha_1 \text{ and}$$

$$V_{2w} = V_2 \cos\alpha_2$$

Using cosine rule, we have

$$V_{r1}^2 = V_1^2 + u_1^2 - 2u_1 V_1 \cos\alpha_1$$

$$V_{r2}^2 = V_2^2 + u_2^2 - 2u_2 V_2 \cos\alpha_2$$

so that

$$u_1 \cos\alpha_1 = \frac{1}{2}\left(u_1^2 + V_1^2 - V_{r1}^2\right)$$

$$u_2 \cos\alpha_2 = \frac{1}{2}\left(u_2^2 + V_2^2 - V_{r2}^2\right)$$

Substituting in equation (4.11)

$$E = \underset{\text{I}}{\frac{V_2^2 - V_1^2}{2g}} + \underset{\text{II}}{\frac{u_2^2 - u_1^2}{2g}} + \underset{\text{III}}{\frac{V_{r1}^2 - V_{r2}^2}{2g}} \quad .....(4.13)$$

In this expression the first term I denotes the increase of kinetic head of fluid in the impeller due to change in absolute velocities. The second term II represents energy used in setting fluid into circular motion about impeller axis. The third term III is to regain static head due to reduction in relative velocity.

From the mode of derivation it is clear that Euler's equation is applicable to a pump and also to a turbine. However, the equation would change its sign. Thus

$$E = \frac{u_1 V_{1w} - u_2 V_2 w}{g} \quad \text{(Turbine)}$$

$$E = \frac{u_2 V_{2w} - u_1 V_{1w}}{g} \quad \text{(Pump)}$$

For axial flow machines $u_1 = u_2 = u$ and

$$E = \frac{u\left(V_{1w} - V_{2w}\right)}{g} \quad \text{(Turbine)}$$

$$E = \frac{u\left(V_{2w} - V_{1w}\right)}{g} \quad \text{(Pump)}$$

CHAPTER - 5

Pelton Turbine

One of the two 260 MW Pelton turbines in the Sellerin-Sitz power station, Austria.
The operating head is 1233 m.

Courtesy : Sulzer Ester Wyss, Zurich, Switzerland.

5.1 Introduction

Turbines are used for converting hydraulic energy into mechanical energy. The capital cost of hydraulic power plants, i.e., reservoir, pipelines, turbines, etc., is higher than thermal power station but they have many advantages and some of them are given below.

- higher efficiency
- operational flexibility
- ease of maintenance
- long wear and tear
- potentially inexhaustible source of energy
- no atmospheric pollution
- an attraction for tourism

Pelton turbine is chosen when operating head is more than 300 m. One of the largest single unit installed at Newcolgate Power Station, California, USA has rating of 170 MW.

5.2 Description of Pelton Turbine Installation

Pelton turbine is an impulse turbine as there is no pressure drop across the buckets. The flow is axial, i.e., there is no change in peripheral velocity and water enters and leaves the buckets at the same radius.

Water supplied is from a high head through a long conduit called penstock. The water is accelerated in the nozzle and the head is converted into velocity and discharges at high speed in the form of a jet at atmospheric pressure. The jet strikes deflecting buckets attached to the rim of a rotating wheel (runner) as shown in Fig. 5.1. The kinetic energy of the jet is lost to the buckets and water discharged at relatively low speed falls into lower reservoir or tail race. The tail race is set to avoid submerging the wheel during floded conditions. When large amount of water is available the power can be obtained by connecting two wheels to a single shaft or by arranging two or more jets to a single wheel.

The buckets are double hemispherical in shape. The water strikes the bucket in the centre and flows, out at both sides making a U turn. The surface inside the buckets is polished and smooth to reduce hydraulic losses. A costly material like broonze or stainless steel is generally used for the buckets. The buckets are detachable.

When the load is removed the water is suddenly cut off from the nozzle but it is directed to deflector plate. The deflector plate that comes into operation cuts off water supply to the wheel. The water from deflector plate goes to the tail race.

The nozzle spear moving inside the nozzle controls water to the turbine. Its operation is explained in the regulation of turbine.

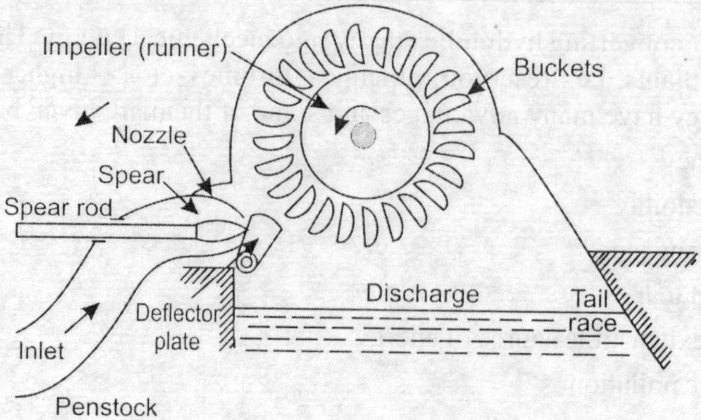

Fig. 5.1 Diagrammatic arrangement of a Pelton wheel.

Fig. 5.2 shows two jets for a single runner. The penstack is bifurcated into two pipes leading to two nozzles. The two jets are directed to the runner. All the peripherals, deflector plate, spear are there as in single jet. Fig. 5.3(a) shows large Pelton wheel runner, at Colgate power station Fig. 5.3(b) shows 4100 mm pelton runner at zurich, Switzerland.

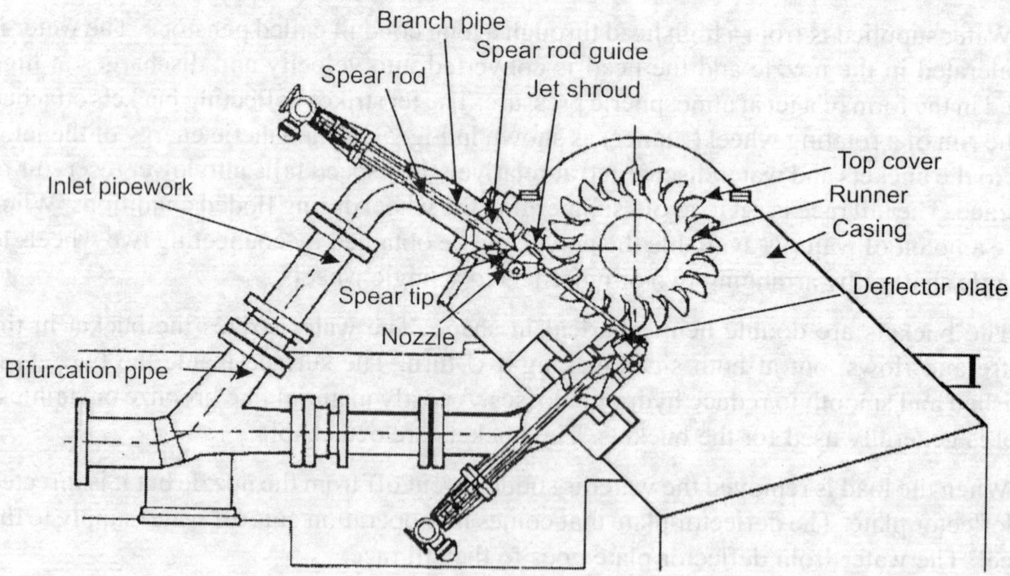

Fig. 5.2 Pelton Wheel with 2 jets.

Fig. 5.3 (a) New the Pelton runner in Colgate Power Station,U.S.A, (Courtesy Voith Hydro. Inc).

Fig. 5.3(b) Pelton turbine Runner diameter 4100 mm Zurich, Switzerland.

5.3 Analysis

Pelton wheel installation is shown in Fig 5.4. The water supply is from a constant head reservoir at an elevation H_1 above the centre line of the jet.

A surge tank is installed to dump out any fluctuations of pressure in the penstock. At the end of the penstock is the nozzle which converts head into velocity as jet.

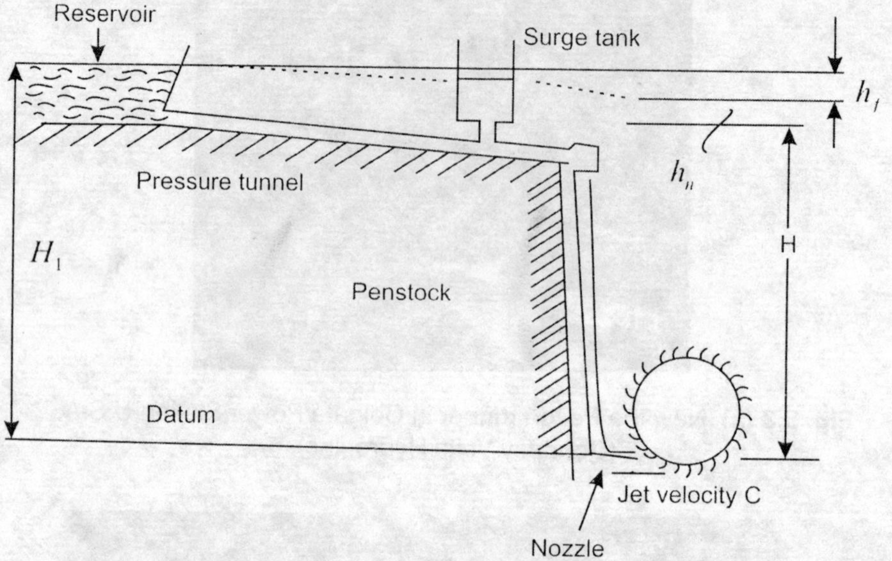

Fig. 5.4 Pelton Wheel Hydroelectric Installation.

Total head available from the reservoir above nozzle is H_1

Head loss in pressure tunnel and penstock due to friction = h_f

Head loss in the nozzle = h_n

Net head available for power generation at exit of nozzle = H

$$\therefore \qquad H = H_1 - h_f - h_n$$

where $$h_f = \frac{flv^2}{2gd}$$

where

l = length of penstock

v = Velocity in penstock

d = diameter of penstock

f = coeff. of friction

In practice the penstock is usually sized so that at rated power the net head is usually 85-95% of the total head. The net head is taken to calculate hydraulic efficiency of turbine.

The jet strikes the bucket at the centre and takes a turn of almost 180° and leaves on both sides of bucket as shown in Fig, 5.5(a), (b).

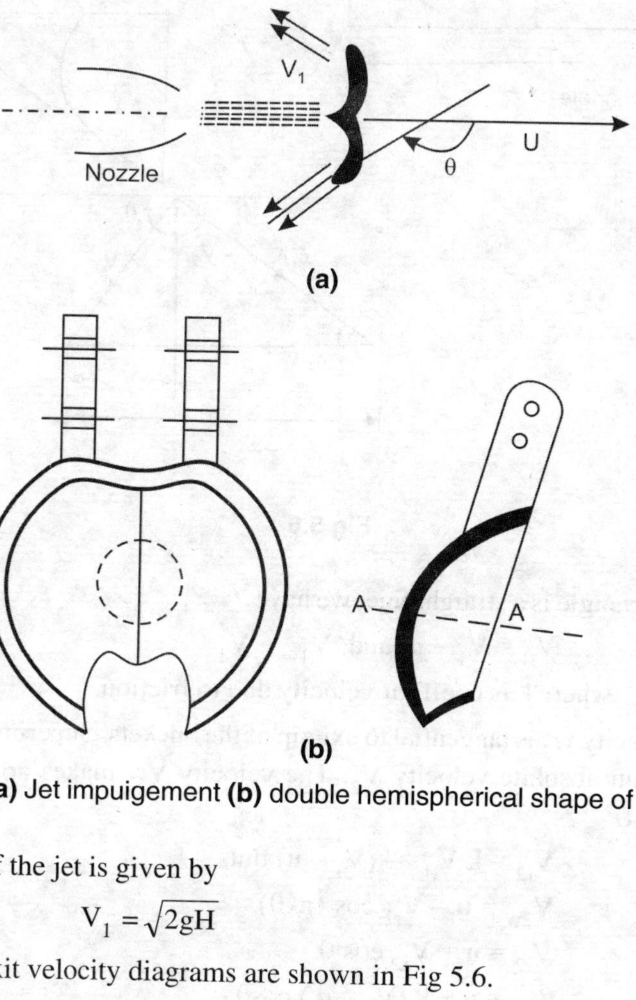

Fig. 5.5 (a) Jet impuigement **(b)** double hemispherical shape of buckets.

The velocity of the jet is given by

$$V_1 = \sqrt{2gH} \qquad \text{..... (5.1)}$$

The inlet and exit velocity diagrams are shown in Fig 5.6.

The total energy transferred to the wheel is given by Euler's Equation.

$$E = \frac{(u_1 V_{1w} - u_2\ V_{2w})}{g} \qquad \text{..... (5.2)}$$

As the turbine is axial the tangential velocity is same at inlet and exit

$u_1 = u_2 = u$ so that eq. 5.2 becomes

$$E = \frac{u(V_{1w} - V_{2w})}{g}$$

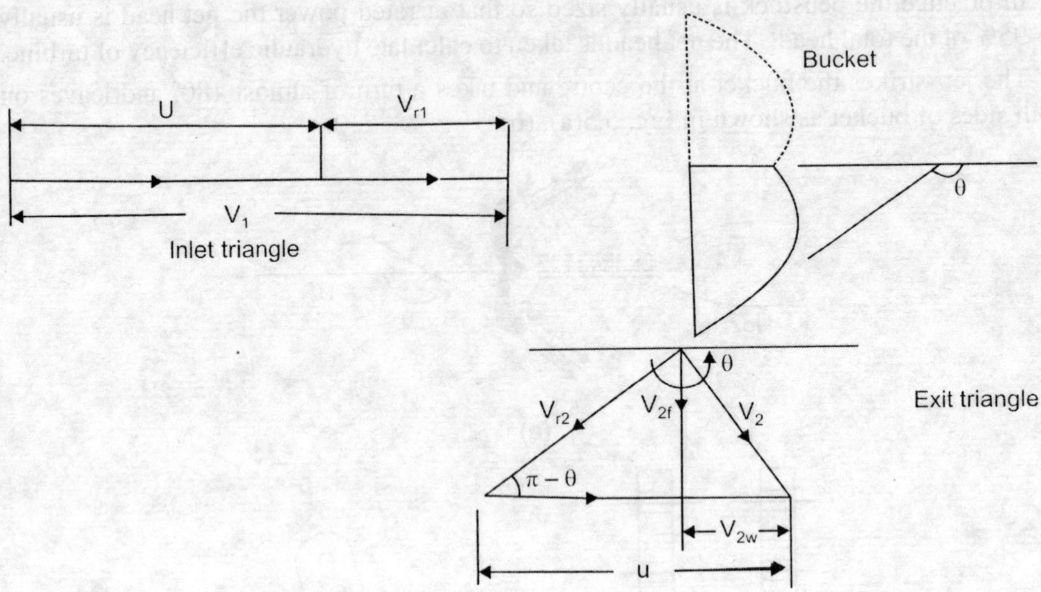

Fig 5.6

The inlet velocity triangle is a straight line, we have

$$V_{rl} = V_1 - u \text{ and } V_{1w} = V_1$$

Also, $V_{r2} = k\ V_{ri}$, where k is coeff. of velocity due to friction.

The relative velocity vr_2 is tangential to exit tip of the buckets. Superimposing peripheral velocity u we obtain absolute velocity V_2. The velocity Vr_2 makes an angle θ with the centreline of bucket.

$$V_{r2} = k\ V_{rl} = k(V_1 - u) \text{ thus}$$

$$V_{2w} = u - V_{r2} \cos(\pi - \theta)$$

$$V_{r2} = u + V_{r2} \cos\theta$$

$$\therefore \quad V_{2w} = u + k\,(V_1 - u)\cos\theta$$

Writing Euler's equation

$$E = \frac{u\,(V_{1w} - V_{2w})}{g} \qquad \text{.... (5.3)}$$

Substituting $V_{2w} = u + k(V_1 - u)\cos\theta$; as $V_{1w} = V_1$, we have

$$E = \frac{[u\,(V_1 - u - k\,(V_1 - u)\cos\theta]}{g}$$

$$E = \left(\frac{u}{g}\right) [\ V_1 - u - k(V_1 - u)\cos\theta]$$

$$\boxed{E = \frac{u}{g}\ [\ (V_1 - u)\ (1 - k\cos\theta]} \quad \text{..... (5.4)}$$

The equation shows that there is no energy transfer when the bucket velocity u is either zero or equal to jet velocity V_1. It is reasonable to expect therefore the maximum energy transfer will occur at some intermediate velocity of the bucket velocity.

Thus differentiating E with respect to u and equating to zero for maximum energy transfer

$$\frac{dE}{du} = \frac{(1 - k\cos\theta)(V_1 - 2u)}{g} = 0$$

Hence, $\quad V_1 - 2u = 0$ as $\frac{(1 - k\cos\theta)}{g}$ cannot be zero

we have $\quad \boxed{\frac{u}{V_1} = \frac{1}{2}}$

Thus tangential velocity is half the jet velocity for maximum energy transfer.
Substituting this value in eq 5.4

$$E_{max} = \left(\frac{V_1}{2g}\right)\left(V_1 - \frac{V_1}{2}\right)(1 - k\cos\theta)$$

$$E_{max} = \left(\frac{V_1^2}{4g}\right)(1 - k\cos\theta)$$

Inlet kinetic energy to the jet $= V_1^2 / 2g$

Thus maximum theoretical hydraulic efficiency of Pelton wheel,

$$\eta_{max} = \frac{E}{\text{K.E of jet}}$$

$$\eta_{max} = \frac{\left(\frac{V_1^2}{4g}\right)(1 - k\cos\theta)}{\frac{V_1^2}{2g}}$$

$$\boxed{\eta_{max} = \frac{(1 - k\cos\theta)}{2g}} \quad \text{..... (5.6)}$$

In an ideal case when $\theta = 180$, $k = 1$; $\eta_{max} = 100\%$. In practice friction exists and K value is in the region of 0.85 - 0.9 and also the value of $\theta = 165^0$ to avoid interference between incoming and outgoing jets. Therefore $\frac{u}{V_1}$ is always less than 0.5. For $\frac{u}{V_1} = 0.46$ and $\theta = 165^o$, the maximum efficiency is around 90% . Rewriting equation 5.4,

$E = \frac{u}{g}(V_1 - u)(1 - k\cos\theta)$ and also K.E of jet $= V_1^2/2g$ and hydraulic efficiency as

$$\eta = \frac{\left(u/g\right)(V_1 - u)(1 - k\cos\theta)}{V_1^2/2g}$$

$$\eta_h = (2)\left(\frac{u}{V_1}\right)\left(1 - \frac{u}{V_1}\right)(1 - k\cos\theta) \qquad ..... (5.7)$$

Fig. 5.7 shows the variation of Pelton wheel efficiency with speed ratio $\frac{u}{V_1}$ theoritical and actual.

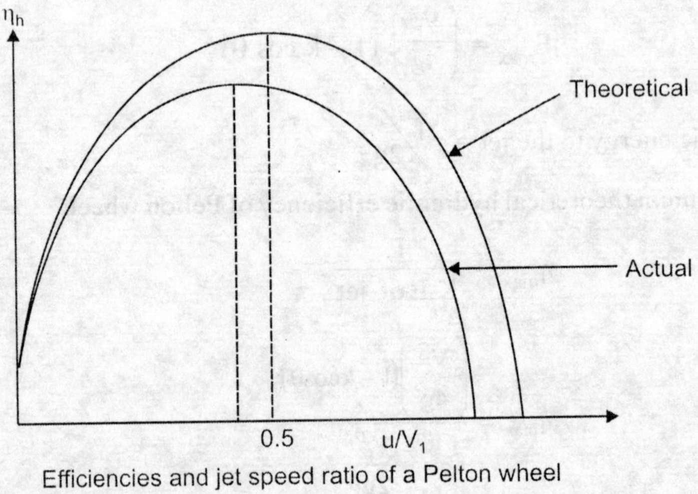

Fig. 5.7 Graphs of theoretical and actual hydraulic efficiency with u/V_1 ratio.

Fig. 5.8 shows variation of load with overall efficiency. At low loads less than 35% the efficiency is low but at higher loads the efficiency is fairly constant around 90%.

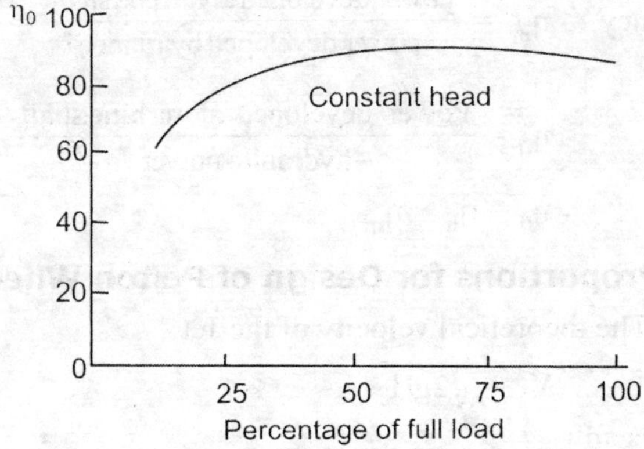

Fig. 5.8 Overall efficiency against turbine load (%).

5.4 Pelton Turbine Losses and Efficiencies

The diagram shown in Fig 5.9 gives Pelton turbine losses in various components. The reservoir read is H_I.

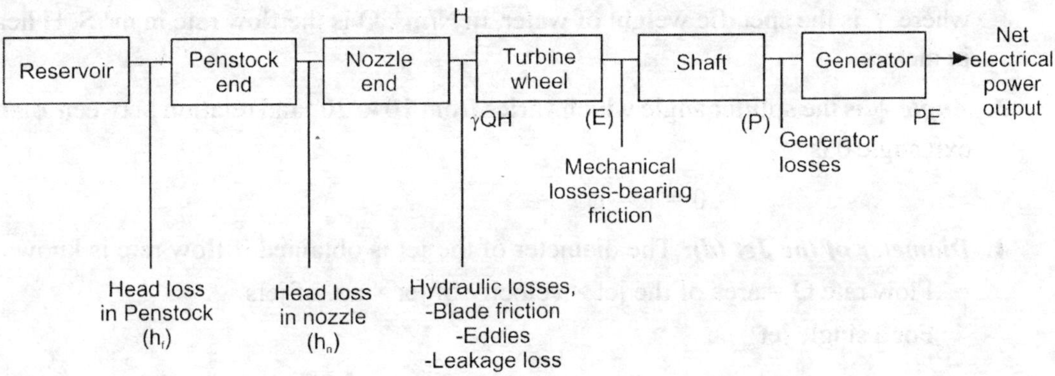

Fig 5.9 Impulse turbine losses and efficiency.

The hydraulic losses in penstock is h_f, head loss in nozzle is h_n. The head before the turbine inlet is H and hydraulic power input is γQH. There are losses like eddives and leakage in the turbine. Head available at the runner is E. There are mechanical losses and as a result shaft power is P. There are transmission and generator losses and net electrical power generated by generator P_E.

$$H = H_I - (h_n + h_f)$$

Hydraulic efficiency $\eta_h = \dfrac{\text{power developed by runner}}{\text{hydraulic power}} = \dfrac{\gamma QE}{\gamma QH}$

Mechanical efficiency $\eta_m = \dfrac{\text{power developed at turbine shaft}}{\text{power developed by runner}} = \dfrac{P}{\gamma QE}$

Overall efficiency $\eta_0 = \dfrac{\text{Power developed at turbine shaft}}{\text{hydraulic power}} = \dfrac{P}{\gamma QH}$

thus $\eta_0 = \eta_h \times \eta_m$

5.4.1 Working Proportions for Design of Pelton Wheel

1. ***Velocity of jet:*** The theoretical velocity of the Jet

$$V_1 = \sqrt{2gH}$$

where H = net head

Actual Velocity of Jet

$$V_a = C_v \sqrt{2gH}$$

where C_v is the coefficient of velocity of the jet which varies from 0.98 to 0.99.

2. ***Power available to the Turbine***

$$P = \gamma QH$$

where γ is the specific weight of water, in N/m^3, Q is the flow rate in m^3/S, H head in meters.

3. ***Angle*** ϕ is the splitter angle which varies from 10 to 20^0 and relation between ϕ and exit angle θ is

$$\theta = \pi - \phi$$

4. ***Diameter of the Jet (d):*** The diameter of the jet is obtained if flow rate is known.

Flow rate Q = area of the jet × velocity of jet × no. of jets

For a single jet

$$Q = \frac{\pi}{4} d^2 \times V_1$$

$$Q = \frac{\pi}{4} d^2 \times C_v \sqrt{2gH}$$

$$d = \left(\frac{4Q}{\pi C_v \sqrt{2gH}}\right)^{1/2}$$

5. ***Speed ratio*** $\left(\frac{u}{V_1}\right)$: The speed ratio is the ratio of the velocity (u) of the wheel at pitch circle to theoretical velocity of the jet. In practice the value is between 0.44 and 0.46 and average is 0.45.
6. ***Mean Diameter of the Wheel (D):*** It is the diameter between centres of the buckets. The diameter can be obtained from peripherial velocity (u)

$$u = \frac{\pi D N}{60}$$

or $$D = \frac{60u}{\pi N}$$

where N = speed of the wheel in revolutions/min.

7. ***Jet ratio (m):*** The ratio of mean diameter of the wheel to diameter of the jet.

$$m = D/d$$

The Jet ratio varies between 10 to 14 and average value of m is 12.

8. ***Size of the buckets:*** The length, width and depth of buckets in terms of diameter of jet 'd' is shown in Fig. 5.10.

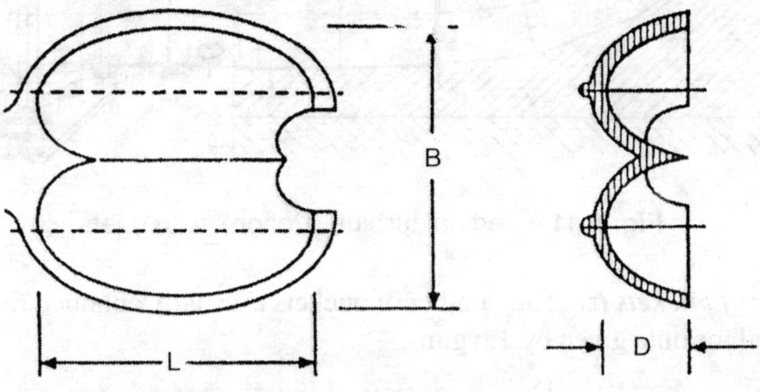

Fig. 5.10 Dimensions of bucket.

- Radial length of bucket L = 2 to 3d
- Axial width of bucket B = 3 to 5d
- Depth of bucket D = 0.8 to 1.2d

9. ***Number of Jets (n):*** Pelton wheels are single jet. When large power is required the flow rate required also increases and then number of jets required is also more than one jet. The jet should have sufficient spacing so that jet strikes one bucket at a time. Ordinarily not more than four jets are provided for horizontal turbine. A vetical Pelton turbine with six jets is shown in Fig. 5.11.

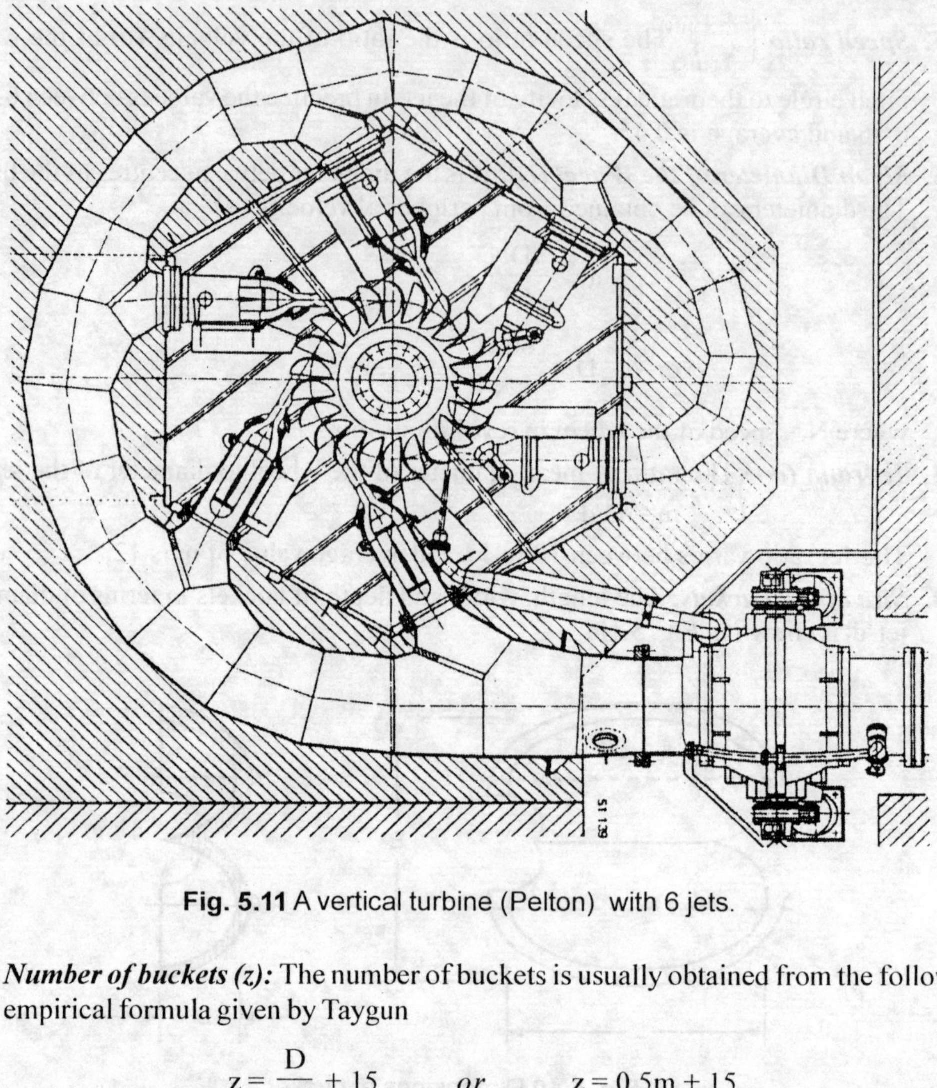

Fig. 5.11 A vertical turbine (Pelton) with 6 jets.

10. ***Number of buckets (z):*** The number of buckets is usually obtained from the following empirical formula given by Taygun

$$z = \frac{D}{2d} + 15 \qquad or \qquad z = 0.5m + 15$$

where m is jet ratio

5.5 Regulation of Pelton Wheel

Hydraulic turbines are usually coupled to an electric generator and the generator must run at constant speed to maintain frequency of supply constant. The speed of generator N in rev/min, the frequency of supply (f) in Hertz and number of poles of the generator P are related by the equation

$$f = \frac{NP}{120}$$

The peripheral velocity u of turbine wheel must remain constant as speed is constant. The velocity u and speed N are connected by the formula

$$u = \frac{\pi DN}{60}$$

where D is mean diameter of the wheel.

It is also desirable to run turbine at maximum efficiency and therefore speed ratio $\frac{u}{V_1}$ must remain same which means the jet velocity must not change as head available H is constant. The only way to adjust the load is to change hydraulic power input given by

$$P = \gamma QH$$

As γ, specific weight of water and H are constant, the only variable factor is Q volume flow rate of water entering the turbine. The flow rate Q is

$$Q = \text{Area of nozzle} \times \text{velocity of jet}$$

Thus flow rate will change by changing the area of the jet or more closely the diameter of the jet. This is accomplished by a spear valve and deflector plate shown in Fig. 5.12. The spear alters the cross-sectioned area of the jet. The position of spear is controlled by a servo mechanism that senses the load change. For a sudden loss of load when the turbine is shut down, a deflector plate rises to remove the jet totally from the buckets and to allow time for the spear to move to new position.

As seen in Fig. 5.12 for high load the spear valve has moved out, then increasing the area of the jet, at low loads the spear has moved in, decreasing the area of the jet. Deflector plate in normal position and fully deflected jet are also seen in the figures.

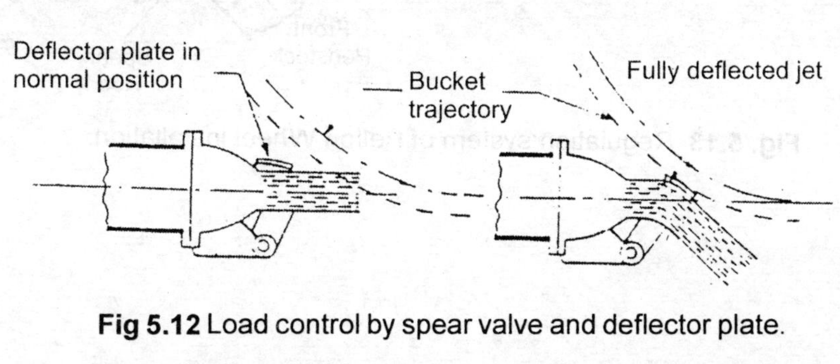

Fig 5.12 Load control by spear valve and deflector plate.

5.6 Regulating System of Pelton Wheel Power Station

The speed change of turbine is first sensed by the governor. When the speed increases fly balls of governor fly apart and when speed decreases they come closer. The sleeve moves up or down due to change of speed. The movement of the sleeve is transmitted to relay which moves the piston in the cylinder. When downward piston uncovers the port, the oil pushes the piston in the servo motor to the right which pushes the spear to move forward to affect the area of the jet. After relay action the oil from the relay cylinder returns to the oil sump. (Fig. 5.13)

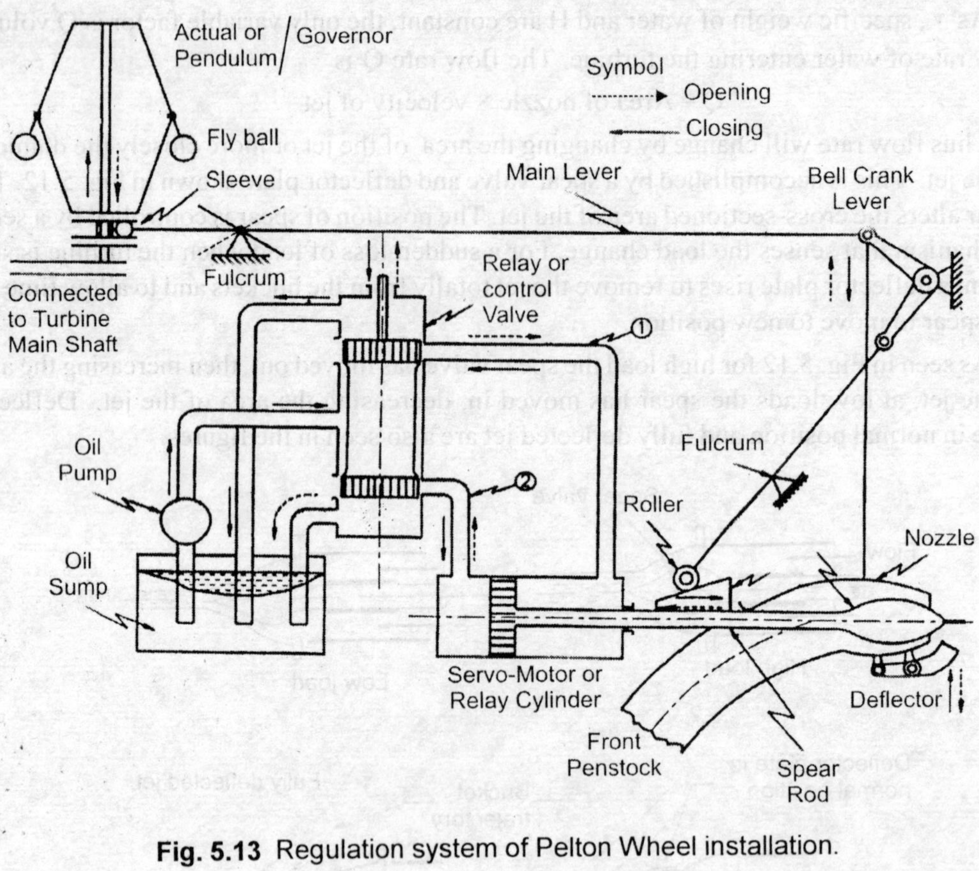

Fig. 5.13 Regulation system of Pelton Wheel installation.

Solved Examples

E.5.1 A Pelton wheel develops 67.5 kw under a head of 60 m of water. It rotates at 400 rev/min. The diameter of penstock is 200 mm. The ratio of bucket speed of jet velocity is 0.46 and overall efficiency of the installation is 83%. Calculate.

(a) Volumetic flow rate

(b) Diameter of the jet

(c) Wheel diameter

Solution

- Overall efficiency $\eta_0 = \dfrac{P}{\gamma QH}$; $Q = \dfrac{P}{\eta_0 \times \gamma H}$

$$\therefore \quad Q = \frac{67.5 \times 1000}{0.83 \times 9800 \times 60} = 0.138 \text{ m}^3/\text{s}$$

- Velocity of the jet $V_1 = \sqrt{2gH}$

$$= \sqrt{2 \times 9.8 \times 60} = 34.2 \text{ m/s}$$

- Flow rate Q = area of nozzle × velocity of jet

$$Q = \frac{\pi}{4} d^2 \times V_1$$

$$\therefore \quad d^2 = \frac{0.138 \times 4}{\pi \times 34.2} = 5.14 \times 10^{-3}$$

$$d = 0.0716 \text{ m} = 71.7 \text{ mm}$$

$$\frac{u}{V_1} = 0.46, \ u = 0.46 \times 34.2 = 15.7 \text{ m/s}$$

$$u = \frac{\pi DN}{60}$$

$$\therefore \quad D = \frac{60 \times u}{\pi \times N} = \frac{60 \times 15.7}{\pi \times 400} = 0.75 \text{ m}$$

Specific speed of turbine

$$w_T = \frac{\omega \left(P/\rho \right)^{\frac{1}{2}}}{(gH)^{5/4}}$$

where

$$\omega = \frac{2N\pi}{60} = \frac{2 \times 400 \times \pi}{60} = 41.8 \text{ rad/s}$$

$$P = 67.5 \times 10^3 \text{ watt}$$

$$\rho = 1000 \text{ kg/m}^3$$

$$H = 60 \text{ m}$$

Substituting,

$$\omega_T = \frac{41.8\left(\frac{67.5\times10^3}{10^3}\right)^{\frac{1}{2}}}{(9.8\times60)^{5/4}}$$

$$\omega_T = 0.11$$

E.5.2 A Pelton wheel works on a head of 400 m. The diameter of the jet is 80 mm. The head loss in penstock and nozzle is 23.6 m. The bucket speed is 40 m/s. The buckets deflect the jet through 165^0. The bucket friction reduces relative velocity at exit by 15% of relative velocity at inlet. The mechanical efficiency of turbine is 90%. Find the flow rate and shaft power developed by the turbine.

Solution

Velocity of the jet $V_1 = \sqrt{2g(H - h_f)}$

$$V_1 = \sqrt{2\times9.8(400 - 23.6)} = 85.8 \text{ m/s}$$

Euler's head $E = \frac{u}{g}(V_1 - u)(1 - k\cos\theta)$

$$= \frac{40}{9.8}(85.8\text{–}40)(1\text{–}0.85 \times \cos 165^0)$$

$$= \frac{40}{9.8}(85.8\text{–}40)(1{+}0.82)$$

$$E = 340.2 \text{ m}$$

Flow rate $Q = \text{area} \times \text{velocity} = \frac{\pi}{4} d^2 \times V_1$

$$Q = \frac{\pi}{4} \times 80^2 \times 10^{-6} \times 85.8 = 0.43 \text{ m}^3/\text{s}$$

Power developed by the runner = γ QE

$$P_E = \frac{\gamma QE}{1000} = \frac{9800 \times 0.43 \times 340.2}{1000} = 1432 \text{ kw}$$

$$\eta_m = \frac{P}{P_E};\ 0.9 = \frac{P}{1432} \quad \therefore P = 1288 \text{ kw}$$

E.5.3 A Pelton wheel is driven by two similar jets transmits 3750 kW to the shaft running at 375 rev/min. The total head available is 200 m and losses is 0.1% of the total head. The diameter of the wheel is 1.45 m, the relative velocity coefficient of the bucket is 0.9, the deflection of the jet is 165^0. Find the hydraulic efficiency, overall efficiency and the diameter of each jet, if the mechanical efficiency is 90%.

Solution

$$\text{Peripherial velocity } u = \frac{\pi DN}{60} = \frac{\pi \times 1.45 \times 375}{60} = 28.4 \text{ m/s}$$

Total head = 200 m, h_f = 200 × 0.1 = 20 m

Effective head H = total head – losses

= 200 – 20 = 180 m

$$\text{Velocity of the jet } V_1 = \sqrt{2gH} = \sqrt{2 \times 9.8 \times 180} = 59.4 \text{ m/s}$$

$$\text{Speed ratio} = \frac{u}{V_1} = \frac{28.4}{59.4} = 0.478$$

$$\text{Hydraulic efficiency } \eta_h = 2\frac{u}{V_1}\left(1 - \frac{u}{V_1}\right)(1 - k\cos\theta)$$

$$= 2 \times 0.478\,(1 - 0.478)\,(1 - 0.9 \times \cos 165^0) = 0.932$$

$$\eta_h = 93.2\%$$

$$\text{Euler's head } E = \frac{u}{g}(V_1 - u)(1 - k\cos\theta)$$

$$E = \frac{28.4}{9.8}(59.4 - 28.4)(1 - 0.9 \times \cos 165^o) = 167.93 \text{ m}$$

Relation between η_0, η_h, η_m is

$$\eta_0 = \eta_m \times \eta_h \ \therefore\ \eta_0 = 0.9 \times 0.932 = 0.838$$

$$\text{hydraulic power} = \frac{P}{\eta_0} = \frac{3750}{0.838} = 4474 \text{ kw}$$

also $$\frac{\gamma QH}{1000} \times 2 = 4474$$

$$Q = \frac{1000 \times 4474}{2 \times 9800 \times 180} = 1.268 \text{ m}^3/\text{s}$$

Flow rate Q = area × velocity of jet

$$Q = \frac{\pi}{4} d^2 \times V_1$$

$$d^2 = \frac{4Q}{\pi \times V_1} = \frac{4 \times 1.268}{\pi \times 59.4} = 0.0272$$

$$d = 164 \text{ mm}$$

E.5.4 In a Pelton wheel the diameter of the wheel is 2 m and angle of deflection is 162^0. The jet diameter is 165 mm and pressure behind the nozzle is 1000 kN/m^2 and wheel rotates at 320.rev/min. Find the hydraulic power developed and hydraulic efficiency.

Solution

$$\text{Pressure } P = \gamma H$$

$$\therefore \quad H = \frac{1000 \times 10^3}{9800} = 102 \text{ m}$$

$\therefore$ Velocity of the jet $V_1 = \sqrt{2gH} = \sqrt{2 \times 9.8 \times 102} = 44.7$ m/s

Flow rate $$Q = \frac{\pi}{4} d^2 \times V_1 = \frac{\pi}{4} \times 165^2 \times 10^{-6} \times 44.7$$

$$Q = 0.955 \text{ m}^3/\text{s}$$

$$\text{hydraulic power} = \frac{\gamma QH}{1000} = \frac{9800 \times 0.955 \times 102}{1000} = 954.6 \text{ kW}$$

$$u = \frac{\pi DN}{60} = \frac{\pi \times 2 \times 320}{60} = 33.4 \text{ m/s}$$

Speed ratio $$\frac{u}{V_1} = \frac{33.4}{44.7} = 0.747$$

$$\text{hydraulic efficiency } \eta_h = 2\left(\frac{u}{V_1}\right)\left(1-\frac{u}{V_1}\right)(1-\cos\theta)$$

$$\eta_h = 2 \times 0.747\,(1-0.747)\,(1-\cos 162^0) = 0.737$$

E.5.5 A Pelton turbine develops 8 MW under a head of 130 m at a speed of 200 rev/min. The following are the particulars of Pelton wheel.

- Coefficient of velocity (C_v) of the nozzle 0.98
- Speed ratio 0.46
- jet diameter 1/9 of diameter of the wheel
- overall efficiency 87%

Determine

- flow required
- diameter of the wheel
- diameter of the jet
- number of jets
- number of buckets

Solution

$$\text{Velocity of the jet} = C_v\sqrt{2gH} = 0.98\sqrt{2\times 9.8\times 130} = 49 \text{ m/s}$$

$$\text{Speed ratio } \frac{u}{V_1} = 0.46;\ u = 0.46 \times 49 = 22.54 \text{ m/s}$$

$$\text{Peripherial Velocity } u = \frac{\pi DN}{60}$$

$$\therefore \quad D = \frac{60\times u}{\pi\times N} = \frac{60\times 22.5}{\pi\times 200}$$
$$= 2.15 \text{ m}$$

$$\frac{d}{D} = \frac{1}{9}$$

$$\therefore \quad d = \frac{D}{9} = \frac{2.15}{9} = 0.238 \text{ m};\quad d = 238 \text{ mm}$$

$$\text{Overall efficiency } \eta_0 = \frac{P}{\gamma QH};\quad Q = \frac{P}{\eta_0\times\gamma\times H}$$

$$\therefore \qquad Q = \frac{8\times 10^3 \times 10^3}{0.87 \times 9800 \times 130} = 7.2 \text{ m}^3/\text{s}$$

Flow rate Q = area of jet × velocity × no.of jets

$$7.2 = \frac{\pi}{4} \times 0.238^2 \times 49 \times n$$

$$\therefore \qquad n = 3$$

Number of buckets $\quad z = \dfrac{D}{2d} + 15 = \dfrac{2.15}{2\times 0.238} + 15 = 20$

E.5.6 (Design)

The particulars are taken from JOR hydropower station situated at Cameron Highlands in Malaysia.
Installed capacity 100 MW, number of units 4, rated speed 428 rev/min, rated head 580 m, rated flow rate 6.85 m^3/s, type of turbine is horizontal - Pelton 2 jets. Design the Pelton turbine completely and determine all the important efficiencies.

Solution

Power output of each unit $P = \dfrac{100}{4} = 25$ MW

hydraulic power $= \gamma QH = \dfrac{9800 \times 6.85 \times 580}{1000 \times 1000} = 38.9$ MW

Overall efficiency $= \dfrac{P}{\gamma QH} = \dfrac{25}{38.9} = 0.642$

Assuming speed ratio $\dfrac{u}{V_1} = 0.46$

Velocity of the jet $V_1 = \sqrt{2gH} = \sqrt{2\times 9.8 \times 580} = 106$ m/s

$$\frac{u}{V_1} = 0.46, \; u = 0.46 \times 106 = 48.7 \text{ m/s}$$

Peripherial velocity $u = \dfrac{\pi DN}{60}$

$$\therefore D = \frac{60 \times u}{\pi N}$$

$$= \frac{60 \times 48.7}{\pi \times 428} = 2.17 \text{ m}$$

Flow rate Q = area of jet × velocity × no of jets $= \frac{\pi}{4} d^2 \times V_1 \times n$

$$6.85 = \frac{\pi}{4} d^2 \times 106 \times 2 \quad \therefore\ d = 0.202 \text{ m}$$

Number of buckets $z = \frac{D}{2d} + 15 = \frac{2.17}{0.202} + 15 = 25$

$$\text{Jet ratio } m = \frac{D}{d} = \frac{2.17}{0.202} = 10.75$$

Radial length of bucket L = 2.5d = 2.5 × 0.202 = 0.5 m

Width of bucket B = 4d = 4 × 0.202 = 0.8 m

Depth of bucket D = d = 1 × 0.202 = 0.202 m

Hydraulic efficiency

$$\eta_h = 2\left(\frac{u}{V_1}\right)\left(1 - \frac{u}{V_1}\right)(1 - k\cos\theta)$$

assume k = 0.95; $\theta = 160^0$

$$\eta_h = 2(0.46)(1 - 0.46)(1 - 0.95 \times \cos 160^0) = 0.94$$

we have $\eta_0 = \eta_h \times \eta_m$

$$\eta_m = \eta_0/\eta_h = 0.642/0.94 = 0.68$$

E.5.7 A Pelton wheel develops 4.5 MW under a head of 120 m at a speed of 200 rev/min. The wheel diameter is 8 times the jet diameter. Use the experimental data of Fig. 5.14 at maximum efficiency to determine the flow rate, wheel diameter of each jet, number of jets required, and the specific speed.

Solution

From the Fig. 5.14

Speed ratio = 0.42 at maximum efficiency of 80%.

$$\text{Overall efficiency } \eta_0 = \frac{P}{\gamma QH}$$

$$Q = \frac{P}{\eta_0 \times \gamma \times H} \quad \text{substituting properly,}$$

$$Q = \frac{4.5 \times 10^6}{0.8 \times 9800 \times 120} = 4.78 \text{ m}^3/\text{s}$$

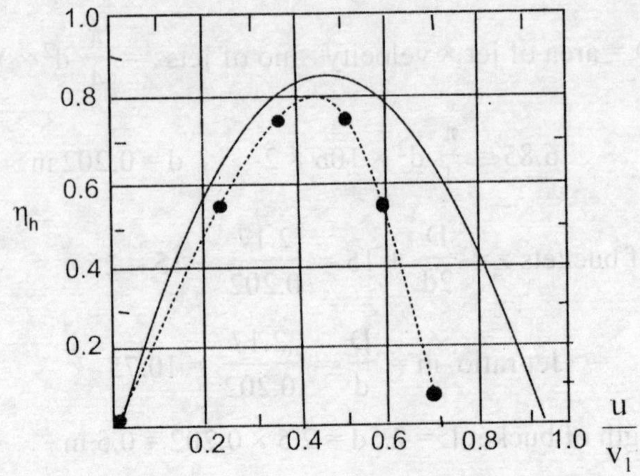

Fig. 5.14 Speed ratio versus efficiency for a laboratory-scale Pelton turbine: solid line, ($c_v = 0.94$, $\theta = 168^0$); dashed line, experimental data.

Velocity of the jet $V_1 = \sqrt{2gH} = \sqrt{2 \times 9.8 \times 120} = 48.5$ m/s

Also $\frac{u}{V_1} = 0.42 \therefore u = 0.42 \times 48.5 = 20.37$ m/s

Peripherial velocity $u = \frac{\pi DN}{60}$; $D = \frac{60 \times u}{\pi \times N}$

$$D = \frac{60 \times 20.37}{\pi \times 200} = 1.95 \text{ m}$$

Diameter of jet = $\frac{D}{8} = \frac{1.95}{8} = 0.243$ m

Number of jets n can be obtained by

$$Q = \text{area of jet} \times \text{velocity} \times \text{no. of jets}$$

$$Q = \frac{\pi}{4} d^2 \times V_1 \times n$$

$$4.78 = \frac{\pi}{4} \times 0.243^2 \times 48.5 \times n$$

$$\therefore \quad n = 2$$

Specific speed $\omega_T = \dfrac{\omega\left(\frac{P}{\rho}\right)^{\frac{1}{2}}}{(gH)^{5/4}}$

$$\omega = \frac{2N\pi}{60} = \frac{2\times 200\times \pi}{60} = 20.9$$

$$P = 4.5 \times 10^3 \times 10^3 \text{ watt}$$

$$\rho = 1000 \text{ kg/m}^3$$

$$H = 120 \text{ m}$$

$$g = 9.8 \text{ m/s}^2$$

$$\omega_T = \frac{20.9\left(\frac{4.5\times 10^6}{1000}\right)^{\frac{1}{2}}}{(9.8\times 120)^{5/4}} = 0.2$$

E.5.8 Technical Information of Sungai Piah Power Station

Sungai Piah Power Station (Upper Scheme)

1.	Catchment area (km^2)	118
2.	Average flow (m^3/s)	5.0
3.	Gross head (m)	160
4.	Intakes (number)	2
5.	Power house type	surface
6.	Totol tunnel length (km)	7.7
7.	Station installed capacity (MW)	14.6
8.	Turbine type	2-Jet horizontal type Pelton
9.	Turbine rated output (KW)	7500
10.	Generated rated output (kw)	7275
11.	Rated net head (m)	255
12.	Generator rating 11 KVA / 0.85 pf / 50 Hz	
13.	Average Energy output (GWH) year	80
14.	Transmission line	132 KVA

Lower Scheme

1.	Catchment area (km^2)	246
2.	Average flow (m^3/s)	11.4
3.	Gross head (m)	403
4.	Intakes (number)	7
5.	Power house type	underground
6.	Total tunnel length (km)	13.8
7.	Station installed capacity (MW)	55.4
8.	No.of units	2
9.	Turbine rated output (KW)	28250
10.	Turbine type	4-Jet horizontal type Pelton
11.	Rated net head (m)	400
12.	Generated rated output (Kw)	27680
13.	Average Energy output (GWH) / year	300

Case Study

The technical information of upper scheme and lower scheme of two hydro power stations one surface and another underground is given below. Essential details are to be noted.

- Station installed capacity = Generated rated capacity of each unit × no. of units.
- There is small difference between Gross head and rated net head, which is hydraulic losses. In the upper scheme percentage loss of head is 3% and lower scheme about 1%.
- The generator efficiency is electrical power output of generator by mechanical output of turbine. In upper scheme generator efficiency is 97% and lower scheme it is 98%.
- The generators work with very high efficiency.
- For any hydropower scheme the head remains almost constant, but the flow rate changes and therefore average value is taken into calculations.
- The flow rate of upper and lower schemes are different as number of intakes is two in upper scheme and seven in lower schemes and naturally the upper scheme works on 5 m^3/s and lower scheme on 11.4 m^3/s, and
  - the number of jets in upper scheme is two and lower scheme it is four.
  - the underground lower scheme has a head of 400 m and surface upper scheme has head 160 m and both use Pelton turbines.
  - The power generated in lower scheme is approximately four times that generated by upper scheme.
  - Energy output (GWH)/year for the upper scheme

- Station installed capacity in Watts × number of hours/year

$$= \frac{14.6 \times 10^3 \times 10^3 \times 8760}{10^9} = 127.89$$

(GWH)/year = 127.89

Average energy output given is 80(GWH)/year

$$\text{Generating efficiency} = \frac{80}{127.89} = 62\%$$

- Energy output (GWH)/year for the lower scheme
= station installed capacity in Watts × no.of hours/year

$$= \frac{55.4 \times 10^3 \times 10^3 \times 8760}{10^9} = 485$$

$$= \text{(GWH)/year} = 485$$

- Average energy output given is 300 (GWH)/year

$$\text{Generating efficiency} = \frac{300}{485} = 62\%$$

- Some of the reasons for this deficiency in generating efficiency is due to shut down of the units for repair and maintenance during the year, fall short of water level in the reservoir or power not required by the main grid and hence some units are shut down.

- The most important parameters are frequency of supply which must be 50 HZ and may fluctuate within very narrow limits and also the power factor (pf) which must be 0.85 - 0.9.
- Electrical charges are given per unit of electricity which is kWh.
Thus units of electrical energy generated for upper scheme.

$$80 \text{ GWH/year} = \frac{80 \times 10^9}{10^3} = 80 \text{ million units/year}$$

Electrical energy generated for lower scheme

$$300\text{(GWH)/year} = \frac{300 \times 10^9}{10^3}$$

$$= 300 \text{ million units/year}$$

CHAPTER - 6

Francis Turbine

New world-record operating head pf 734 m for the two high pressure Francis turbine for Hisling, Australia. The turbines have an output of 180 MW each. The model runner used for laboratory investigation is shown in the photograph.

Courtesy : Sulzer, Escher Wyss, Zurich, Switzerland.

6.1 Introduction

The hydraulic turbines are classified into two types, impulse and reaction.

As explained earlier in impulse turbines, there is no pressure drop across the moving blades, whereas in reaction turbines the pressure drop is divided in the guide vanes and moving blades.

The reaction turbines are low head high flow rate machines. For raction turbines, the rotor is surrounded by a casing (or volute), which is completely filled with the working fluid. Turbines are manufactured in a variety of configurations, radical flow, axial flow and mixed flow.

Typical radial and mixed flow hydraulic turbine is Francis turbine, named after James B. Francis, an American engineer. In this turbine the energy available in water is transfered to the shaft by means of a rotating runner and resulting torque transferred by rotating shaft can drive the eletric generator.

6.2 Description of Francis Turbine

A sketch of a Francis turbine is shown in Fig. 6.1. The flow is contained in a spiral casing called volute that channel the water into the runner. The volute has decreasing area to maintain uniform velocity, to the row of stationary vanes.

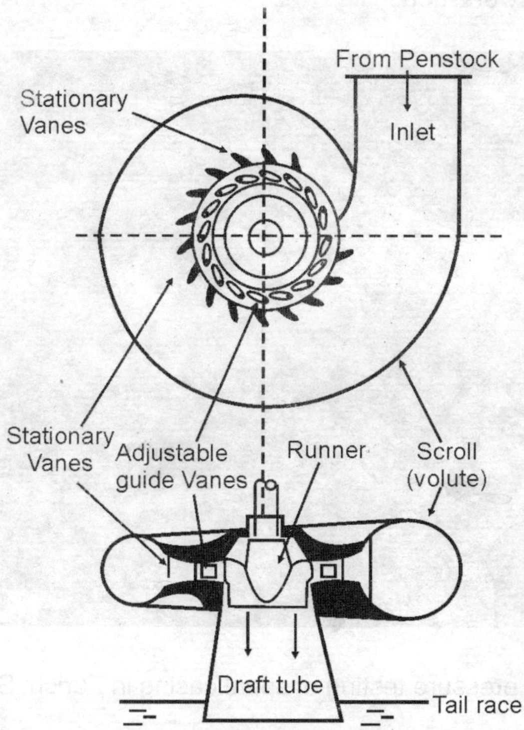

Fig. 6.1 Main components of Francis tubine.

The water passes through row of fixed guide vanes followed by adjustable guide vanes. The flow can be varied when the turbine is working at partial loads by changing the cross-sectional area between the guide vanes. The water then passes through the runner with radial vanes. The water enters the runner at large radius and leaves the runner blades at a smaller radius. The interaction between the fluid and runner blades results in torque applied to the runner. The runner is connected to the driving shaft to drive an electric generator. The turbine shown in the Fig. 6.1 is vertical type.

The water after doing the work leaves through the draft tube. It is essentially a diffuser whose area increases in the direction of the fluid flow. As area increases velocity decreases and pressure rises.

It produces a negative pressure at turbine exit and thus increases the head over the turbine which means more power.

There is energy loss at various components from the reservoir to the tail race. There is energy loss in the penstock conveying water to the turbine losses in fixed guide vanes, and also adjustable guide vanes, and runner vanes. There is also head loss in the draft tube and residual kinetic energy loss at exit from the draft tube. Fig. 6.2 shows a large spiral casing of Francis turbine for pressure testing in the workshop. Fig. 6.3 shows assembly of guide vanes and runner in Zurick workshop.

Fig. 6.2 Workshop pressure testing of spiral casing in Zurich, Switzerland.

Fig. 6.3 Runner and guide vane system in Zurich works, Switzerland.

6.3 Analysis

Let

H	-	Total head available to the turbine
V_o	-	Absolute velocity of water at inlet to stationary vanes
V_1	-	Absolute velocity of water at exit to ajustable guide vanes
V_2	-	Absolute velocity of water at exit to runner vanes
V_{r1}	-	Relative velocity at inlet to runner vane
V_{r2}	-	Relative velocity at exit to runner vane
u_1	-	Peripheral velocity at inlet to runner vane
u_2	-	Peripheral velocity at exit to runner vane
V_{1w}, V_{2w}	-	Whirl velocities at inlet and exit of runner vane
V_{1f}, V_{2f}	-	Flow velocities at inlet and exit of runner vane
α_1	-	Guide vane angle
β_1	-	Runner blade inlet angle
β_2	-	Runner blade exit angle

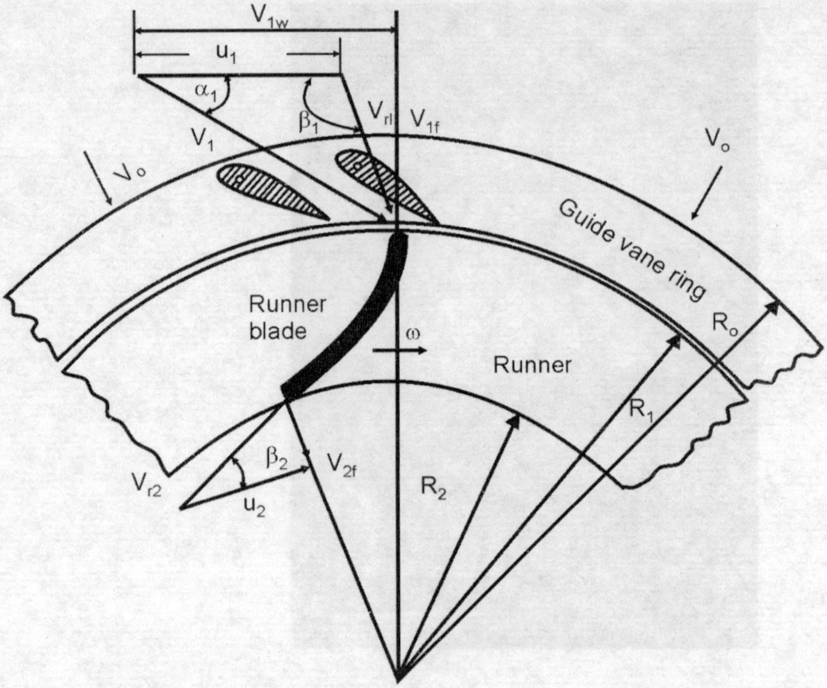

Fig. 6.4 Inlet and exit velocity diagram.

The inlet and exit velocity diagrams of the runner vane is shown in Fig. 6.4.

we have,

$$u_1 = \omega R_1;\ u_2 = \omega R_2;\ \text{and } \omega = \frac{2N\pi}{60}$$

The water comes out from the guide vanes at absolute velocity V_1 at an angle α_1 to the direction of rotation. The peripheral velocity u_1 is subtracted from V_1 to give relative velocity V_{r1} at angle β_1 to the direction of rotation is obtained.

At exit the water leaves the runner blade at relative velocity V_{r2} which makes an angle β_2 with the direction of rotation. Superimposing u_2 absolute velocity V_2 is obtained.

Euler's head is given by

$$E = \qquad \text{..... (6.1)}$$

If the whirl velocity at exit is zero, $V_{2w} = 0$, which means that velocity V_2 has no horizontal component or $\alpha_2 = 90^o$, then Euler's eq. 6.1 for maximum efficiency is given by

$$E = \frac{u_1 V_{1w}}{g} \qquad \text{.....(6.2)}$$

In such a case flow velocity at exit $V_{2f} = V_2$, $\tan\beta_2 = \dfrac{V_2}{u_2} = \dfrac{V_{2f}}{u_2}$ so that β_2 can be determined.

The energy distribution through a hydraulic reaction turbine is shown in Fig. 6.5.

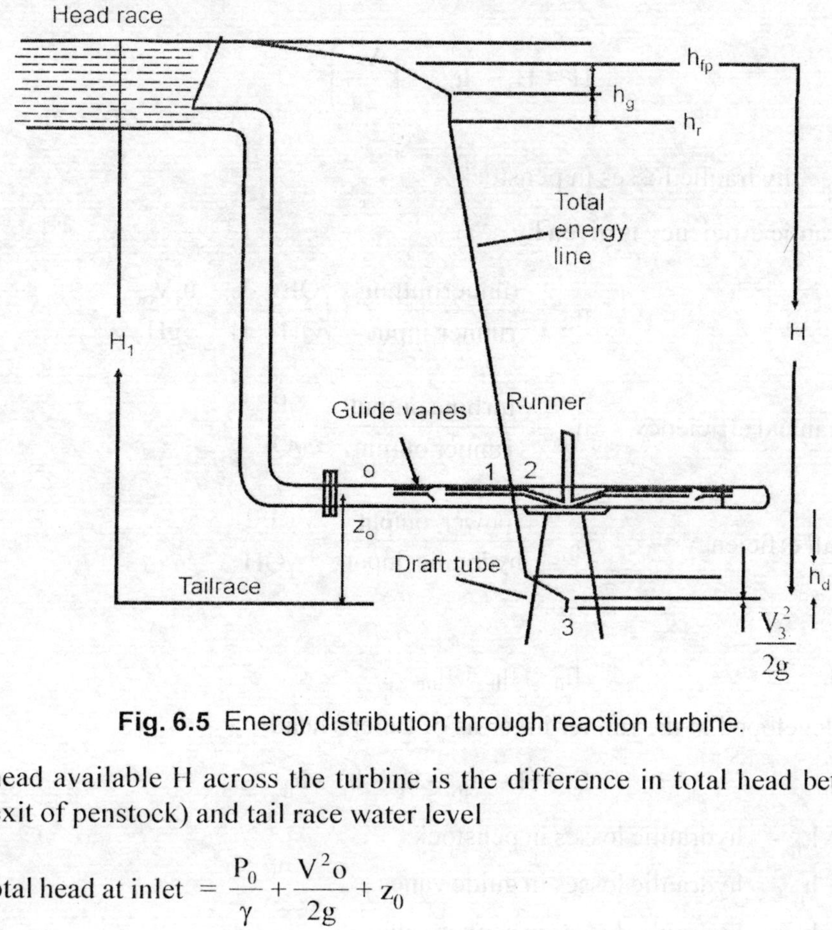

Fig. 6.5 Energy distribution through reaction turbine.

Net head available H across the turbine is the difference in total head between inlet flange (exit of penstock) and tail race water level

- Total head at inlet $= \dfrac{P_0}{\gamma} + \dfrac{V^2 o}{2g} + z_0$

- Total head at exit $= \dfrac{P_3}{\gamma} + \dfrac{V_3^2}{2g} + z_3$

- Net head across the turbine

$$H = \left(\frac{P_o}{\gamma} + \frac{V_0^2}{2g} + z_o\right) - \left(\frac{P_3}{\gamma} + \frac{V_3^2}{2g} + z_3\right) \quad \text{..... (6.3)}$$

But P_3 = atmospheric pressure = 0; z_3 is tail race taken as datum $z_3 = 0$, thus eq. 6.3 becomes

$$H = \left(\frac{P_o}{g} + \frac{V_o^2}{2g} + z_o\right) - \left(\frac{V_3^2}{2g}\right)$$

$$H = H_1 - h_{fp} - \left(\frac{V_3^2}{2g}\right)$$

where h_{fp} = hydraulic losses in penstock

The hydraulic efficiency is given by,

$$\eta_R = \frac{\text{runneroutput}}{\text{runner input}} = \frac{\gamma QE}{\gamma QH} = \frac{E}{H} = \frac{u_1 V_{1w}}{gH} \quad \text{..... (6.4)}$$

Mechanical efficiency $\quad \eta_m = \dfrac{\text{turbine output}}{\text{runner output}} = \dfrac{P}{\gamma QE}$

Overall efficiency $\quad \eta_o = \dfrac{\text{power output}}{\text{hydraulic input}} = \dfrac{P}{\gamma QH}$

thus $\quad \eta_o = \eta_h \times \eta_m \quad$ ..... (6.5)

Energy developed in the runner in terms of Euler's head

$$E = H - h_{fp} - h_g - h_r - h_d \quad \text{.... (6.6)}$$

where
- h_{fp} - hydraulic losses in penstock
- h_g - hydraulic losses in guide vanes
- h_r - hydraulic losses in runner vanes
- h_d - hydraulic losses in draft tube

6.4 Draft Tube

A draft tube is connected between runner exit and tail race to obtain continuous stream of water between them. It is diverging tube. The pressure increases and velocity decreases in the tube. The tail race pressure is atmospheric and runner exit pressure is negative (below atmospheric). Then the net head acting on the turbine increases. The turbine works with a larger head and more power is developed by the turbine. This is the main advantage of installing a draft tube. All Francis turbines will have a draft tube.

Analysis

With references to Fig. 6.5 and applying Bernoulli's equation between point (2) and (3) we get

$$\frac{P_2}{\gamma}+\frac{V_2^2}{2g}+Z_2=\frac{P_3}{\gamma}+\frac{V_3^2}{2g}+Z_3+h_d \quad .....(6.7)$$

where h_d represents losses in the diffuser also P_3 = atmospheric = 0; the tail race is taken as datum and therefore $Z_3 = 0$.

Re-writing eq. 6.7 with the above assumptions, we have

$$\frac{P_2}{\gamma}=\frac{V_3^2-V_2^2}{2g}-Z_2+h_d \quad .....(6.8)$$

Also $V_3 < V_2$, and if hd is neglected, $\frac{P_2}{\gamma}$ in negative.

The draft tube produces negative pressure at exit which increases the pressure head over the turbine.

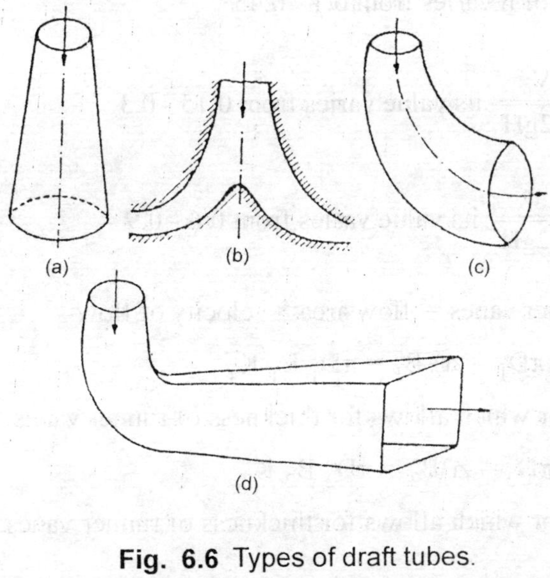

Fig. 6.6 Types of draft tubes.

Some of the types of draft tubes are shown in Fig. 6.6.

(a) Straight divergent tube

(b) Moody spreading tube

(c) Simple elbow tube

(d) Elbow tube with circular inlet section and exit rectangular.

6.5 Working Proportions of Francis Turbine

Let

B	-	breadth/width of runner vane
D	-	diameter of runner
z	-	number of runner vanes
t	-	thickness of runner vane
n	-	ratio of width to diameter of runner
χ	-	Flow ratio
ϕ	-	speed ratio
V_f	-	flow velocity
$\sqrt{2gH}$	-	Jet velocity

– $n = \frac{B}{D}$ The value of n varies from 0.1 - 0.45

– Flow ratio $\chi = \frac{V_f}{\sqrt{2gH}}$ its value varies from 0.15 - 0.3

– Speed ratio $\phi = \frac{u}{\sqrt{2gH}}$ its value varies from 0.6 - 0.9

– Flow through runner vanes = flow area × velocity of flow

$$\text{Area (inlet)} = (\pi D_1 - zt)\, B_1 = \pi D_1\, B_1\, K_1$$

where k_1 is a factor which allows for thickness of runner vanes.

$$\text{Area (exit)} = (\pi D_2 - zt) B_2 = \pi D_2\, B_2\, K_2$$

where K_2 is a factor which allows for thickness of runner vanes.

Flow rate

$$Q = (\pi D_1 - zt_1)\, B_1\, V_{1f} = (\pi D_2 - zt)\, B_2\, V_{2f}$$

$$Q = \pi D_1 B_1\, K_1\, V_{1f} = \pi D_2\, K_2\, V_2\, V_{2f}$$

$$Q = \pi D_1^2\, n_1 K_1 V_{1f} = \pi D_2^2\, n_2\, K_2\, V_{2f} \qquad \text{..... (6.9)}$$

if $K_1 = K_2$; $V_{1f} = V_{2f}$; $n_1 = n_2$, then equation becomes

$$B_1\, D_1 = B_2\, D_2$$

The number of runner vanes varies from 16 to 24. The number of runner vanes should be either one more or less than the number of guide vanes to avoid periodic impact.

Fig. 6.7 shows the runner of Francis turbine. As indicated B is the breadth of runner and D the diameter.

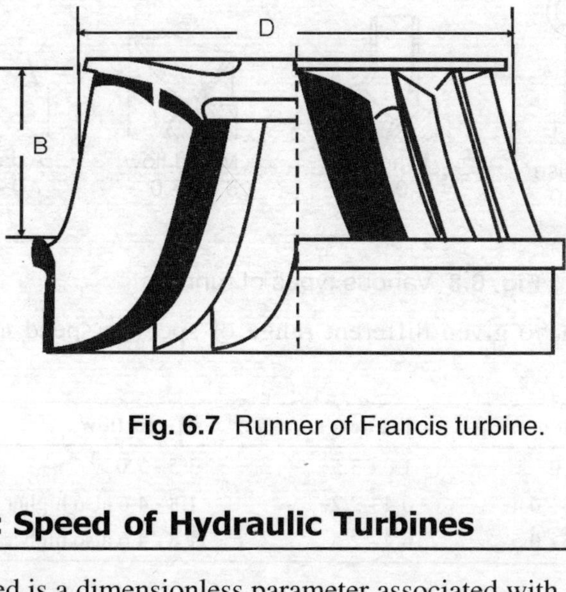

Fig. 6.7 Runner of Francis turbine.

6.6 Specific Speed of Hydraulic Turbines

The specific speed is a dimensionless parameter associated with a given family of turbines operating at maximum efficiency with known values of angular velocity ω head H, and power output P.

The specific speed is given by

$$\omega_T = \frac{\omega \left(P/\rho \right)^{\frac{1}{2}}}{(gH)^{5/4}} \qquad \text{..... (6.9)}$$

where

ω = angular velocity in rad/s

P = power output in Watt

ρ = density of water in kg/m^3

H = head over the turbine in meters

g = acceleration due to gravity in m/s^2

A preliminary selection of the appropriate type of turbine for given installation is based on specific speed ω_T. Fig. 6.8 shows type of the runner for different ranges of ω_T.

Impulse 0 – 1; Francis 1 – 3.5; Mixed flow 3.5 – 7; Axial flow 7 – 14

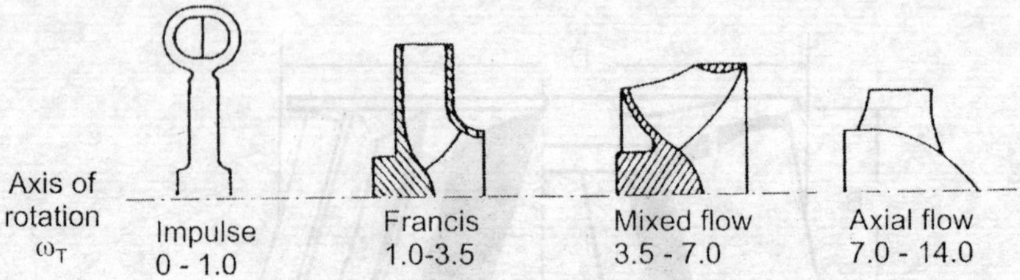

Fig. 6.8 Various types of runners.

The various authors have given different range of specific speed ω_T and some are summarised below.

Author	Pelton	Francis	Mixed flow	Axial flow
Potter (1977)	0- 1.0	1.0 - 3.5	3.5 - 7.0	7.0 - 14.0
Douglas (1995)	0.05 - 0.4	0.4 - 2.2	1.8 - 4.6 also higher	
Shames (1992)	0.05 - 0.5	0.4 - 2.5	1.8 - 4.6 also higher	

For turbines homologous specific speed N_s is also used, given by the following equation.

$$(Ns)_T = \frac{NP^{\frac{1}{2}}}{H^{5/4}} \qquad \text{..... (6.10)}$$

where H is in meters, P the power output in kw, and speed N in rev/min of runner.

On this basis specific speeds of different turbines is given in Table 6.1 based the book of Fluid Mechanics by Arora (2005).

Table 6.1 Specific Speed Ns of different turbines.

S.No	Range of head (m)	sp. speed N_s	Type of turbine
1	10 - 20	290 - 860	Propeller and Kaplan
2	30 - 60	215 - 340	Francis low speed
3	150 - 500	70 - 130	Francis high speed
4	150 - 500	24 - 70	Pelton 4 nozzle
5	500 - 1500	17 - 50	Pelton 2 nozzles
6	500 - 2000	12 - 30	Pelton 1 nozzle

6.7 Regulation of Francis Turbine

Francis turbine usually drives an electric generator, and hence the speed must remain constant. Since the total head available is constant it is not desirable to control flow rate by a valve due to hydraulic losses.

The flow rate in Francis turbine is controlled by varying the flow area in between the adjustable guide vanes. The guide vanes are hinged at the centre to a circular ring. The area in between the vanes is varied by varying the guide vane angle α_1. Refering to inlet velocity diagram of Fig.6.4 change in α_1 results in change of whirl velocity and flow velocity components. Such a change also changes inlet angle of the blade β_1 which means deviation from 'no shock entry' conditions.

Thus efficiency is reduced at partial loads.

Similarly the exit velocity diagram also changes and whirl component produces vortex motion in draft tube which may cause cavitation phenomena in turbine.

The regulation of guide vanes is done by servo mechanism as shown in Fig. 6.9. As load on the turbine decreases the piston of servo mechanism moves to the right and this causes the movement necessary to close the gates.

Fig. 6.10 shows the positions of guide vanes during fully open position (maximum flow) and close position (no flow).

Fig. 6.10 shows the position of the gates when fully open and fully closed.

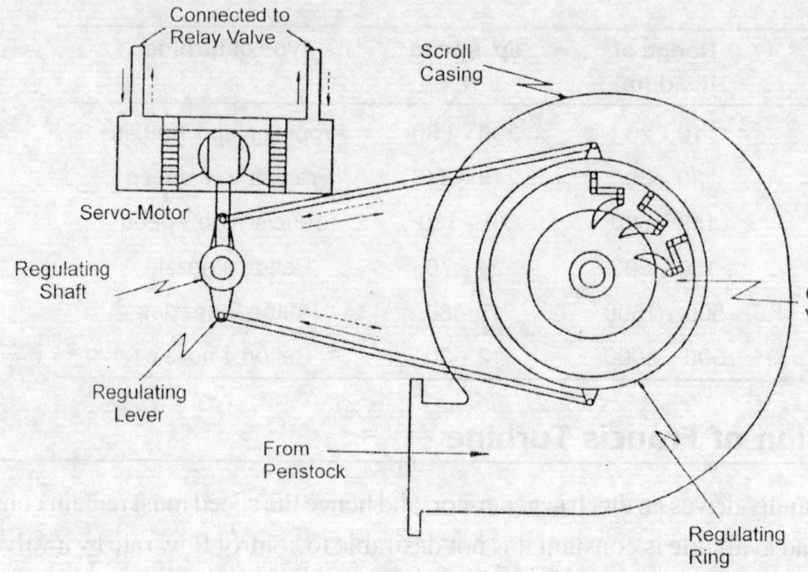

Fig. 6.9 Regulating mechanism of Francis turbine.

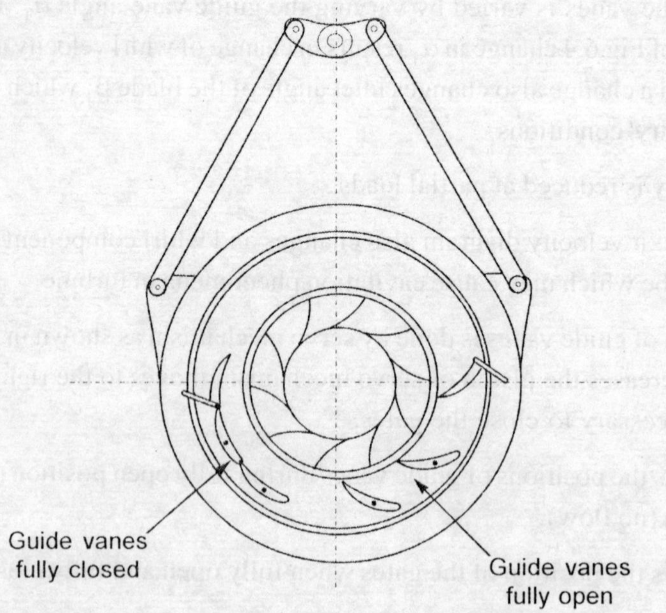

Fig. 6.10 Position of guide vanes during open and close position.

6.7.1 Comparison between Pelton and Francis Turbines

S.No	Pelton turbine	Francis turbine
1	Impulse type	Reaction type
2	Axial flow	Radial flow
3	Jet produced by nozzle - a fixed element	Water suppled by adjustable guide vanes
4	High head	Medium head
5	Low discharge	Medium flow
6	Specifc speed $\omega_T < 0 - 1$	Specific speed $\omega_{T,}$ 1 - 3.5
7	Turbine does not run full of water	Turbine runs full of water

Fabrication of bifurcation no.1 inlet diameter 10.98 m and bifurcation no.2 of diameter 7.47 m supplying water to six Francis turbines from the mian inlet diameter of 12.32 m to the works largest bifurcation at Tarbela power station Pakistan. It is shown in 6.11 and 6.12.

Fig. 6.11 Fabrication of bifurcation no.1 inlet diameter 10.98 m and bifurcation no.2 of diameter 7.47 m supplying water to six Francis turbines from the mian inlet diameter of 12.32 m to the works largest bifurcation at Tarbela power station Pakistan.

Courtesy : Zurich works Switzerland.

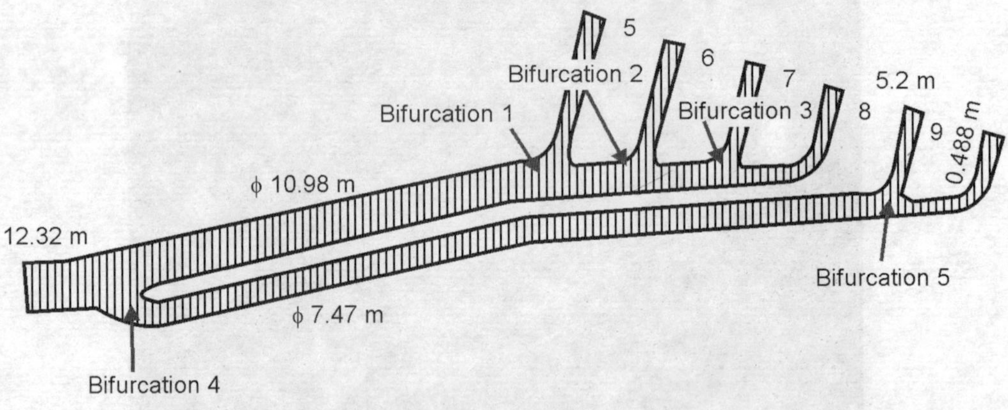

Fig. 6.12 Shows butterfly valves serve as safety shut off devices for 340 MW Francis turbine in Karakaya Power Station Turkey. The closing time is 120 s in dead water and about 40 s in emergency shut down for flow rate of 240 m^3/s.

Fig. 6.13 Shows butterfly valves serve as safety shut off devices for 340 MW Francis turbine in Karakaya Power Station Turkey. The closing time is 120 s in dead water and about 40 s in emergency shut down for flow rate of 240 m^3/s.

Courtesy : Sulzer Escher, Zurich, Switzerland.

Solved Examples

E.6.1 An inward flow turbine with radial discharge has an overall efficiency of 80% and develops 150 kw. The head is 8 m and the peripheral velocity at inlet is $0.96\sqrt{2gH}$ and flow velocity is $0.36\sqrt{2gH}$. The runner speed is 150 rev/min; the hydraulic efficiency is 85%.

Determine.

(a) velocity of whirl at inlet

(b) diameter of the wheel at inlet

(c) flow rate

(d) guide vane angle

Solution

– Peripheral velocity $u_1 = 0.96\sqrt{2gH} = 0.96\sqrt{2\times9.8\times8} = 12.02$ m/s

– Flow velocity $v_{1f} = 0.36\sqrt{2gH} = 0.36\sqrt{2\times9.8\times8} = 4.5$ m/s

– Hydraulic efficiency

$$\eta_h = \frac{(u_1 V_{1w} - u_2 V_{2w})}{gH} \text{ as it is radial discharge } V_{2w} = 0$$

$$\eta_h = \frac{u_1 V_{1w}}{gH}, \text{ substituting proper values}$$

$$\therefore \quad 0.85 = \frac{12.02 \times V_{1w}}{9.8 \times 8}$$

$$V_{1w} = 5.54 \text{ m/s}$$

$$\text{inlet angle } \tan \alpha_1 = \frac{V_{1f}}{V_{1w}} = \frac{4.5}{5.54} = 0.812$$

$$\alpha_1 = 39^o$$

$$u_1 = \frac{\pi D_1 N}{60}$$

$$\therefore \quad D_1 = \frac{60 \times u_1}{\pi \times N} = \frac{60 \times 12.02}{\pi \times 150} = 1.53 \text{ m}$$

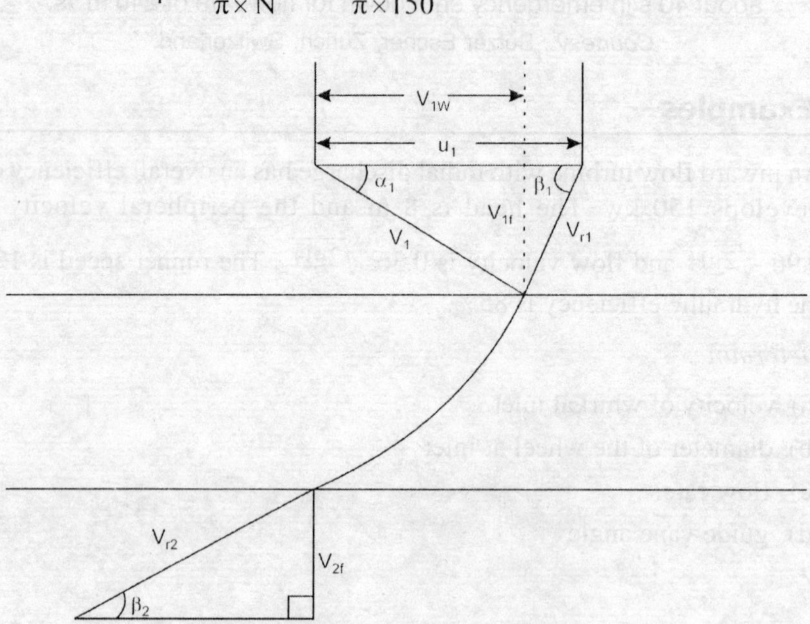

Fig. 6.14

overall efficiency $\eta_o = \dfrac{P}{\gamma QH}$

$$\therefore \qquad Q = \frac{P}{\gamma H \times \eta_o} = \frac{150 \times 1000}{9800 \times 8 \times 0.8} = 2.4 \text{ m}^3/\text{s}$$

$$Q = 2.4 \text{ m}^3/\text{s}$$

E.6.2 A Francis turbine has the following specifications.

Inlet radius 300 mm, outer radius 150 mm, flow rate 0.05 m^3/s, inlet guide blade 30°, angle the absolute velocity at exit makes an angle of 80° with the axis inlet absolute velocity 6 m/s, exit absolute velocity 3 m/s; overall efficiency 80%, hydraulic efficiency 90%. Determine head and power output if angular velocity is 25 rad/s.

Solution

Refering to velocity diagrams shown in Fig. 6.15, we have

$R_1 = 300$ mm, $R_2 = 150$ mm, $Q = 0.05 \text{ m}^3/\text{s}$

$\alpha_1 = 30^o$, $\alpha_2 = 80^o$, $V_1 = 6$ m/s, $V_2 = 3$ m/s

$\eta_o = 80\%$, $\eta_h = 90\%$, $\omega = 25$ rad/s

$$u_1 = \omega R_1 = \frac{300}{1000} \times 25 = 7.5 \text{ m/s}$$

$$u_2 = \omega R_2 = \frac{150}{1000} \times 25 = 3.75 \text{ m/s}$$

$$V_{1w} = V_1 \cos \alpha_1 = 6 \times \cos 30 = 6 \times 0.866 = 5.2 \text{ m/s}$$

$$V_{2w} = V_2 \text{ Cos } \alpha_2 = 3 \times \cos 80 = 3 \times 0.172 = 0.52 \text{ m/s}$$

$$\text{Euler's head } E = \frac{u_1 V_{1w} - u_2 V_{2w}}{g}$$

$$E = \frac{7.5 \times 5.2 - 3.75 \times 0.52}{9.8} = 3.7$$

$$E = 3.7 \text{ m}$$

$$\eta_h = \frac{E}{H}$$

$$H = \frac{3.7}{0.9} = 4.1 \text{ m}$$

$$\text{Power input} = \gamma QH = \frac{9800 \times 0.05 \times 4.1}{1000} = 2 \text{ kw}$$

$$\text{Power output} = \eta_o \times \text{ power input} = 2 \times 0.8 = 1.6 \text{ kw}$$

$$P = 1.6 \text{ kw}$$

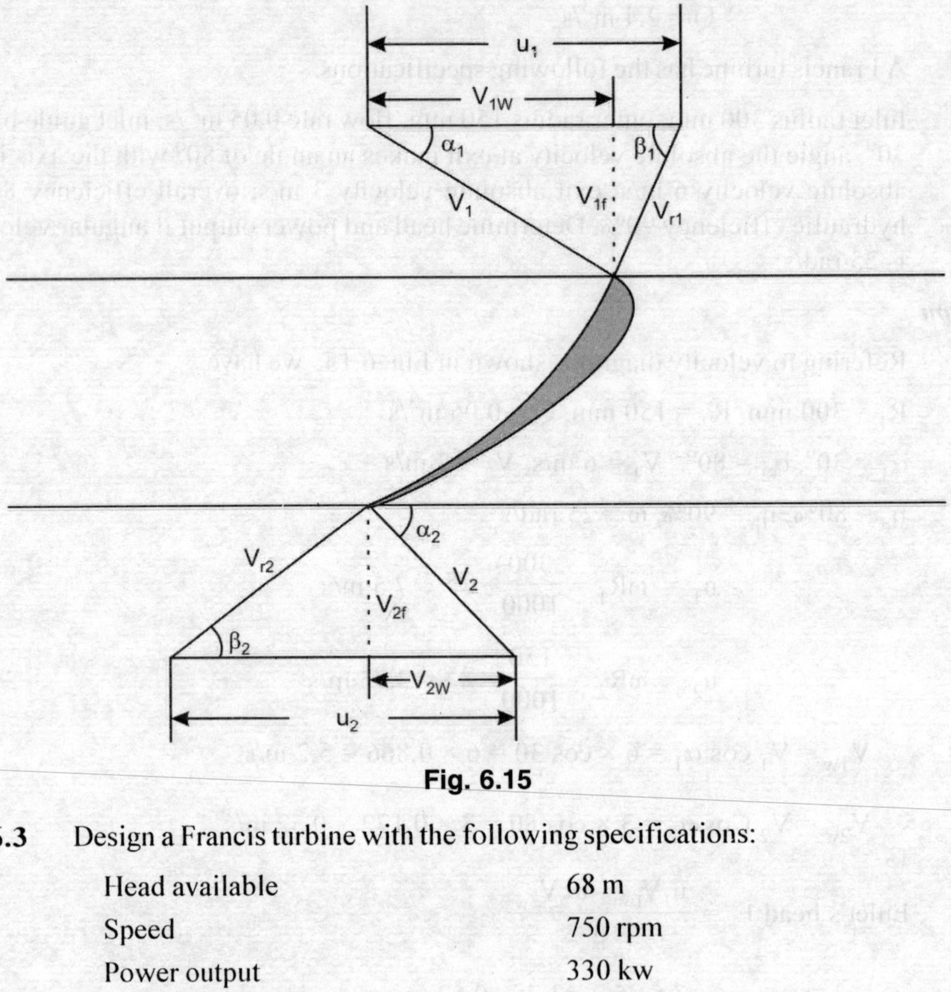

Fig. 6.15

E.6.3 Design a Francis turbine with the following specifications:

Head available	68 m
Speed	750 rpm
Power output	330 kw
hydraulic efficiency	94%
overall efficiency	85%
Flow ratio χ	0.15
Breadth to diameter ratio at inlet	0.1
outer to inner diameter ratio	$\frac{1}{2}$

Assume 6% of circumferential area of runner occupied by thickness of vanes and flow velocity remains constant and flow is radial at exit.

Solution

Given H = 68 m; χ = 0.15; N = 750 rpm, n_1 = 0.1

P = 330 kw; $D_2/D_1 = \frac{1}{2}$; η_h = 94%; η_o = 85%; area reduction = 6%; k_1 = 0.94;

overall efficiency $\eta_o = \frac{P}{\gamma QH}$; $0.85 = \frac{330 \times 1000}{9800 \times Q \times 68}$

$$\therefore \quad Q = 0.582 \text{ m}^3/\text{s}$$

$$\chi = \frac{V_f}{\sqrt{2gH}};$$

$$V_f = 0.15\sqrt{2 \times 9.8 \times 68}$$

$$V_f = 5.47 \text{ m/s}$$

$$V_f = V_{1f} = V_{2f} = 5.47 \text{ m/s}$$

From eq. 6.9 $Q = (k\,\pi\,n_1\,D_1^2)\,V_{1f}$ and substituting proper values

$$0.582 = 0.94 \times \pi \times 0.1 \times D_1^2 \times 5.47$$

$$D_1 = 0.6 \text{ m} = 600 \text{ mm}$$

$$\frac{B_1}{D_1} = 0.1$$

$$\therefore \quad B_1 = 600 \times 0.1 = 60 \text{ mm}$$

$$u_1 = \frac{\pi D_1 N}{60}$$

$$\therefore \quad u_1 = \frac{\pi \times 0.6 \times 750}{60} = 23.5 \text{ m/s}$$

$$\eta_h = \frac{u_1 V_{1w} - u_2 V_{2w}}{gH}$$

as $V_{2w} = 0$ beause radial discharge

$$\eta_h = \frac{u_1 V_{1w}}{gH}$$

$$\therefore \quad V_{1w} = \frac{0.94 \times 9.8 \times 68}{23.5}$$

$$= 26.6 \text{ m/s}$$

From Fig. 6.16 we have

$$\therefore \quad \tan \alpha_1 = \frac{V_{1f}}{V_{1w}} = \frac{5.47}{26.6} = 0.2$$

$$\alpha_1 = 11.6^o$$

outer diameter $D_2 = \frac{1}{2} D_1 = \frac{1}{2} \times 600 = 300$ mm

$$u_2 = \frac{\pi D_2 N}{60}$$

$$\therefore \quad u_2 = \frac{\pi \times 0.3 \times 750}{60} = 11.7 \text{ m/s}$$

$$\tan \beta_2 = \frac{V_{2f}}{u_2} = \frac{5.47}{11.7} = 0.46$$

$$\beta_2 = 25^0$$

$$Q = k_1 \pi D_1^2 n_1 V_{1f} = k_2 \pi D_2^2 n_2 V_{2f}$$

assume $k_1 = k_2$; $V_{1f} = V_{2f}$

$$\therefore \quad 0.6^2 \times 0.1 = n_2 \times 0.3^2$$

$$n_2 = 0.4$$

$$n_2 = \frac{B_2}{D_2}$$

$$\therefore \quad B_2 = 300 \times 0.4 = 120 \text{ mm}$$

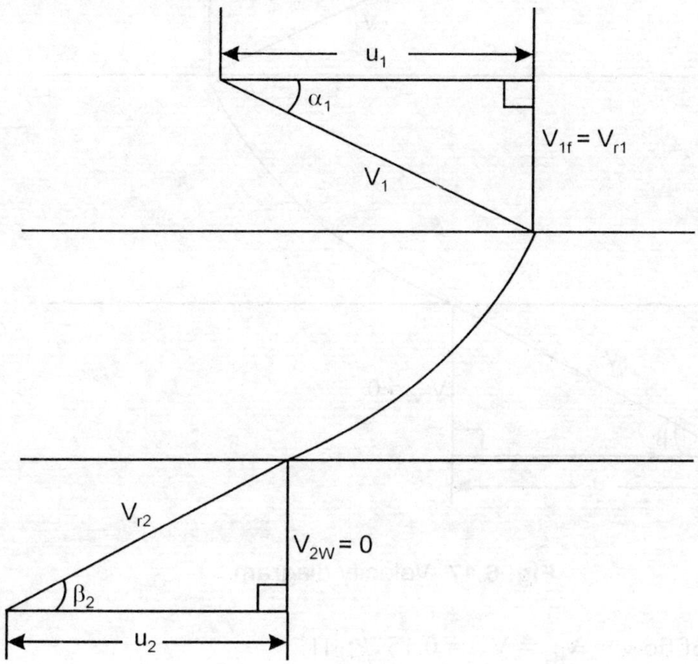

Fig. 6.16 Inlet and exit velocity diagram.

E.6.4 In a Francis turbine the supply head is 12 m and flow rate is 0.28 m^3/s, outer diameter is half the inner diameter 12 m. The velocity of flow is $0.15\sqrt{2gH}$. The inner vanes are radial at inlet and runner rotates at 300 rpm. The hydraulic efficiency is 80%. Determine guide vane angle and runner vane angle at exit for radial discharge.

Solution

Given

$$H = 12 \text{ m}, Q = 0.28 \text{ m}^3/\text{s} ; V_f = 0.15 \sqrt{2gH}$$

$$N = 300 \text{ rpm}, \eta_h = 80\%, \alpha_1 = ?, \beta_2 = ?$$

Referring to inlet and exit velocity diagram shown in Fig. 6.17.

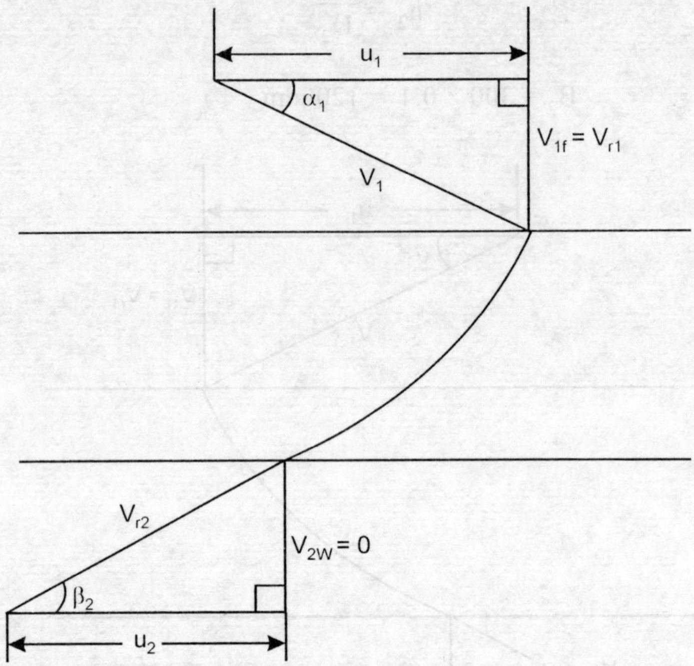

Fig. 6.17 Velocity diagram.

Velocity of flow $V_{1f} = V_{2f} = 0.15\sqrt{2gH}$

$$V_{1f} = 0.15\sqrt{2 \times 9.8 \times 12} = 2.3 \text{ m/s}$$

$$\eta_h = \frac{u_1 V_{1w} - u_2 V_{2w}}{gH} \quad \text{as } V_{2w} = 0$$

$$\eta_h = \frac{u_1 V_1 w}{gH} \quad \text{also } V_{1w} = u_1$$

$$0.8 = \frac{V_{1w}^2}{9.8 \times 12}$$

$$V_{1w} = 9.7 \text{ m/s}$$

$$u_1 = V_{1w} = 9.7 \text{ m/s} ; \quad \text{also } u_1 = \omega R_1,\ u_2 = \omega R_2$$

$$\therefore \qquad u_2 = u_1 \times \frac{R_2}{R_1} = 9.7 \times \frac{1}{2} = 4.85 \text{ m/s}$$

$$\tan \beta_2 = \frac{V_{2f}}{u_2} = \frac{2.3}{4.85} = 0.474$$

$$\beta_2 = 25^o$$

$$\tan \alpha_1 = \frac{V_{1f}}{u_1} = \frac{2.3}{9.7} = 0.237$$

$$\alpha_1 = 13^o$$

E.6.5 A Francis turbine has the following data:

Flow rate 0.4 m^3/s, head = 92 m, runner speed 1260 rev/min. The guide vane angle 20°, the radius at inlet = 600 mm, width of vanes 30 mm. Determine the shaft power, hydraulic efficiency and specific speeds (ω_T, N_T). Assume radial discharge.

Solution

Given N = 1260 rpm, Q = 0.4 m^3/s, H = 92 m, $\alpha_1 = 20^o$; R_1 = 600 mm, B_1 = 30 mm

Torque produced by the runner

$$T = \dot{m}\ V_{1w} R_1 - \dot{m} V_{2w} R_2$$

$$T = Q\rho\ V_{1w} R_1 \qquad \text{as } V_{2w} = 0$$

also $\qquad Q = \pi D_1 B_1 V_{1f}$

$$\therefore \qquad 0.4 = \pi \times \frac{2 \times 600}{1000} \times \frac{30}{1000} \times V_{1f}$$

$$\therefore \qquad V_{1f} = 3.5 \text{ m/s}$$

From inlet diagram Fig. 6.18

$$\tan \alpha_1 = \frac{V_{1f}}{V_{1w}}; \tan 20 = \frac{3.5}{V_{1w}}$$

$$\therefore \qquad V_{1w} = 9.61 \text{ m/s}$$

$$T = Q\rho V_{1w} R_1 = 0.4 \times 1000 \times 9.61 \times \frac{600}{1000}$$

$$T = 2304 \text{ N-m}$$

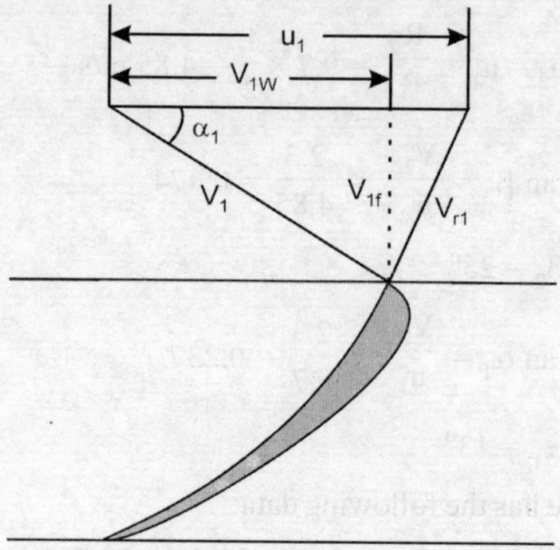

Fig. 6.18 Inlet diagram.

Shaft power $= T \times \omega$

where $\omega = \dfrac{2N\pi}{60}$; $\omega = \dfrac{2 \times 1260 \times \pi}{60} = 131.1$ rad/s

Shaft power $= \dfrac{2304 \times 2 \times 1260 \times \pi}{60} = 304$ kw

Overall efficiency $= \dfrac{\text{shaft power}}{\text{hydraulic power}} = \dfrac{304}{360} = 0.84$

$= 84\%$

Specific speed $\omega_T = \dfrac{\omega\sqrt{P/\rho}}{(gH)^{5/4}}$

$\omega = \dfrac{2 \times 1260 \times \pi}{60} = 131.8$ rad/s, substituting proper values

$$\omega_T = \frac{131.8\sqrt{\dfrac{304 \times 10^3}{1000}}}{(9.8 \times 92)^{5/4}}$$

$$\omega_T = 0.46$$

$$N_s = \frac{N\sqrt{P}}{H^{5/4}} = \frac{1260\sqrt{304}}{92^{5/4}} = 76.9$$

Problems

P.6.1 Turbines are designed to develop 20,000 kw while operating under a head of 20 m and speed of 60 rev/min. What type of turbine is best suited for thier purpose. Estimate the flow rate needed.

P.6.2 Draft tubes as shown in the following Fig. 6.19 often installed at exit of Kaplan and Francis turbines. Explain why such draft tubes are advantageous.

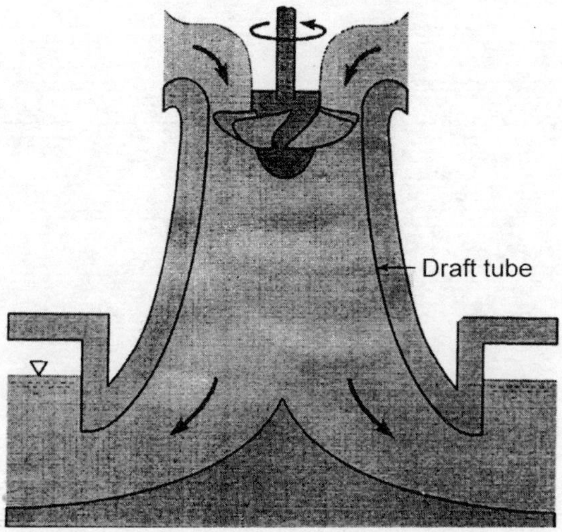

Fig. 6.19

CHAPTER - 7

Propeller and Kaplan Turbines

Photograph of fixed blade runner in workshop assembly.
***Courtesy:* Sulzer Escher Wyss, Zurich, Switzerland.**

7.1 Introduction

It has been mentioned in the previous chapters that the power developed by a hydraulic turbine is the product of head available and flow rate. Pelton turbine is suitable for high head and low flow rates. Francis turbine is suitable for medium head and medium discharge. Pelton turbine is classified as impulse and Francis as reaction. Pelton is axial flow and Francis is radial flow. Now we deal with two other axial flow turbines, low head and high discharge, namely, Propeller and Kaplan turbines. Basically there is not much difference between the two turbines. In kaplan turbine both the guide vanes and runner blades are adjustable with load thus maintaining high efficiency. The blade adjustments are made simultaneously to accommodate changing conditions. Kaplan turbines have reached efficiencies between 90-95%. Also more than 100 MW can be developed from a single unit.

In the propeller type only guide vanes are adjustable with fixed runner blades. Both the turbines are reaction type and axial flow.

A large hydro elective power generator unit is shown in Fig. 7.1. A propeller type of turbine axial flow is seen in the picture. A common vertical shaft connected the turbine runner and electric generator. The electric generator is air cooled. As clearly visible adjustable guide vanes (wicket gates) and runner blades 6 in number are installed. The guide vanes and runner blades are not visible from outside, but one can see the electric generator and listen to its humming sound.

7.2 Description of Propeller Turbine

The propeller type consists of axial flow runner with 4 to 6 blades of an aerofoil shape as shown in Fig.7.2. The spiral casing and guide vanes are similar to Francis turbine. The flow enters the runner through guide vanes which can be set to any desired angle (within limit) to accommodate changes in power output demand. The runner blades are fixed and cannot change their position. The guide vanes ring is in a plane perpendicular to the shaft so that flow is radial. The runner is situated further downstream so that between guide vanes and the runner the fluid turns through a right angle into axial direction. The runner blades are long in order to accommodate large flow rate and therefore pitch/chord ratio of runner blades is 1 to 1.5 and hence number of blades is small. The propeller type has low head between 5-80 m. Fig. 7.2(a) shows the plan view of guide vanes and Fig.7.2(b) shows profile of the system.

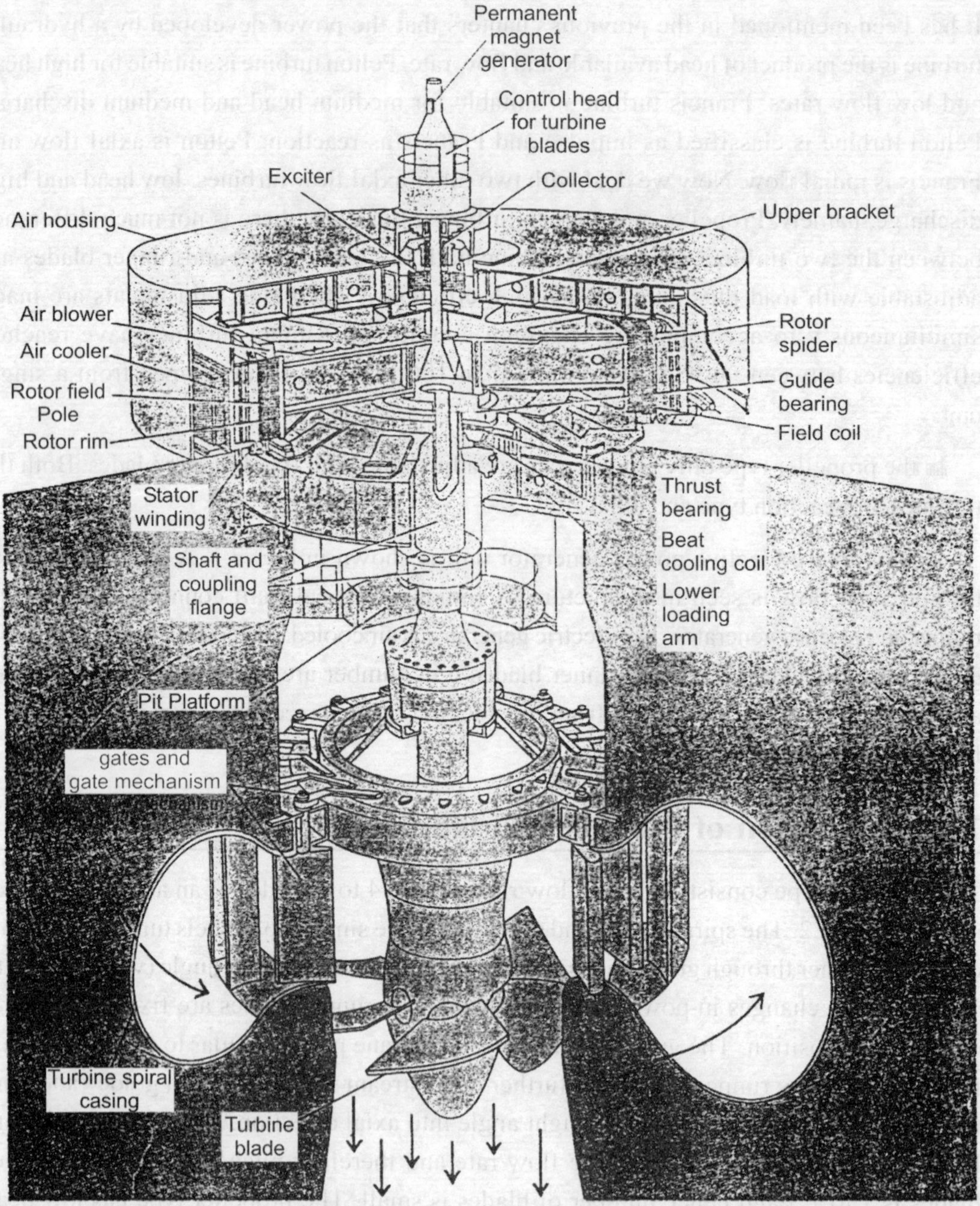

Fig. 7.1 A large hydroeletric power generator.

Courtesy : Westing house eletric corp.

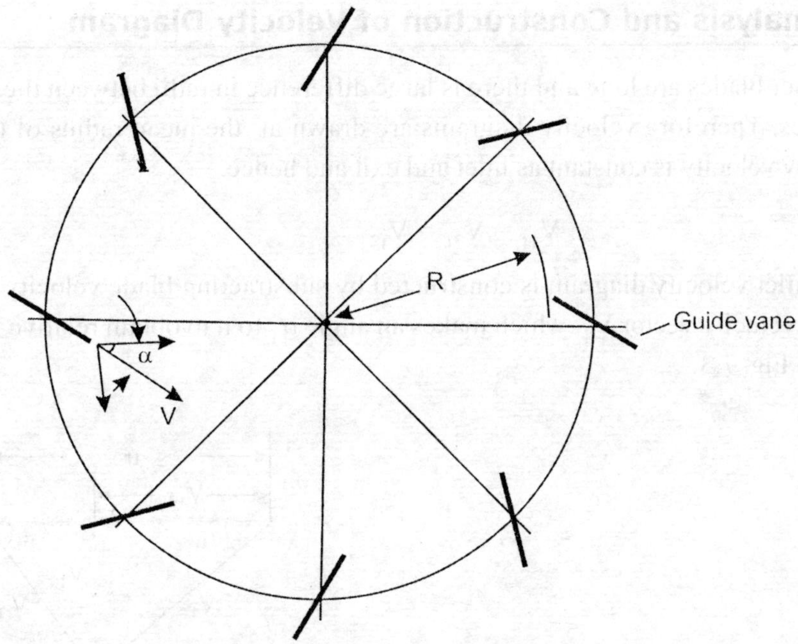

Fig. 7.2(a) Plan view of guide vanes.

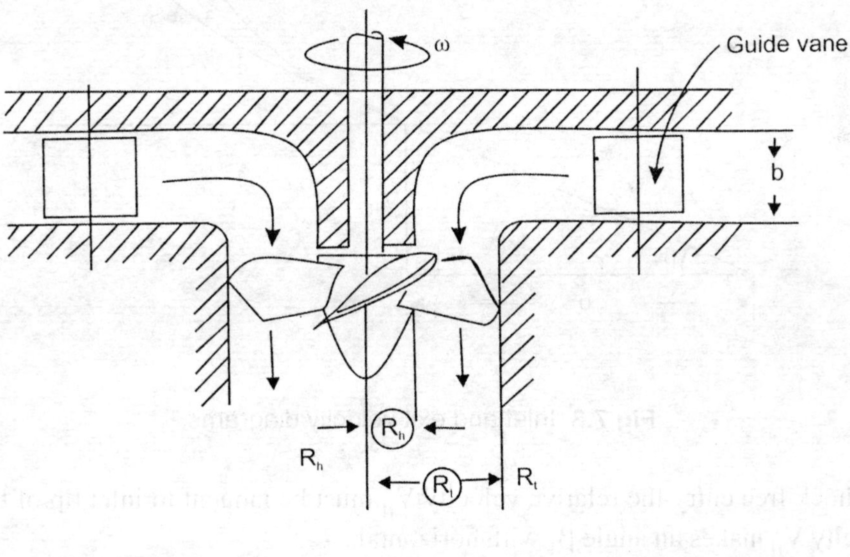

Fig. 7.2(b) Axial-flow propeller type turbine, guide vanes and runner.

7.3 Analysis and Construction of Velocity Diagram

The runner blades are long and there is large difference in radii between the hub and tip of the blades. Therefore velocity diagrams are drawn at the mean radius of the blade. The axial flow velocity is constant as inlet and exit and hence

$$V_{1f} = V_{2f} = V_f$$

The inlet velocity diagram is constructed by substracting blade velocity vector u from absolute velocity vector V_1, which makes an angle α_1 to u to obtain relative velocity V_{rl} as shown in Fig. 7.3.

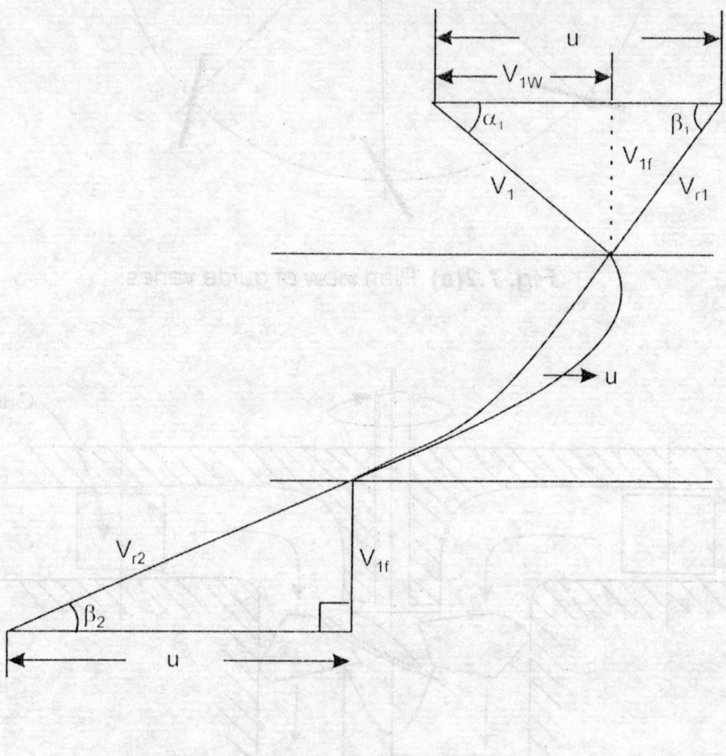

Fig 7.3 Inlet and exit velocity diagrams.

For shock free entry the relative velocity V_{rl} must be tangent to inlet tip of the blade. The velocity V_{rl} makes an angle β_1 with horizontal.

The exit velocity diagram is constructed by drawing relative velocity at exit V_{r2} tangential to exit tip of the blade, superimposing peripheral velocity u, we obtain absolute velocity V_2 which is axial. The velocity diagrams are shown in Fig. 7.4.

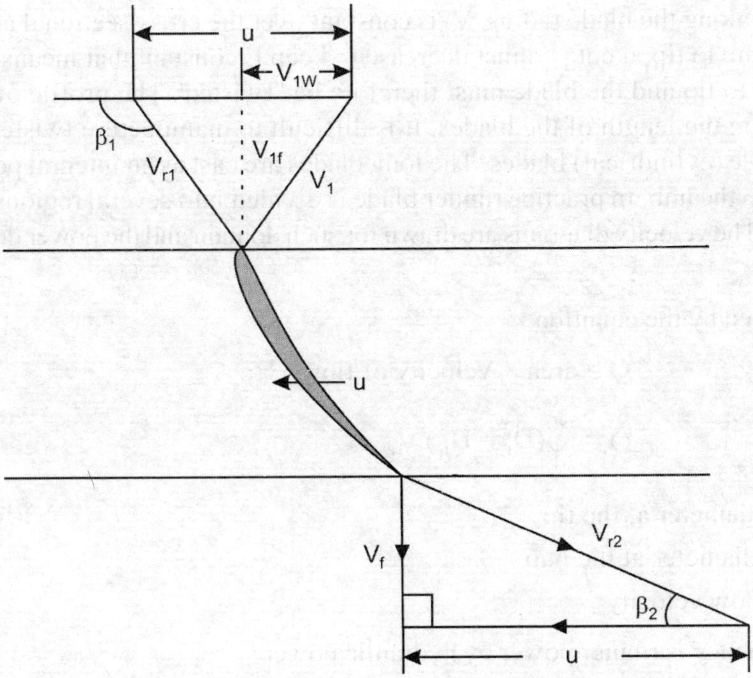

Fig. 7.4 Inlet and exit velocity diagram.

For maximum efficiency the whirl component V_{2w} at exit must be zero because velocity V_2 is axial and also

$$V_2 = V_{2f}$$

Writing Euler's equation as

$$E = \frac{u(V_{1w} - V_{2w})}{g} \quad \text{as } V_{2w} = 0 \qquad .....(7.1)$$

$$E = \frac{uV_{1w}}{g} \qquad .....(7.2)$$

From inlet diagram, we have

$$V_{1w} = u - V_f \cot(180 - \beta_1) = u + V_f \cot\beta_1$$

Substituting this value of V_{1w} in eq. 7.2

$$E = \frac{u(u + V_f \cot\beta_1)}{g} = \frac{u^2 + uV_f \cot\beta_1}{g}$$

$$E = \frac{u^2 + uV_f \cot\beta_1}{g} \qquad .....(7.3)$$

If E is constant along the blade radius, V_f is constant over the cross-sectional area, then u increases from hub to tip, u cot β_1 must decrease t keep E constant that means β_1 must increase from hub to tip and the blade must therefore be 'Twisted'. The profile of twisted blade changes along the length of the blades. It is difficult to manufacture twisted blades than constant profile (cylindrical) blades. The long blades are cast as an integral part of the runner or welded to the hub. In practice runner blade is divided into several regions of flow around the blades. The velocity diagrams are drawn for such domain and the power developed computed.

Flow rate is given by the equation

$$Q = \text{area} \times \text{Velocity of flow}$$

$$Q = \frac{\pi}{4}(D_t^2 - D_h^2)\,V_f \qquad \text{.....(7.4)}$$

where D_t = diameter at the tip

D_h = diameter at the hub

V_f = flow velocity

Hydraulic efficiency is runner power by hydraulic power

$$\eta_h = \frac{E}{H} = \frac{\gamma QE}{\gamma QH} \qquad \text{.....(7.5)}$$

$$\text{Mechanical efficiency } \eta_m = \frac{\text{shaft power}}{\text{runner power}} = \frac{P}{\gamma QE}$$

$$\eta_m = \frac{P}{\gamma QE} \qquad \text{.....(7.6)}$$

$$\text{Overall efficiency} = \frac{\text{shaft power}}{\text{hydraulic power}} = \frac{P}{\gamma QH}$$

$$\eta_o = \frac{P}{\gamma QH} \qquad \text{.....(7.7)}$$

From eqns. 6.6, 6.7 and 6.8 we get,

$$\eta_o = \eta_m \times \eta_h \qquad \text{.....(7.8)}$$

H is effective head $H = H_1 + H_2$ as shown in Fig. 7.4 of Kaplan turbine installation.

Fig.7.5 shows overall efficiency against percentage of design power for various turbines.

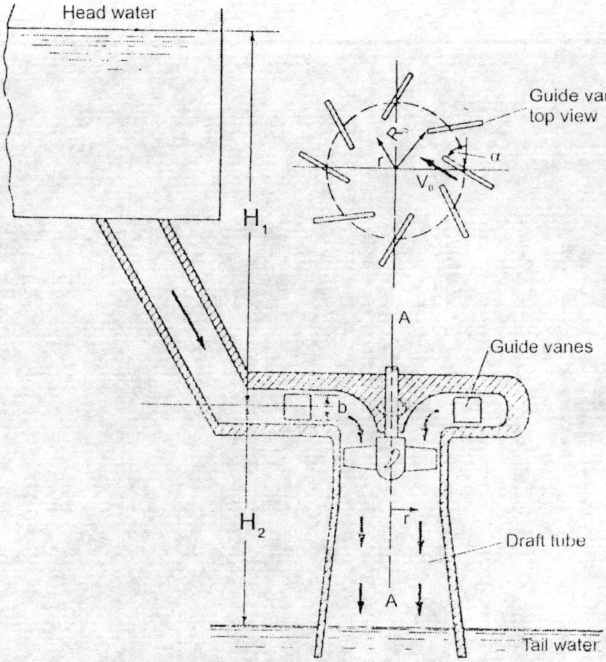

Fig. 7.5 Axial flow turbine

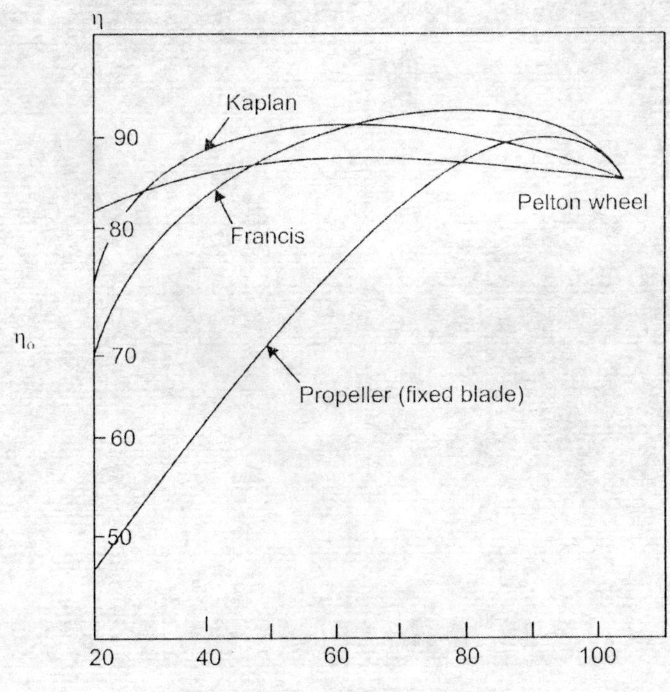

Fig. 7.6 Graph overall efficiency against percentage of design power.

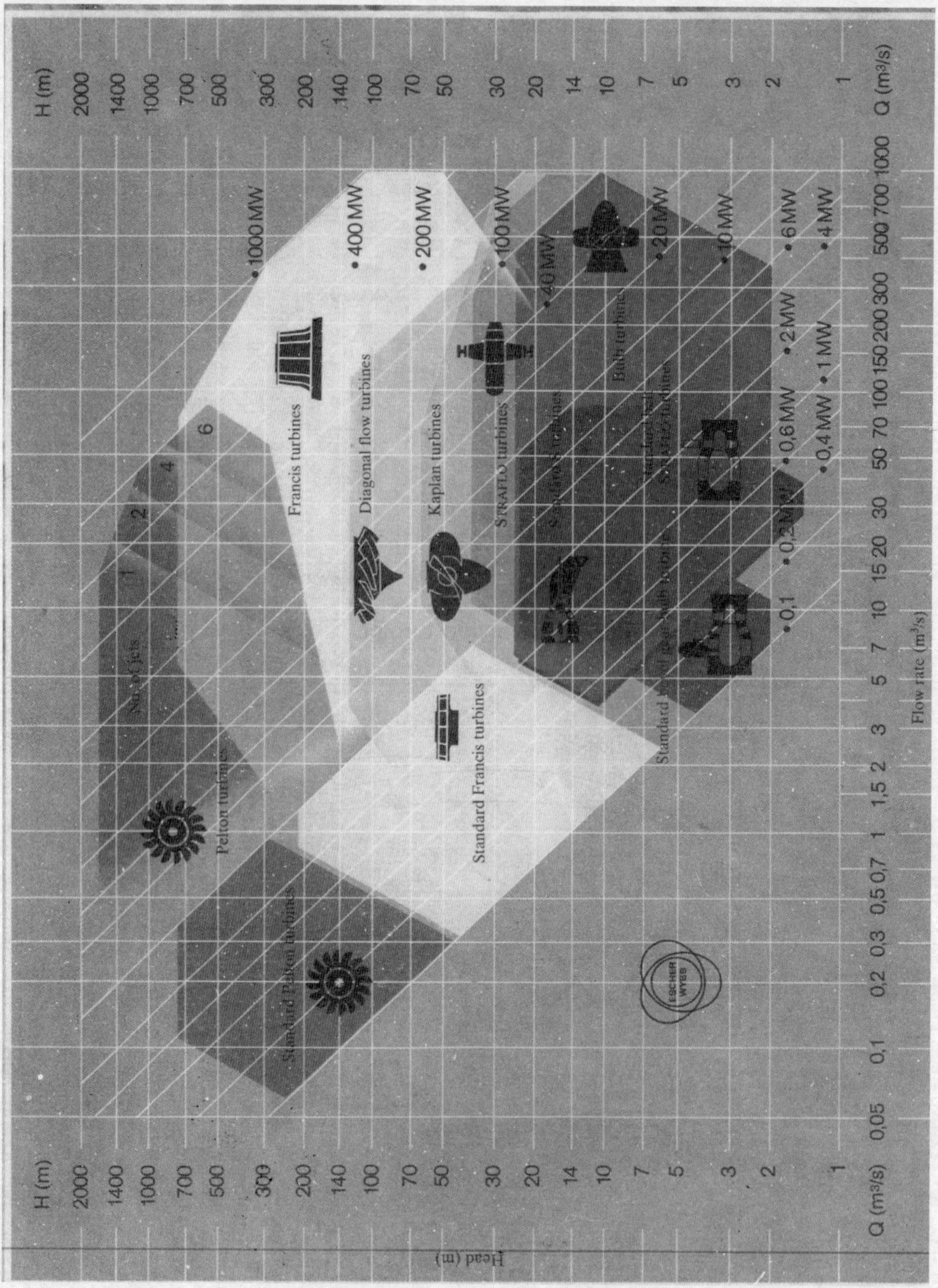

Fig. 7.7 Graphs show application ranges of Escher Wyss water turbines.

The characteristic curve for the axial flow Kaplan turbine is similar to radial flow Francis turbine. The Pelton efficiency curve is flatter but maximum efficiency is lower than Francis turbine. Kaplan has better characteristics than propeller type.

The two methods of determining specific speed of propeller/Kaplan turbine is given below:

$$\omega_T = \frac{\omega\sqrt{\frac{P}{\rho}}}{(gH)^{5/4}}$$

and $$N_s = \frac{N\sqrt{P}}{H^{\frac{5}{4}}}$$

Fig. 7.6 shows application ranges of Escher water turbines. The Pelton turbines are divided into two ranges. The minimum head of 50-700 m and head of 300-1400 m with low flow rate. Kaplan turbine works from 2-20 m with high flow rate developing maximum power of about 100 MW. The Francis turbine has a big range from 20-300 m and maximum power of 100 MW.

7.4 Twisted Blades

The Kaplan turbine aerofoil type propeller blades are long and the radius at the hub and tip varies considerably. The inlet and exit velocity diagrams change at every section of the blading. Therefore blade is divided into several domain and calculations made for every section with the inlet angle α_1 remaining same. Inlet and exit blade angles β_1 and β_2 change from hub to tip.

Euler's equation is re-written as

$$E = \frac{u(V_{1w} - V_{2w})}{g} \text{ as } V_{2w} = 0,$$

we have $$E = \frac{u\,V_{1w}}{g} = \frac{\omega R}{g}.V_{1w} = \left(\frac{\omega}{g}\right)(R\,V_{1w})$$

$$E = \left(\frac{\omega}{g}\right)(R\,V_{1w}) \quad .....(7.9)$$

The blades are designed in such a way to keep E = constant at every section which means, RV_w is constant. The law of twisted blades is therefore RV_w = constant.

The mean diameter, of the blade is given by

$$D = \frac{D_t + D_h}{2} \qquad .....(7.10)$$

where D_t, D_h are the diameters, of tip and hub, respectively

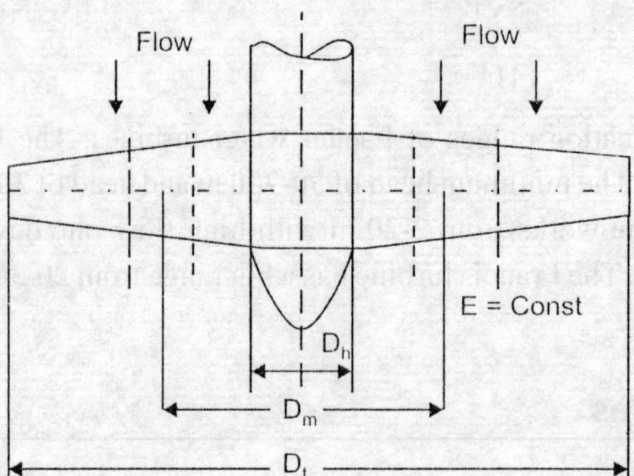

Fig. 7.8 Twisted blades.

7.5 Description of Kaplan Turbine

The Propeller turbine is suitable when the load on turbine remains constant. It has low efficiency at part load, as blade angles do not change and water enters with shock accompanied with losses. The Kaplan turbine is fitted with adjustable runner blades and both guide vanes and runner blades act simultaneously. The blade angles changes automatically by servo motor as load changes. Thus Kaplan has high efficiency as part loads. Kaplan turbine installation with draft tube is shown in Fig. 7.9. Governing equations of Kaplan turbine are similar to propeller turbines.

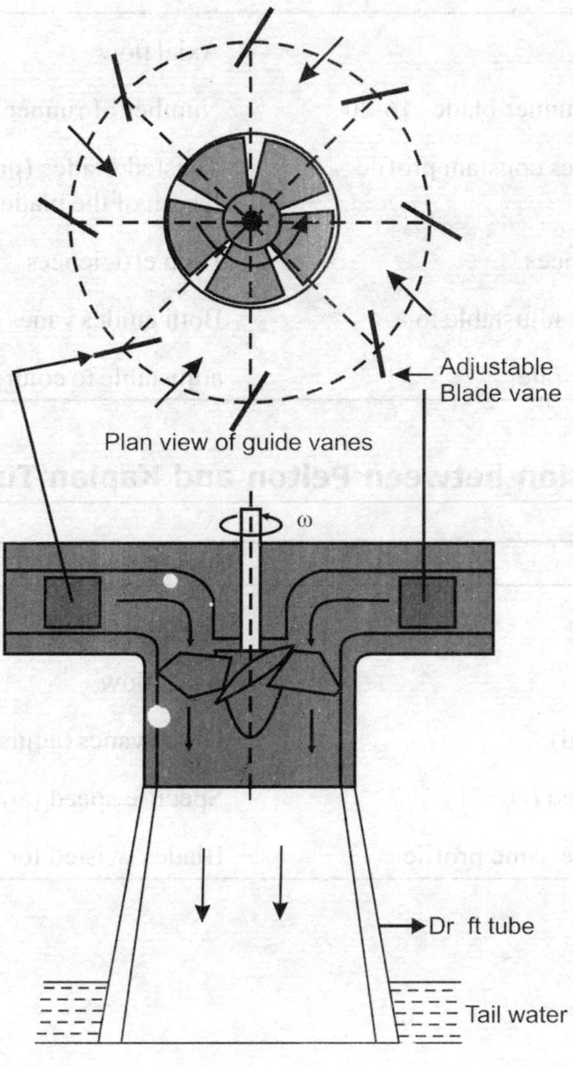

Fig. 7.9 Kaplan Turbine with draft tube.

7.6 Comparision between Francis and Kaplan Turbine

Francis	Kaplan
1. Radial flow	Axial flow
2. Number of runner blades 16-20	Number of runner blades 4-6
3. Runner blades constant profile	Twisted blades (profile changes along length of the blade
4. Low efficiences	High efficiences
5. Guide vanes adjustable to change flow rate	Both guides vanes and propeller blades adjustable to control flow rate

7.7 Comparision between Pelton and Kaplan Turbine

Pelton	Kaplan
1. Impulse type	Reaction type
2. Axial flow	Axial flow
3. Nozzle (fixed)	Guide vanes (adjustable)
4. Specific speed ($\omega_s < 1$)	Specific speed ($\omega_T > 2.3$)
5. Buckets have same profile	Blades twisted for higher efficiency

Solved Examples

E.7.1 An axial flow turbine operates under a head of 21.8 m and develops 21 MW when running at 140 rpm. The tip diameter is 4.5 m and hub diameter is 2.0 m. The hydraulic efficiency is 94%. Determine inlet and exit angles of blades mean diameter if the overall efficiency is 88%.

Solution

Given H = 21.8 m, P = 21 MW; N = 140 rpm; $D_t = 4.5$ m, $D_h = 2.0$m,

$\eta_h = 94\%$, $\eta_n = 88\%$

$$\text{Mean diameter} \quad = \frac{D_t + D_h}{2} = \frac{4.5 + 2.0}{2} = 3.25 \text{ m}$$

$$\omega = \frac{2N\pi}{60}; \ \omega = \frac{2 \times 140 \times \pi}{60} = 14.65 \text{ rad/s}$$

$$u = \omega\, r; \ u = \frac{14.65 \times 3.25}{2} = 23.8 \text{ m/s}$$

$$\eta_h = \frac{uV_{1w}}{gH};$$

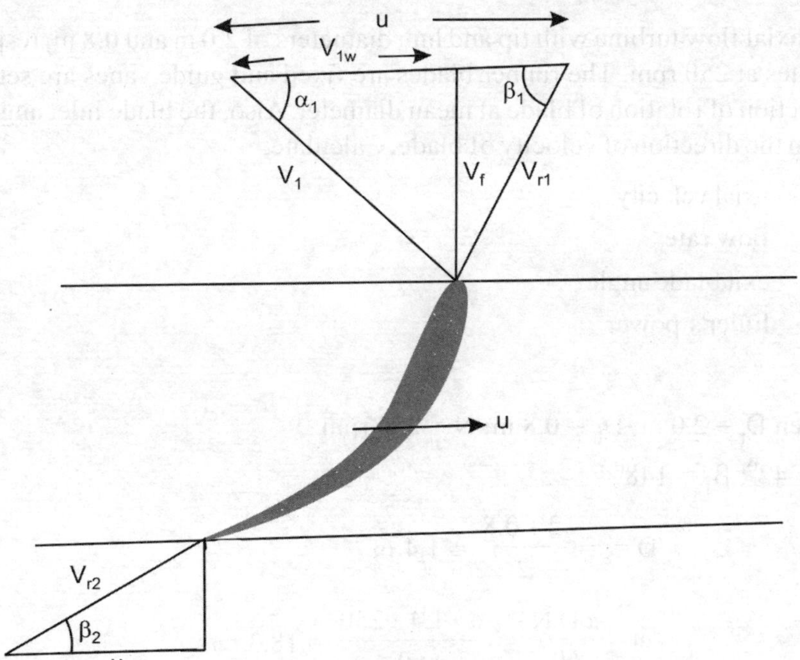

Fig. 7.10

$$\therefore \qquad V_{1w} = \frac{0.94 \times 9.8 \times 21.8}{23.8} = 8.43 \text{ m/s}$$

$$\eta_0 = \frac{P}{\gamma Q H}\ ; Q = \frac{21 \times 1000 \times 1000}{0.88 \times 9800 \times 21.8} = 111.7 \text{ m}^3/\text{s}$$

$$Q = \frac{\pi}{4}\left(D_t^2 - D_h^2\right) \times V_f$$

$$111.7 = \frac{\pi}{4}\,(4.5^2 - 2^2)\,V_f$$

$$\therefore \qquad V_f = 8.75 \text{ m/s}$$

$$\tan\beta_1 = \frac{V_f}{u - V_{1w}} = \frac{8.75}{23.8 - 8.43} = \frac{8.75}{15.37} = 0.56$$

$$\beta_1 = 30^o$$

$$\tan\beta_2 = \frac{V_f}{u} = \frac{8.75}{23.8} = 0.36$$

$$\beta_2 = 20^0$$

E.7.2 An axial flow turbine with tip and hub diameters of 2.0 m and 0.8 m, respectively, rotates at 250 rpm. The runner blades are fixed and guide vanes are set at 42° to direction of rotation of blade at mean diameter. Also, the blade inlet angle is 148° from the direction of velocity of blade. Calculate,

- axial velocity
- flow rate
- exit blade angle
- Euler's power

Solution

Given $D_t = 2.0$ m; $D_h = 0.8$ m; N = 250 rpm

$\alpha_1 = 42^o$; $\beta_1 = 148^o$

$$D = = \frac{2 + 0.8}{2} = 1.4 \text{ m}$$

$$u = \frac{\pi D N}{60} = \frac{\pi \times 1.4 \times 250}{60} = 18.3 \text{ m/s}$$

From inlet triangle of velocities diagram of Fig. 7.11, we have

$$V_f = \tan(\pi - \beta_1)(u - v_{1w}) = \tan \alpha_1 V_{1w}$$

$$\therefore \quad \tan(\pi - 148)(18.3 - V_{1w}) = \tan 42 V_{1w}$$

$$\therefore \quad V_{1w} = 7.5 \text{ m/s}$$

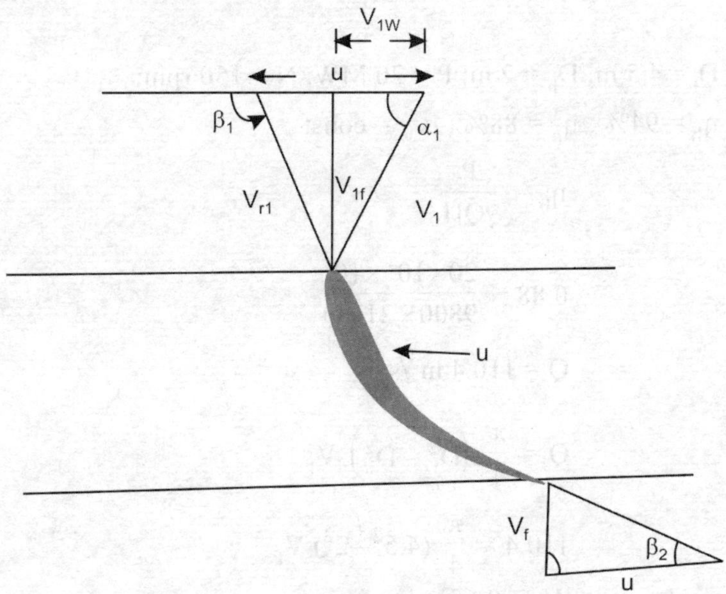

Fig. 7.11 Inlet and exit velocity diagrams.

$$\tan \alpha_1 = \frac{V_f}{V_{1w}},$$

$$\therefore \quad V_f = 7.5 \times \tan 42 = 6.75 \text{ m/s}$$

$$Q = \frac{\pi}{4}\left(D_t^2 - D_h^2\right) V_f = \frac{\pi}{4}(2^2 - 0.8^2)\, 6.75 = 17.8 \text{ m}^3/\text{s}$$

Euler's head $\quad E = \dfrac{u V_{1w}}{g} = \dfrac{18.3 \times 7.5}{9.8} = 14 \text{ m}$

Euler's power $\quad \gamma QE = \dfrac{9800 \times 17.8 \times 14}{1000} = 2.4 \text{ kW}$

$$\tan \beta_2 = \frac{V_f}{u} = \frac{6.75}{18.3} = 0.368$$

$$\beta_2 = 20^o$$

E.7.3 A propeller turbine runner has a tip diameter of 4.5 m and hub diameter of 2 m. It is required to develop 20 MW when running at 150 rpm. Assuming hydraulic efficiency of 94% and overall efficiency of 88%, determine blade angles at hub, mean and tip diameters. Assume that runner blades are designed according to the law rv_w = constant, where r is radius and V_w is whirl velocity. The head available is 21 m.

Solution

Given $D_t = 4.5$ m, $D_h = 2$ m; P = 20 MW; N = 150 rpm;

$$\eta_h = 94\% \; ; \; \eta_o = 88\% \; ; \; rv_w = \text{const}$$

$$\eta_0 = \frac{P}{\gamma Q H}$$

$$\therefore \quad 0.88 = \frac{20 \times 10^3 \times 10^3}{9800 \times 21 \times Q}$$

$$\therefore \quad Q = 110.4 \text{ m}^3/\text{s}$$

$$Q = \frac{\pi}{4}\left(D_t^2 - D_h^2\right) V_f$$

$$110.4 = \frac{\pi}{4}(4.5^2 - 2^2)\, V_f$$

$$\therefore \quad V_f = 8.65 \text{ m/s}$$

$$\eta_h = \frac{uV_w}{gH} \; ; \; 0.94 = \frac{2 \times 150 \times \pi}{60} \times \frac{1}{9.8} \times \frac{1}{21}(rV_w)$$

$$\therefore \quad \boxed{rV_w = 12.32}$$

$$D = \frac{D_t + D_h}{2} = \frac{4.5 + 2}{2} = 3.25; \quad r_m = 1.625$$

$$r_m = 1.625 \qquad (V_w)_m = \frac{12.32}{1.625} = 7.58 \text{ m/s}$$

$$r_t = 2.25 \qquad (V_w)_t = \frac{12.32}{2.25} = 5.47 \text{ m/s}$$

$$r_h = 1.0 \qquad (V_w)_R = \frac{12.32}{1} = 12.32 \text{ m/s}$$

$$u_h = \frac{\pi D_h N}{60} = \frac{\pi \times 2 \times 150}{60} = 15.7 \text{ m/s}$$

$$u_m = \frac{\pi D_m N}{60} = \frac{\pi \times 3.25 \times 150}{60} = 25.5 \text{ m/s}$$

$$u_t = \frac{\pi D_t \times N}{60} = \frac{\pi \times 4.5 \times 150}{60} = 35.3 \text{ m/s}$$

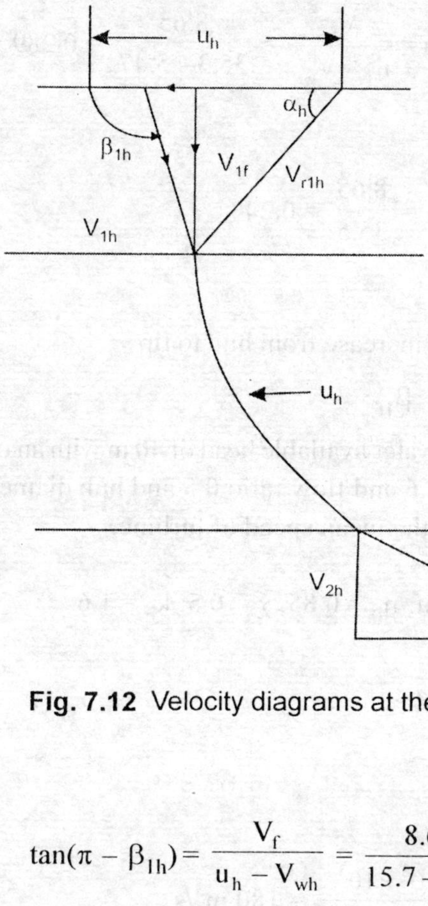

Fig. 7.12 Velocity diagrams at the hub of the blade.

Hub:

$$\tan(\pi - \beta_{1h}) = \frac{V_f}{u_h - V_{wh}} = \frac{8.65}{15.7 - 12.3} = 2.54$$

$$\pi - \beta_{1h} = 68.5; \qquad \beta_{1h} = 111.5^0$$

$$\tan\beta_{2h} = \frac{V_f}{u_h} = \frac{8.65}{15.7} = 0.55 ;$$

$$\beta_{2h} = 28.8^o$$

Mean:

$$\tan(\pi - \beta_{1m}) = \frac{V_f}{u_m - V_{wm}} = \frac{8.65}{25.5 - 7.58} = 0.48$$

$$\pi - \beta_{1m} = 25.6; \qquad \beta_{1m} = 154.4^0;$$

$$\tan\beta_{2m} = \frac{V_f}{u_m} = \frac{8.65}{25.5} = 0.33 \qquad \beta_{2m} = 18.7^0$$

Tip:

$$\tan(\pi - \beta_{1t}) = \frac{V_f}{u_t - v_{wt}} = \frac{8.65}{35.3 - 5.47} = 0.289$$

$$\beta_{1t} = 164^o$$

$$\tan\beta_{2t} = \frac{V_f}{ut} = \frac{8.65}{35.5} = 0.243$$

$$\beta_{2t} = 13.7^o$$

Thus the inlet angle β_1 must increase from hub to tip

$$\beta_{1h} < \beta_{1m} < \beta_{1t}$$

E.7.4 A Kaplan produces 60 MW, water available head of 40 m with an overall efficiency of 85%. The speed ratio is 1.6 and flow ratio 0.5 and hub diameter is 0.35 times the tip diameter. Determine the mean speed of turbine.

Solution

Given P = 60 MW; H = 40 m; $\eta_0 = 0.85$, $\chi = 0.5$; $k_u = 1.6$

$$\text{Overall efficiency } \eta_0 = \frac{P}{\gamma QH}$$

$$\therefore \qquad Q = \frac{P}{\eta_0 \cdot \gamma\gamma \cdot}$$

$$Q = \frac{60 \times 10^3 \times 10^3}{0.85 \times 9800 \times 40} = 180 \text{ m}^3/\text{s}$$

$$\chi = \frac{V_f}{\sqrt{2gH}}$$

$$\therefore \qquad V_f = \chi\sqrt{2gH} = 0.5\sqrt{2 \times 9.8 \times 40}$$

$$= 14 \text{ m/s}$$

Flow in Kaplan turbine $Q = \dfrac{\pi(D_t^2 - D_h^2)}{4} V_f$

$$180 = \frac{\pi(D_t^2 - 0.35\,D_t^2)}{4} \times 14$$

$$D_t = 4.3 \text{ m}$$

$$D_h = 0.35\,D_t = 0.35 \times 4.3 = 1.5 \text{ m}$$

Mean diameter $D = \dfrac{D_t + D_h}{2} = \dfrac{4.3 + 1.5}{2} = 2.9 \text{ m}$

$$u = \frac{\pi DN}{60},\ k_u = \frac{u}{\sqrt{2gH}}$$

$$k_u\sqrt{2gH} = \frac{\pi DN}{60}$$

$$1.6\sqrt{2 \times 9.8 \times 40} = \frac{\pi \times 2.9 \times N}{60}$$

$$N = 295 \text{ rev/min}$$

E.7.5 Water is supplied to an axial flow turbine under a head of 35 m. The mean diameter of runner is 2 m and rotates at 145 rev/min. Water leaves the guide vanes at 30° to the direction of rotation and blade angle at exit is 28°, losses is guide vanes is 7% of the head and the flow of exit is axial. Determine blade inlet angle and Euler's head.

Solution

Given H = 35 m, D = 2 m, N = 145 rev/min; $\alpha_1 = 30^o$, $\beta_2 = 28^o$, h_g = 7% of H,

- Head available H = 0.93 × 35 = 32.6 m
- inlet velocity $V_1 = \sqrt{2gH} = \sqrt{2 \times 9.8 \times 32.6} = 25.3$ m/s
- $u = \dfrac{\pi DN}{60} = \dfrac{\pi \times 2 \times 145}{60} = 15.2$ m/s
- From inlet triangle of velocities

$$V_{r1}^2 = V_1^2 + u^2 - 2\,u\,v_1 \cos\alpha_1 \text{ in Fig. 7.13}$$

$$= 25.3^2 + 15.2^2 - (2 \times 15.2 \times 25.3 \cos 30)$$

$$V_{r1} = 14.3 \text{ m/s}$$

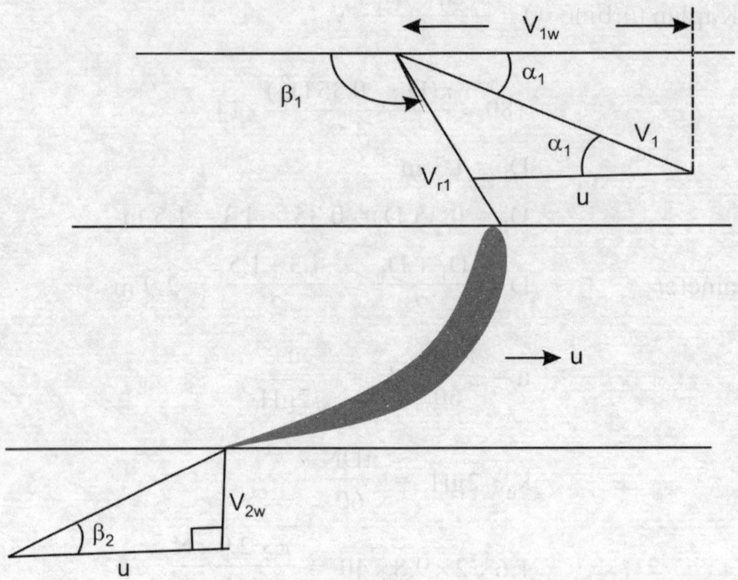

Fig. 7.13 Inlet and exit velocity diagrams.

Again $u^2 = V_{r1}^2 + V_1^2 - (2 \times V_{r1} \times V_1 \cos(\pi - \beta_1))$

$$15.2^2 = 14.3^2 + 25.3^2 - (2 \times 14.3 \times 25.3 \cos(\pi - \beta_1))$$

$$231 = 204.5 + 640 - 723.5 \cos(\pi - \beta_1)$$

$$613.5 = 723.5 \cos(\pi - \beta_1)$$

$$0.8479 = \cos(\pi - \beta_1)$$

$$\therefore \quad \beta_1 = 148^o$$

$$V_{1w} = V_1 \cos\alpha_1 = 25.3 \times 0.866 = 21.9 \text{ m/s}$$

$$E = \frac{u\,V_{1w}}{g} = \frac{15.2 \times 21.9}{9.8} = 33.9 \text{ m}$$

Table 7.1 gives technical specification of Pelton, Francis and Kaplan turbines installed in power stations. **For each power station the specific speeds ω_T, N_s and overall efficiency η_o calculated and checked with ranges of values given in the text.**

Table 7.1 The Technical specification of some power stations installing Pelton, Francis, and Kaplan turbine.

S.No.	Power Station	Installed Capacity	No.of Units	Unit rated output MW	Manufacture	Type	Rated speed	Type	Rated power MW	Head m	Flow rate $m^{3/s}$
1.	Termingor	348	4	87	Hitachi	vertical	214.3	Francis	90	101	125.4
2.	Bersia	72	3	24.7	Seimon	vertical	187.5	Kaplan	24.7	26.5	164.1
3.	JOR	100	4	26.1	Le Material Electriche	Horizontal	428	Pelton 2 Jets	26.1	587.3	6.85
4.	Pergau	600	4	150	Boving	Vertical	429	Francis	150	495	138.5
5.	Piah	35.36	2	27.68	BHEL	Vertical	428	Pelton 4-Jets	28.25	400	11.4
6.	Woh	150	3	50	Fuji Electric	Vertial	600	Francis	51.4	406	19.4

E.7.6 Bersia power station

$P = 24.7$ MW

$H = 26.5$ m

$N = 187.5$ rev/min

$Q = 104\ m^3/s$

Solution

$$\omega = \frac{2N\pi}{60} = \frac{2 \times 187.5 \times \pi}{60} = 19.6 \text{ rad/s}$$

$$\omega_T = \frac{\omega\sqrt{P/\rho}}{(gH)^{5/4}}$$

$$\omega_T = \frac{19.6\sqrt{\frac{24.7 \times 10^6}{10^3}}}{(9.8 \times 26.5)^{5/4}} = \frac{19.6 \times 157.2}{1042.5} = 2.95$$

$$N_s = \frac{N\sqrt{P}}{H^{5/4}} = \frac{187.5\sqrt{24.7 \times 10^3}}{(26.5)^{5/4}} = \frac{187.5 \times 157.1}{60.1} = 490.1$$

$$\text{Overall efficiency } \eta_o = \frac{P}{\gamma QH} = \frac{24.7 \times 10^6}{9800 \times 104 \times 26.5} = 91.4\%$$

Based on specific speed values obtained Kaplan turbine is selected with an overall efficiency of 91.5%

E.7.7 Termengor power station

- Flow rate $Q = 125.4\ m^3/s$
- Head $H = 101$m
- Speed $N = 214.3$ rev/min
- Power $\rho = 90$MW

Solution

Specific speed

$$\omega_T = \frac{\omega\sqrt{P/\rho}}{(gH)^{5/4}} \text{ ; } \omega = \frac{2N\pi}{60} = \frac{2 \times 214.3}{60} \times \pi = 22.4 \text{ rad/s}$$

$$- \quad \omega_T = \frac{22.4\sqrt{\dfrac{90\times10^3\times10^3}{10^3}}}{(9.8\times101)^{5/4}} = \frac{22.4\times300}{5551} = 1.2$$

$$- \quad N_s = \frac{N\sqrt{P}}{H^{5/4}} = \frac{214.3\sqrt{90\times1000}}{(101)^{5/4}} = 200.7$$

$$- \quad \text{Overall efficiency } \eta_o = \frac{P}{\gamma QH} = \frac{90\times10^6}{9800\times125.4\times101} = 72.5\%$$

Based on the values obtanied for specific speeds Francis turbine is selected with an overall efficiency of 72.5 %.

E.7.8 JOR power station

$P = 26.1 MW$

$H = 587.3$ m

$N = 428$ rev/min

$Q = 6.85\ m^3/s$

Solution

$$\omega = \frac{2N\pi}{60} = \frac{2\times428\times\pi}{60} = 44.7 \text{ rad/s}$$

$$\omega_T = \frac{\omega\sqrt{P/\rho}}{(gH)^{5/4}} = \frac{44.7\dfrac{\sqrt{26.1\times10^6}}{10^3}}{(9.8\times587.3)^{5/4}} = \frac{44.7\times161.5}{50131} = 0.144$$

$$Ns = \frac{N\sqrt{P}}{H^{5/4}} = \frac{428\sqrt{26.1\times10^3}}{(587.3)^{5/4}} = \frac{428\times1615}{2891} = 161.5$$

$$- \quad \text{Overall efficiency } \eta_o = \frac{P}{\gamma QH} = \frac{26.1\times10^6}{9800\times6.85\times587.3} = 66.2\%$$

Based on the value of specific speed obtained pelton turbine is selected with an overall efficiency of 66.2%. The power station commisioned in 1963, the efficiency is low and installation requires refurbication which may include complete replacement of buckets, bearings and other components.

CHAPTER - 8

Turbo Pumps

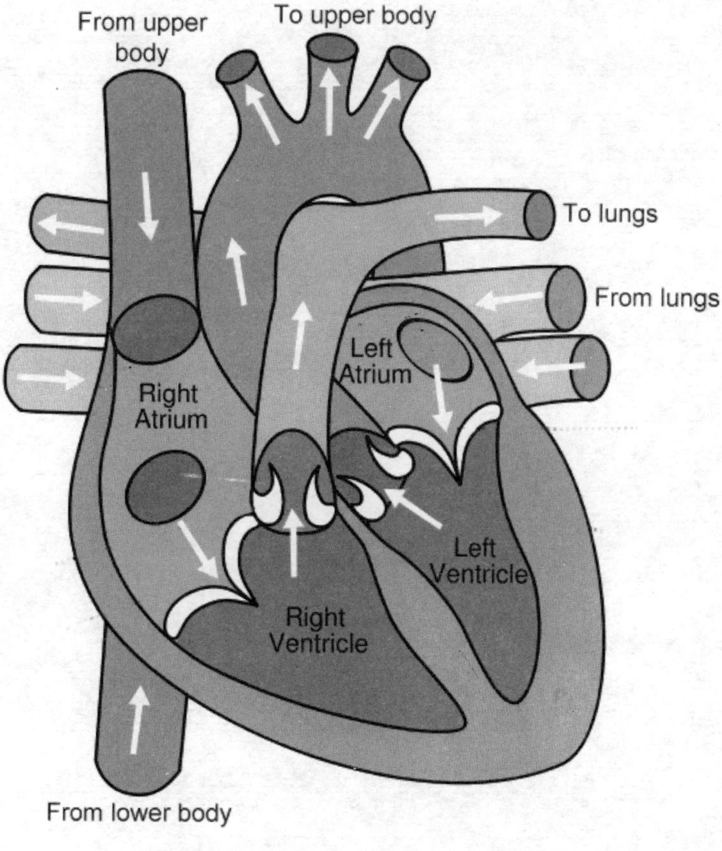

Human Heart pump

8.1 Introduction

Pumps and turbines occur in a wide variety of configurations. In general pumps add energy to the fluid – they do work on the fluid, turbines extract energy from the fluid – the fluid does work on them. Turbo pumps are used to raise the level of potential energy of the fluid and widely used in hydro and thermal power plants, chemical industries, buildings and deep wells. They have relatively few moving parts and reasonable efficiency.

As explained earlier turbo pump is a power absorbing machine which means it requires a driver, an electric motor or an I.C. engine. A turbo pump essentially consists of blades, flow channels around an axis of rotation to form a rotor. Rotation of rotor produces dynamic effects that add energy to the fluid.

8.2 Human Heart (Pump)

Human heart is a wonderful pump which does not require any moving part and does not require any maintenance and yet highly efficeint. The level of persistent, rythmic, decidedly dynamic activity of the pump provoke a sense of awe to a mechanical engineer. It is a muscle which weighs about 300-400 grams, produces a positive pressure of 130 mm of Hg. and negative pressure of 70 mm of Hg; circulates blood about 4-5 L/min, with a velocity of 0.2 m/s.

The flow carries both pressure energy and kinetic energy component $\frac{\rho V^2}{2}$, where V is the velocity of blood and ρ is density. The heart pump has to pump blood through hundreds of kilometers of linked arteries, veins and smaller parts of the body. There is circulation of blood within the heart which has to pass through collection of veins, pipes and valves. The whole process works in such a manner that there is no leakage anywhere in flow system.

In 1960 artificial heart implantable pumps replaced the function of heart. Improved materials as well as advances in electronics and mechanical engineering have played a major role in making artificial heart safe and effective to allow limited clinical applications.

8.3 Description of Centrifugal Pump

One of the most common radial flow turbo machine is centrifugal pump. This type of pump has two main components. An impeller attached to the rotating shaft, and a stationery casing, housing, or volute enclosing the impeller. The impeller consists of a number of blades (usually curved) also sometimes called vanes, arranged in a regular pattern around the shaft. A sketch of centrifugal pump is shown in Fig. 8.1.

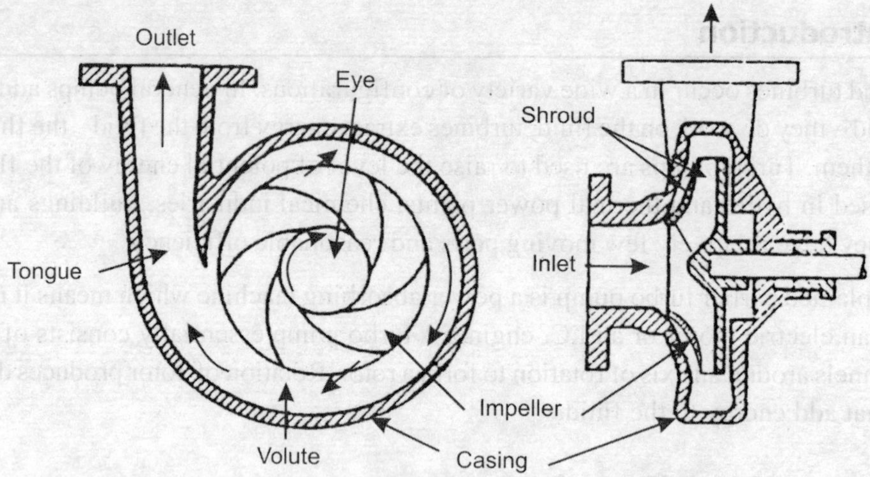

Fig. 8.1 Schematic diagram of basic elements of a centrifugal pump.

Working of Centrifugal Pump

As the impeller rotates the fluid is sucked in through the eye of the impeller and flows radially outward. Energy is added to the rotating blades and both pressure and absolute velocity are increased as the fluid flows from the eye to the periphery of the vanes. The fluid then discharges directly into a volute chamber.

The volute is designed to reduce velocity and increase pressure. The volute casing with an increase in area in the direction of the fluid, is used to produce essentially a uniform velocity distribution as fluid moves around the casing into discharge opening.

Impellers are of two types – open impeller and enclosed or shrouded impeller. An open impeller is shown in Fig. 8.2(a) where blades are arranged on a hub or backing plate and are open on the other (casing or shroud) side. Shrouded impeller is shown in Fig. 8.2(b) where blades are covered on both hub and shroud ends. A shrouded impeller will have no peripherial leakage.

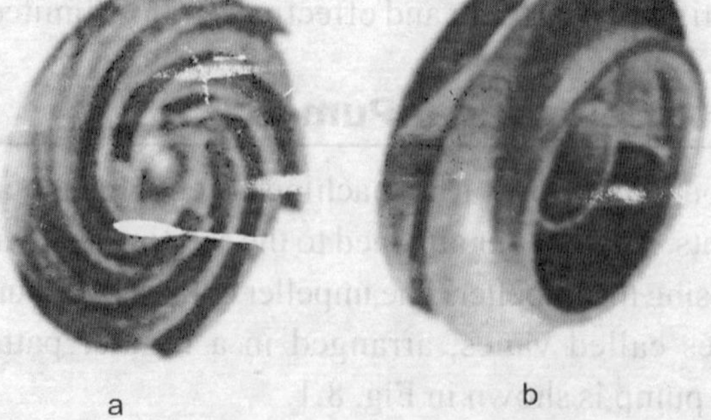

Fig. 8.2 (a) open impeller (b) shrouded impeller.

Pump impellers can be single or double suction. For the single suction impeller the fluid enters through the eye from one side of impeller, whereas in double suction impeller the fluid enters from both sides of the impeller. The double suction type reduces end thrust on the shaft.

Pumps can be single stage or multi-stage. For a single stage pump, only one impeller is mounted on the shaft, whereas for multi-stage pump, several impellers are mounted on the same shaft. The stages are arranged in series, i.e., discharge from one stage enters flows into eye of second impeller, and so on. The flow rate is same from each stage but the pressure rises in each stage and therefore at the end of last stage a very large pressure or head can be developed by multistage.

8.4 Analysis

Fig. 8.3 shows radial flow impeller. The velocity diagram is drawn at the inlet location 1 and exit location 2. The velocity diagrams have the same meaning as given earlier.

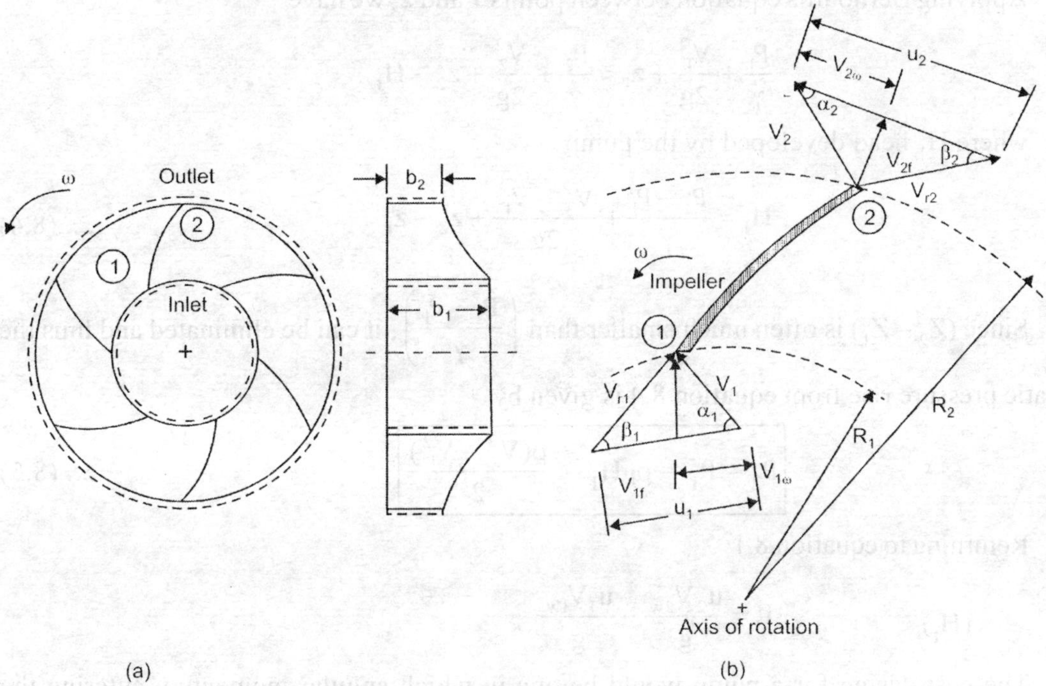

Fig. 8.3 (a) Radial flow impeller (b) velocity diagram.

For the idealised situation in which there are no losses the theoritical pressure head across the pump is given by the Euler's equation.

$$(H_t) \qquad E = \frac{u_2 V_{2w} - u_1 V_{1w}}{g} \qquad .....(8.1)$$

From the law of cosines, we can write

$$V_{r1}^2 = u_1^2 + v_1^2 - 2uV_1 \cos\alpha_1 \quad .....(8.2)$$

$$V_{r2}^2 = u_2^2 + v_2^2 - 2uV_2 \cos\alpha_2$$

Substituting values of $uV_{1w} \cos\alpha_1$ and $u V_{2w} \cos\alpha_2$ in equation 8.1.

$$(H_t) \quad E = \frac{V_2^2 - V_1^2}{2g} + \frac{(u_2^2 - u_1^2) - (V_{r2}^2 - V_{r1}^2)}{2g} \quad .....(8.3)$$

I II

The first term on the right hand represents gain in the kinetic energy as fluid passes through the impeller, the second term accounts for the increase in pressure across the impeller.

Applying Bernoullis equation between points 1 and 2, we have

$$\frac{P_1}{\gamma} + \frac{V_1^2}{2g} + z_1 = \frac{P_2}{\gamma} + \frac{V_2^2}{2g} + z_2 - H_1$$

where H_1 head developed by the pump

$$H_1 = \frac{P_2 - P_1}{\gamma} + \frac{V_2^2 - V_1^2}{2g} + z_2 - z_1 \quad .....(8.4)$$

Since $(Z_2 - Z_1)$ is often much smaller than $\left(\frac{P_2 - P_1}{\gamma}\right)$, it can be eliminated and thus the static pressure rise from equation 8.4 is given by

$$P_2 - P_1 = \rho g H_1 - \frac{\rho(V_2^2 - V_1^2)}{2} \quad .....(8.5)$$

Returning to equation 8.1

$$(H_t) \quad E = \frac{u_2 V_{2w}}{g} - \frac{u_1 V_{1w}}{g}$$

The best design for a pump would be one in which angular momentum entering the impeller is zero, so that maximum pressure rise can take place, thus if

$u_1 V_{1w} = 0$; $u_1 \neq 0$, $V_{1w} = 0$ i.e. $\alpha_1 = 90^0$ then $V_1 = V_{1f}$ and equation (8.1) becomes

$$H_t = \frac{u_2 V_{2w}}{g} = \frac{u_2 V_2 \cos\alpha_2}{g} \quad ..... (8.6)$$

From triangle geometry of Fig. 8.3b

$V_2\cos\alpha_2 = u_2 - V_{2f}\cot\beta_2$, so in eq. (8.6) H_t is written as

$$\boxed{H_t = \frac{u_2^2}{g} - \frac{u_2 V_{2f}\cot\beta_2}{g}} \qquad \text{..... (8.7)}$$

Applying equation of continuity in the region of the impeller, flow rate is given by

$$Q = \pi D_2 b_2\, V_{2f}$$

where D_2 is the diameter of the impeller at exit

b_2 is the width and V_{2f} flow velocity

$$V_{2f} = \frac{Q}{\pi D_2 b_2}$$

substituting this value in eq. (8.7)

$$\boxed{H_t = \frac{u_2^2}{g} - \frac{u_2\cot\beta_2}{\pi D_2 b_2 g}\,.\,Q} \qquad \text{..... (8.8)}$$

Equation 8.8 is of the form

$$H_t = a_1 - a_2 Q$$

where a_1 and a_2 are function of machine geometry.

$$a_1 = \frac{u_2^2}{g} = \frac{\omega^2 R_2^2}{g} \text{ and}$$

$$a_2 = \frac{u_2\cot\beta_2}{\pi D_2 b_2 g} = \frac{\omega\cot\beta_2}{2\pi\, b_2 g}.Q$$

The constant $a_1 = {u_2^2}/{g}$ represents ideal head developed by the pump for zero flow rate and it is referred to as "shut off" head. The slope of curve of head versus flow rate depends on sign and magnitude of a_2.

Radial vanes: for radial vanes $\beta_2 = 90^o$, and $a_2 = 0$. The whirl component of absolute velocity V_{2w} at exit is equal to peripherial velocity u_2 and head is independent of flow rate as shown in Fig 8.4.

Backward curved vanes: for backward curved vanes $\beta_2 < 90^o$ and $a_2 > 0$, then from exit triangle of velocity $V_{2w} > u_2$ and head decreases with flow rate as shown in Fig.8.4.

Formed curved vane: for forward curved vanes $\beta_2 > 90^o$ and and $a_2 < 0$ then from exit velocity traiangle $V_{w2} > u_2$ and head increases with flow rate as shown in Fig. 8.4.

For actual pumps, the blade angle β_2 falls in the range of 15 - 35°, with a nominal range of $20^o < \beta_2 < 25^o$ and with $15^o < \beta_1 < 50^o$. Pumps are not usually designed with forward curved since such pumps tend to suffer unstable flow condition.

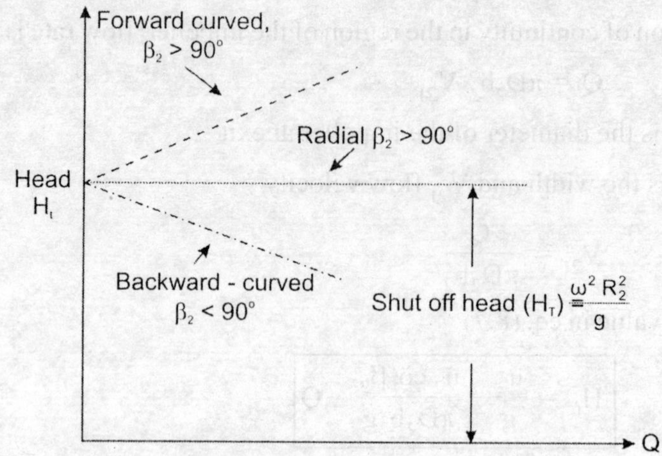

Fig. 8.4 Graphs showing head versus flow rate for various types of pumps.

Fig. 8.5 shows the effect of blade angle β_2 at outlet on exit velocity triangle. For same peripherial velocity u_2, for forward curved vane $V_{2w} > u_2$, for radial vane $u_2 = V_{2w}$ and for backward curved vane $V_{2w} < u_2$.

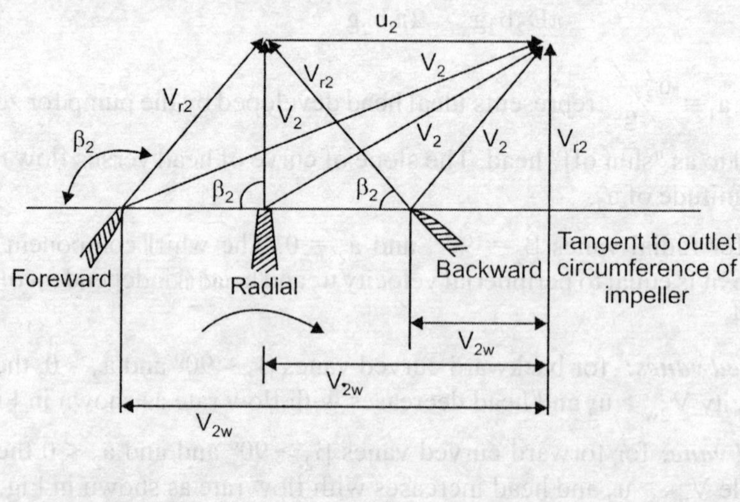

Fig. 8.5 Effect of blade angle β_2 on exit velocity diagram.

For real fluid flow theoretical head cannot be acquired in practice due to losses in the pump

$\therefore \quad H = H_t - h_f$ .....(8.9)

where H = actual head

H_t = theoretical head

h_l = hydraulic losses

Hydraulic efficiency is defined as actual head to theoretical head

$$\eta_h = \frac{H}{H_t} = \frac{\gamma QH}{\gamma QH_t} \quad .....(8.10)$$

Mechanical efficiency is output of pump divided by input shaft power

$$\eta_m = \frac{\gamma QH_t}{T.\omega} \quad .....(8.11)$$

Overall efficiency is defined as power output divided by power input

$$\eta_0 = \frac{\gamma QH}{T\omega} \quad .....(8.12)$$

Following relation holds good

$$\eta_0 = \eta_h \times \eta_m \quad .....(8.13)$$

where T is the torque applied to the shaft

8.4.1 Specific Speed

It is possible to correlate a turbo pump of a given family to a dimensionless number that characterises its operation at maximum condition. Such a number is termed specific speed and is given by

$$\boxed{\omega_p = \frac{\omega Q^{\frac{1}{2}}}{(gH)^{3/4}}} \quad .....(8.14)$$

where ω = angular velocity in rad/s

Q = flow rate in m^3/s

H = head in meters

g = acceleration due to gravity in m/s^2

The value of ω is usually based on motor requirement and values of Q and H are those at maximum efficiency. The type of pump is selected based on value of ω_p. For

$\omega_p < 1$	radial flow pump
$1 < \omega_p < 4$	mixed flow pump
$\omega_p > 4$	axial flow pump

Fig. 8.6 shows various types of impellers. Their shape depends on sp. speed of the pump.

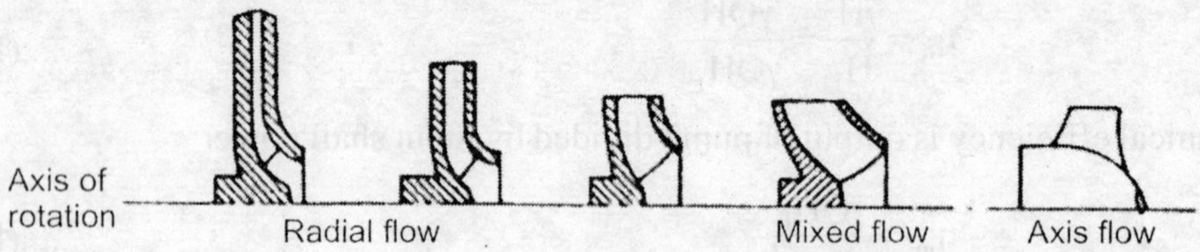

Fig. 8.6 Types of impellers.

8.5 Cavitation and Net Positive Suction Head (NPSH)

On the suction side of the pump low pressures are commonly encountered, with the possibility of cavitation occuring in the pump. Cavitation occurs when the liquid pressure at a given location is reduced to the vapour pressure of the liquid. When this occurs, vapour bubbles form. This phenomena can cause a loss in efficiency as well as structural damage to the pump, when these bubbles collide with the metal surface. The cavitation has to be avoided in the pump. To characterise potential for cavitation the difference between the total head on suction side and vapour pressure head is used. The difference is called net positive suction head (NPSH)

Total head near the pump impeller is

$$\frac{P_s}{\gamma} + \frac{V_s^s}{2g}$$, where P_s is suction pressure and V_s velocity of liquid.

Liquid vapour pressure head is

$$\frac{P_v}{\gamma}$$, where P_v is vapour pressure at the location

$$\boxed{\text{NPSH} = \frac{P_s}{\gamma} + \frac{V_s^2}{2g} - \frac{P_v}{\gamma}} \qquad ..... (8.15)$$

Consider a schematic of pump installation shown in Fig. 8.7 to illustrate NPSH

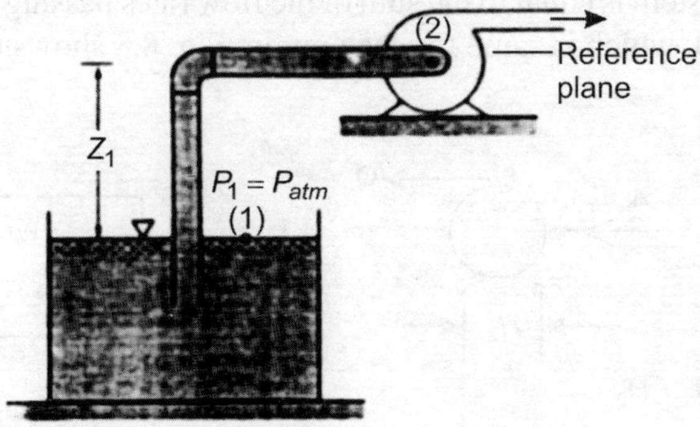

Fig. 8.7 Schematic of pump installation in which pump must raise liquid from one level to another.

For typical flow system shown in the Fig. 8.7 and applying energy equation between free liquid surface, when the pressure is atmospheric and a point on suction side of pump near the impeller yields.

$$\frac{P_{atm}}{\gamma} = \frac{P_s}{\gamma} + \frac{V_s^2}{2g} + z_1 + \Sigma h \qquad ..... (8.16)$$

where h_l represents hydraulic losses between free surface and pump impeller inlet. Thus head available at pump inlet is

$$\frac{P_s}{\gamma} + \frac{V_s^2}{2g} = \frac{P_{atm}}{\gamma} - z_1 - \Sigma h_l$$

Substituting this value in eq. 8.15 of NPSH

$$\boxed{NPSH = \frac{P_{atm}}{\gamma} - z_1 - \Sigma h_l - \frac{P_v}{\gamma}} \qquad ..... (8.17)$$

For this calculation absolute pressures are to be used since vapour pressure is in absolute units.

8.6 Pumps in Series and Parallel

Pumps can be arranged in series or in parallel to provide for additional head or flow capacity. When the pumps are arranged in series the inlet of second pump is connected to the outlet of the first pump so that same flow rate passes through each pump, but the heads generated by the two pumps are added together for a given flow rate.

When the pumps are arranged parallel each pump handles part of the flow rate because the inlets of the pumps as well as the outlets are coupled together. Thus the total flow rate passing through the system is equal to the sum of the flow rates passing through the individual pumps at a given head, which is same for each pump. Fig. 8.8 shows the two arrangements.

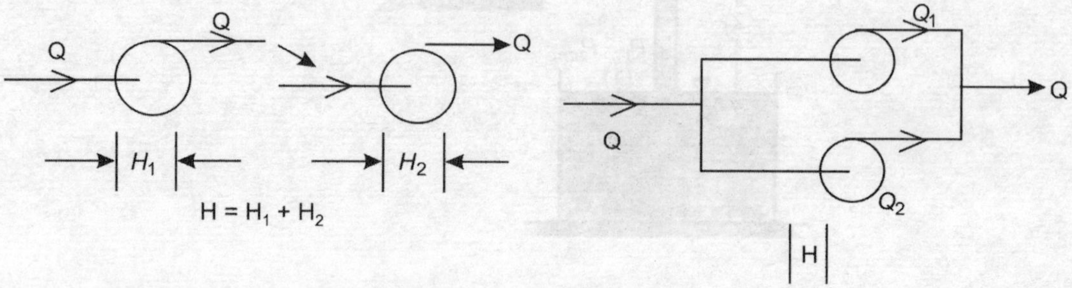

Fig. 8.8 Series and parallel arrangement.

8.7 Matching Pumps to a System Demand

Consider a single pipeline that contains a pump to deliver fluid between two reservoirs 1 and 2 as shown in Fig. 8.9.

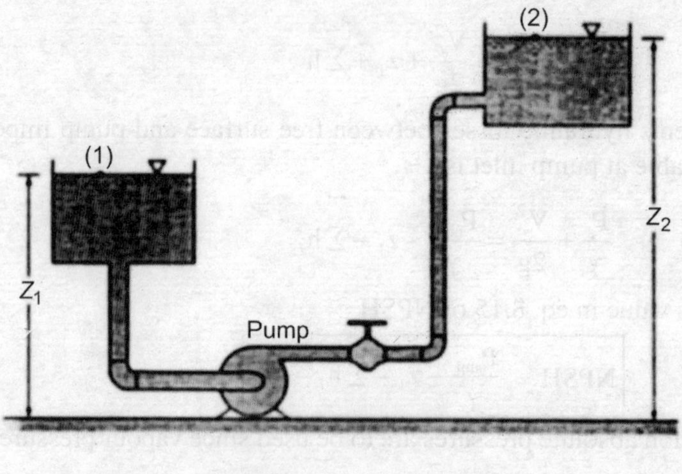

Fig. 8.9 Typical flow system.

The system demand curve is defined aselevation head plus friction and minor losses.

H = elevation head + pipe friction losses + minor losses

$$H = (z_2 - z_1) + \frac{flv^2}{2gD} + \Sigma k\left(\frac{V^2}{2g}\right)$$

$$H = (z_2 - z_1) + \left(\frac{fL}{D} + \Sigma k\right)\frac{Q^2}{2gA^2} \qquad \text{..... (8.18)}$$

For $z_2 > z_1$, $\frac{fLQ^2}{2gDA^2}$ represents friction losses, and $\frac{Q}{2gDA^2}\Sigma k$ k represents minor losses.

Where f = coefficient of fraction, L = length of pipe, D = Diameter of pipe, A = area, and Q = flow rate.

Fig. 8.10 gives performance (H-Q) curve of the pump and also system demand curve. The intersection of pump performance curve and system demand curve is the operating point which gives head and discharge. It is desirable that the intersection occurs as close to the point of maximum efficiency of the pump as the 'best operating point'.

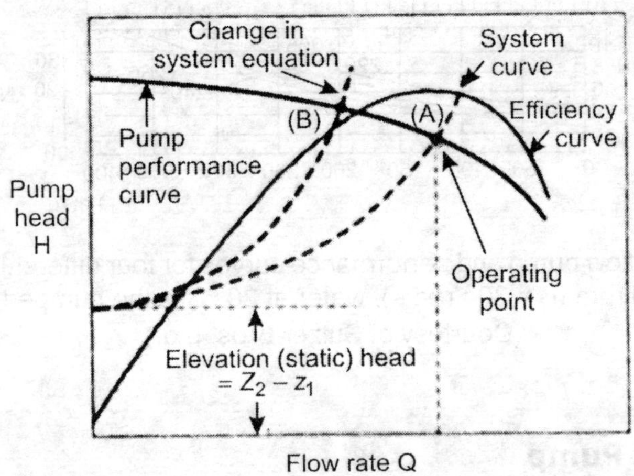

Fig. 8.10 Graphs show system curve and pump performance curve to obtain operating point.

Fig. 8.11 gives the performance curves radial flow pump. The upper part is head (m), against flow rate Q in m^3/h with constant efficiency curves. The middle part is power P in KW against flow rate Q in m^3/h for different impellar diameters, the lower part is NPSH(m) against flow rate Q in m^3/h. The curves drawn for constant speed at 2900 rpm.

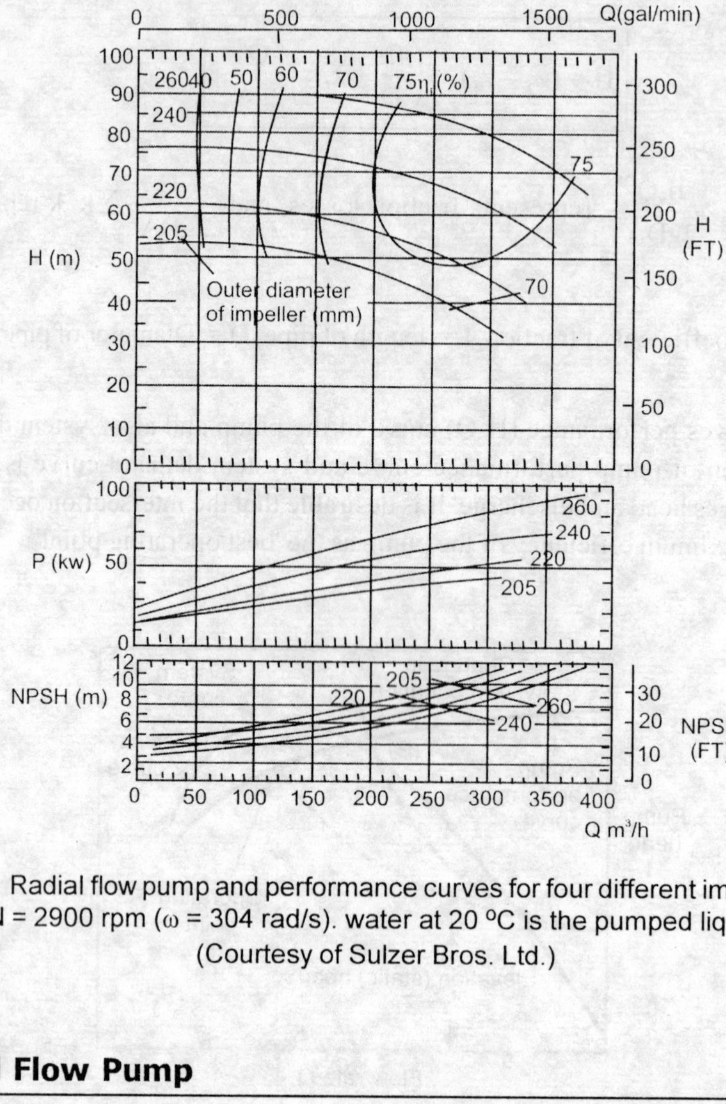

Fig. 8.11 Radial flow pump and performance curves for four different impellers with N = 2900 rpm (ω = 304 rad/s). water at 20 °C is the pumped liquid. (Courtesy of Sulzer Bros. Ltd.)

8.8 Axial Flow Pump

In axial flow pump, there is no radial flow and liquid particles enter and leave the impeller at same radius. Furthermore assuming uniform flow and applying continuity equation, flow velocity at inlet is same as exit. The sketch of axial flow pump is shown in Fig. 8.11a. The rotor is connected to a motor through a shaft, and as it rotates at relatively high speed, the fluid is sucked in through the inlet. The fluid discharges through a row of fixed blades (guide) vanes with high pressure. The inlet and exit velocity diagrams are shown in Fig.8.11b.

For the inlet velocity and exit velocity diagrams

$$u_1 = u_2 = u \text{ and } V_{f1} = V_{f2} = V_f$$

Euler's equation for the axial pump is same for radial pump

$$H_1 = \frac{u_2 V_{2w} - u_1 V_{1w}}{g} \quad \text{as } u_1 = u_2 = u \qquad \text{..... (8.19)}$$

$$H_1 = \frac{u(V_{2w} - V_{1w})}{g}$$

we have the following identities

$$V_{2w} = V_2 \cos\alpha_2 = u - V_f \cot\beta_2 \qquad \text{.....(8.20)}$$

$$V_{1w} = V_1 \cos\alpha_1 = V_f \cot\alpha_1 \qquad \text{..... (8.21)}$$

Substituting in eq. 8.19

$$H_1 = \frac{u(u - V_f \cot\beta_2 - V_f \cot\alpha_1)}{g}$$

$$\boxed{H_1 = \frac{u^2}{g} - \frac{uV_f}{g}(\cot\alpha_1 + \cot\beta_2)} \qquad \text{..... (8.22)}$$

If there is no prewhirl at entrance $\alpha_1 = 90^o$ and $V_{1w} = 0$ the theoretical head eq.8.19 becomes

$$\boxed{H_1 = \frac{u^2}{g} - \frac{uV_f \cot\beta_2}{g}} \qquad \text{.....(8.23)}$$

The radius of impeller vane for axial pump varies from hub to tip of the blade. The flow rate is given by

$$Q = \frac{\pi}{4}(D_t^2 - D_h^2)V_f \qquad \text{..... (8.24)}$$

where D_t = tip diameter, D_h = hub diameter, V_f = flow velocity

Usually calculations are made at the mid-diameter given by

$$D = \frac{D_t + D_h}{2}$$

The axial pumps are very much used in deep wells. Apart from centrifugal and axial pumps, there are other type of pumps such as gear pump, vane pump, rotory pumps and piston pumps, which are used in hydraulic system using oil as working fluid.

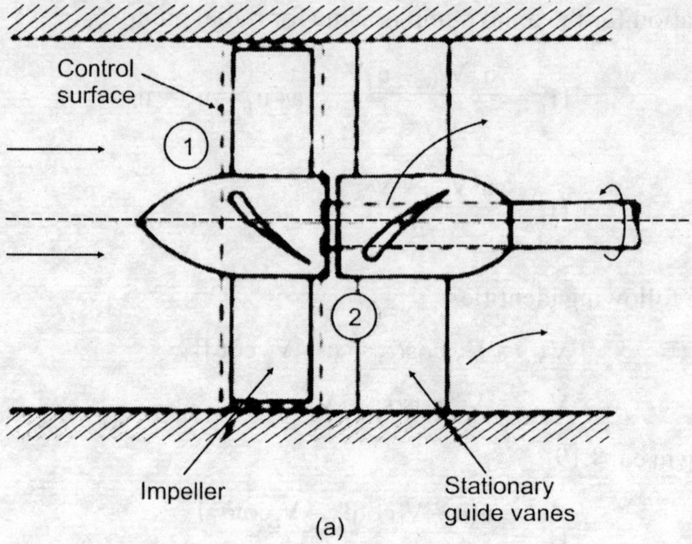

Fig. 8.11(a) Schematic of an axial pump.

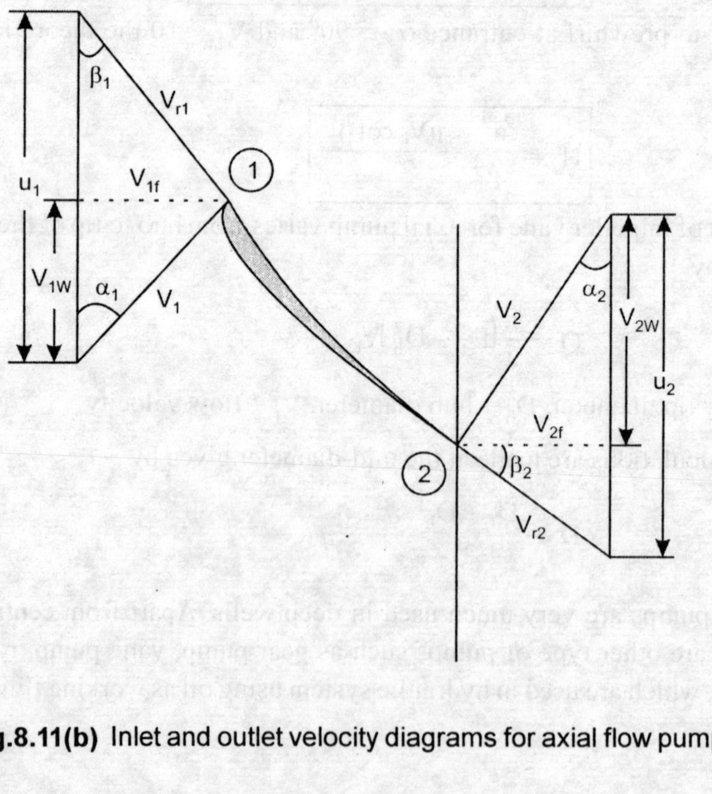

Fig.8.11(b) Inlet and outlet velocity diagrams for axial flow pump.

Solved Examples

E.8.1 Select a pump to deliver 1890 *l*/min with a pressure head of 448 kpa. Assume rotational speed of the pump is 3600 rev/min.

Solution

Given Q = 1890 *l*/min, P = 448 kPa, N = 3600 rev/min

$$\text{speed in rad/s } \omega = \frac{2N\pi}{60} = \frac{2\times3600\times\pi}{60} = 376.8 \text{ rad/s}$$

$$\text{Flow rate} \quad Q = \frac{1890}{60}\times10^{-3} = 0.0315 \text{ m}^3/\text{s}$$

$$\text{head in meters} H = \frac{P}{\gamma} = \frac{448\times10^3}{9800} = 45.7 \text{ m}$$

Specific speed of the pump given by

$$\omega_p = \frac{\omega\sqrt{Q}}{(gH)^{3/4}} = \frac{376.8\sqrt{0.0315}}{(9.8\times45.7)^{3/4}} = 0.68$$

$$\omega_p = 0.68$$

$\omega_p < 1$ therefore radial pump selected

E.8.2 Determine the elevation that the 240 mm diameter pump can be situated above the water surface of suction reservoir without experiencing cavitation. Water at 15 °C is being pumped at 250 m³/hr. Neglect losses in the system. The NPSH value for discharge of 250 m³/hr can be taken as 7.4 m. Use atmospheric pressure = 101kPa.

Solution

Given Q = 250 m³/hr, Pa = 101 kPa, NPSH = 7.4 m

Eq.8.17 of NPSH is used as

$$\text{NPSH} = \frac{P_{atm}}{\gamma} - z_1 - \sum h_l - \frac{P_v}{\gamma}$$

For water at temperature of 15 °C, partial pressure of vapour is 1666 Pa absolute and also $\Sigma h_l = 0$

$$\therefore \quad z_1 = \frac{P_{atm} - P_v}{\gamma} - \text{NPSH} - 0$$

$$z_1 = \frac{101000 - 1666}{9800} - 7.4 - 0 = 2.74 \text{ m}$$

The pump must be placed at approximately 2.7 m above the suction reservoir of water surface.

E.8.3 Water is pumped in between two reservoirs in a pipeline. The radial flow pump characteristic is given by

$$H = 22.9 + 10.7\,Q - 111Q^2$$

The system demand curve is given by

$$H = 15 + 85\,Q^2$$

Determine the operating point of the pump and determine flow rate and head.

Solution

The operating point is the point of intersection of pump characteristic and system demand curve and hence equating both these equations

$$15 + 85\,Q^2 = 22.9 + 10.7\,Q - 111Q^2$$

solving for Q

$$196\,Q^2 - 10.7\,Q - 7.9 = 0$$

The equation in the form of $ax^2 + bx + c = 0$ and its solution is

$$x = \frac{1}{2a}\left[-b \pm \sqrt{b^2 - 4ac}\right]$$

thus

$$Q = \frac{1}{2 \times 196}\left[+10.7 \pm \sqrt{10.7^2 + 4 \times 196 \times 7.9}\right]$$

$$= 0.23 \text{ m}^3/\text{s}$$

$$\therefore \quad H = 15 + 85 \times Q^2 = 15 + 85 \times 0.23^2$$

$$= 19.49 \text{ m}$$

At operating point $Q = 0.23$ m^3/s and $H = 19.49$ m

E.8.4 A radial flow pump has the following dimensions:

inlet blade angle = 44^0, inlet radius 21 mm, width 11 mm, exit blade angle = 33^0, exit radius 66 mm, width 5 mm. The speed of the pump is 2500 rev/min. Assume ideal conditions (frictionless flow and negligible thickness of vanes). Assume no prewhirl at inlet. Determine (a) flow rate (b) theoretical head and (c) required power (d) pressure across the impeller.

Solution

Given

$\beta_1 = 44^0$, $R_1 = 21$ mm; $b_1 = 11$ mm, $\beta_2 = 30^0$, $R_2 = 66$ mm, $b_2 = 5$ mm, N = 2500 rpm, $h_1 = 0$, $\alpha_1 = 90^0$

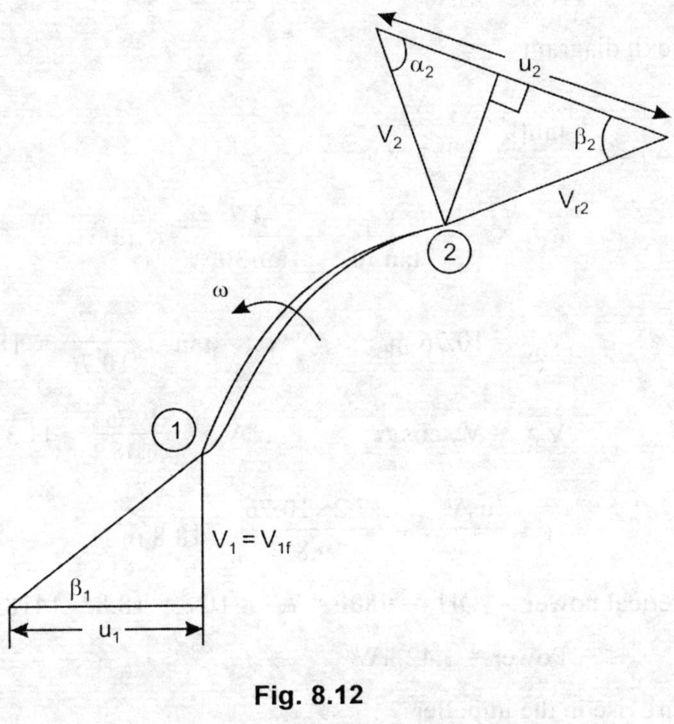

Fig. 8.12

Peripherial velocity at inlet $u_1 = \omega R_1 = \dfrac{2N\pi}{60} \times R_1$

$$= \frac{2 \times 2500 \times \pi \times 21 \times 10^{-3}}{60} = 5.5 \text{ m/s}$$

Peripherial velocity at exit $u_2 = \omega R_2 = \dfrac{2N\pi}{60} \times R_2$

$$u_2 = \frac{2 \times 2500 \times \pi \times 66 \times 10^{-3}}{60} = 17.2 \text{ m/s}$$

From inlet diagram

$$\tan \beta_1 = \frac{V_1 f}{u} \quad \therefore V_1 f = \tan 44 \times 5.5 = 5.3 \text{ m/s}$$

$$Q = \pi D_1 b_1 V_{1f} = \pi \times 2 \times 21 \times 10^{-3} \times 11 \times 10^{-3} \times 5.3$$

$$= 7.7 \times 10^{-3} \text{ m}^3/\text{s}$$

Also $\quad Q = \pi D_2 b_2 V_{2f}$

$$7.7 \times 10^{-3} = \pi \times 2 \times 66 \times 10^{-3} \times 5 \times 10^{-3} \times V_{2f}$$

$\therefore \quad V_{2f} = 3.7$ m/s

From exit diagram

$$\tan\beta_2 = \frac{V_{2f}}{u_2 - V_{2w}}$$

$$\therefore \quad u_2 - V_{2w} = \frac{V_{2f}}{\tan 30^0} = \frac{3.7}{\tan 30^0} = 6.44$$

$$V_{2w} = 10.76 \text{ m/s} ; \qquad \alpha_2 = \tan{-1} \frac{3.7}{10.76} = 18.9^0$$

Also $\quad V_{2w} = V_2 \cos \alpha_2 \qquad \therefore V_2 = \dfrac{10.76}{\cos 18.9} = 11.3$ m/s

$$H_1 = \frac{u_2 V_{2w}}{g} = \frac{17.2 \times 10.76}{9.8} = 18.8 \text{ m}$$

Theoretical power = $\gamma Q H_1 = 9800 \times 7.7 \times 10^{-3} \times 18.8 = 1418$ Watt

Power = 1.42 kW

Pressure rise in the impeller

$$P_2 - P_1 = \rho g H_1 - \frac{\rho}{2} \left(V_2^2 - V_1^2\right)$$

$$P_2 - P_1 = 1000 \times 9.8 \times 18.8 - \frac{1000}{2} (11.37^2 - 5.3^2)$$

$$P_2 - P_1 = 1.33 \times 10^5 \text{ Pa}$$

$$p_2 - p_1 = 1.34 \text{ bar}$$

E.8.5 Water is pumped between two reservoirs in a pipeline with the following characteristics. L = 70 m, D = 300 mm, f = 0.025, $\sum k = 2.5$. The radial flow pump characteristic curve is approximated by the formula

$$H_1 = 22.9 + 10.7\,Q - 111\,Q^2$$

where H_1 is in meters, Q in m^3/s

Determine discharge and head when $z_2 - z_1 = 15$ m with two identical pumps operated in parallel.

Solution

The system demand curve equation is given by

$$H = z_2 - z_1 + \left(f\frac{L}{D} + \sum k\right)\frac{Q^2}{2gA^2}$$

Substituting proper values $z_2 - z_1 = 15$ m, f = 0.025, L = 70 m, D = 0.3 m, k = 2.5

$$H_1 = 15 + \left(\frac{0.025 \times 70}{0.3} + 2.5\right)\frac{Q^2}{2 \times 9.8\left(\frac{\pi}{4} \times 0.3^2\right)^2}$$

$$H_1 = 15 + 85\,Q^2$$

For the two pumps in parallel the characteristic curve is

$$H_1 = 22.9 + 10.7\left(\frac{Q}{2}\right) - 111\left(\frac{Q}{2}\right)^2$$

$$H_1 = 22.9 + 5.35\,Q - 27.75\,Q^2$$

Equating this to system demand curve

$$H_1 = 15 + 85\,Q^2$$

$$\therefore \quad 15 + 85\,Q^2 = 22.9 + 5.35\,Q - 27.75\,Q^2$$

$$112.8\,Q^2 - 5.35\,Q - 7.9 = 0$$

$$\therefore \quad Q = \frac{1}{2 \times 112.8}\left[5.35 \pm \sqrt{5.35^2 + 4 \times 112.8 \times 7.9}\right]$$

$$Q = 0.29\ m^3/s$$

The design calculated head

$$H_1 = 15 + 85Q^2 = 15 + 85 \times 0.29^2 = 22.2 \text{ m}$$

$$\therefore \quad Q = 0.29 \text{ m}^3/\text{s} \; ; \; H_1 = 22.2 \text{ m}$$

E.8.6 An axial flow pump has guide blade angle of 75^0 as the fluid enters the impeller region. The impeller has a speed of 500 rpm with the blade exit angle of 70^0. The inner diameter of the blade is 150 mm and outer diameter of 300 mm. The discharge of the pump is 150 l/s. Determine the velocity of flow, theoretical head and power required to drive the pump.

Solution

Given $\alpha_1 = 75^0$, N = 500 rpm, $\beta_2 = 70^0$

$$D_h = 150 \text{ mm}, \; D_t = 300 \text{ mm}, \; Q = 150 \; l/s$$

Velocity of flow $V_f = \dfrac{Q}{A} = \dfrac{150 \times 10^{-3}}{\frac{\pi}{4}\left(0.3^2 - 0.15^2\right)} = 2.83 \text{ m/s}$

The peripherial velocity is calculated on the mean diameter

$$D = \frac{D_t + D_h}{2} = \frac{0.3 + 0.15}{2} = 0.225 \text{ m}$$

Peripherial velocity $u = \omega R = \dfrac{2 \times 500 \times \pi}{60} \times \dfrac{0.225}{2} = 5.88 \text{ m/s}$

Theoretical head $H_1 = \dfrac{u^2}{g} - \dfrac{uV_f}{g}(\cot\alpha_1 + \cot\beta_2)$

$$= \frac{5.88^2}{9.8} - \frac{2.83 \times 5.88}{9.8}(\cot 75 + \cot 70)$$

$$= 2.44 \text{ m}$$

Required power $P = \gamma Q H_1 = \dfrac{9800 \times 0.15 \times 2.44}{10^3}$

$$= 3.58 \text{ kw}$$

E.8.7 A centrifugal pump is to be placed over a large open water tank and is to pump water at a rate of 3.5×10^{-3} m³/s. At this flow rate, the value of NPSH given by the manufacturer is 4.5 m. If the water temperature is 15°C and atmospheric pressure of 10 kPa, determine the maximum height that the pump can be located above the water surface without cavitation. Assume the major head loss between tank and the pump is due to filter at the pipe inlet having a minor loss coefficient of 20. Other losses being neglected, the pipe on the suction side of the pump has a diameter of 10 cm.

Solution

Given $Q = 3.5 \times 10^{-3}\ m^3/s$; NPSH = 4.5 m

$t = 15^oC$, $P_{atm} = 101$ kPa, $k = 20$

NPSH is given by the equation

$$NPSH = \frac{P_{atm}}{\gamma} - z_1 - \sum h_l - \frac{P_v}{\gamma}$$

$$z_1 = \frac{P_{atm}}{\gamma} - \sum h_l - \frac{P_v}{\gamma} - NPSH$$

Velocity in the suction pipe $V = \frac{Q}{A} = \frac{3.5 \times 10^{-3}}{\frac{\pi}{4} \times 0.1^2} = 0.45$ m/s

$$\sum h_l = k\frac{V^2}{2g} = \frac{20 \times 0.45^2}{2 \times 9.8} = 0.2 \text{ m}$$

Vapour pressure P_v at 15^oC = 1666 Pa

∴ substituting proper values,

$$z_1 = \frac{101 \times 10^3}{9800} - 0.2 - \frac{1666}{9800} - 4.5$$

$$= 10.3 - 0.2 - 0.17 - 4.5 = 5.43\text{m}$$

The pump should be located higher than 5.43 m above the water surface.

Problems

P.8.1 An axial flow pump designed to move 19,000 l/min of water over a head of 1.5 m of water. Estimate the motor power requirement and the $u_2 V_{2w}$ needed to achieve this flow rate on a continuous basis.

P.8.2 Explain why statements "pumps move fluids" and "moving fluids drive turbines" are true.

P.8.3 In a certain application a pump is required to deliver 19,000 *l*/min against a head of 90 m head when operating at 1200 rev/min. What type of pump would you recommend?

P.8.4 A centrifugal pump provides a flow rate of 1900 *l*/min when operating at 1750 rev/min against a head of 60 m. Determine pump's flowrate and developed head if the pump speed is increased to 3500 rev/min.

P.8.5 Water is pumped with a centrifugal pump, and measurement made on the pump indicate that for a flow rate of 910 *l*/min required input power of 4.5 kw. For a pump efficiency of 62%, what is the actual head rise of the water being raised?

P.8.6 A centrifugal pump having an impeller diameter of 0.5 m operates at 900 rpm. The water enters the pump parallel to the pump shaft. If the blade exit angle is 25° determine shaft power required to turn the impeller when the flow through the pump is 0.16 m^3/s. The uniform blade height is 50 mm.

P.8.7 Water is pumped at the rate of 5300 *l*/min through a centrifugal pump operating at a speed of 1750 rev/min. The impeller has a uniform blade height of 5 cm with inner radius of 48 mm and outer radius of 178 mm and exit blade angle of 23°. Assume ideal flow conditions with $\alpha_1 = 90°$. Determine (a) tangential velocity component V_{2w} at exit (b) ideal head (c) power transferred to the fluid.

CHAPTER - 9

Positive Displacement Pumps

A shovel dozer designed for digging and loading can also be used for moving "spoil" over short distances. The crawler has a bucket with holding capacity of 4 cubic meters of soil. It can also remove rocks and tree stumps.

9.1 Introduction

Machines which deliver liquids with pressure are simply called pumps. Earlier we discussed mainly centrifugal pumps with water as a working fluid. In this chapter we shall decribe briefly positive displacement pumps which includes pumps using oil as working fluid. The positive displacement pump designs are as follows.

(a) Reciprocating type

- Piston or Plunger type
- Diaphragm type.

(b) Rotary

- Single rotor such as sliding vane.
- Multiple rotors such as gear, lobe, and screw type.

Many mechanical designs are in wide use and a few of the following are shown in Fig. 9.1 as

(a) Piston/Plunger type

(b) Gear pump

(c) Screw type

(d) Vane pump

(e) Lobe pump.

All the positive displacement pumps deliver a pulsating or periodic flow as the cavity, volume opens, traps, and squeezes the liquid. Their advantage is delivery of any liquid regardless of its viscosity.

Since positive displacement pump compresses mechanically against a cavity filled with liquid. A common feature is that they develop immense pressures if the outlet is shut for any reason. Sturdy construction is required and complete shut off would cause damage if relief valves are not used.

9.2 Description of a Reciprocating Pump

A reciprocating pump essentially consists of a piston moving to and fro in a cylinder. The piston is driven by a crank powered by some prime mover such an electric motor, IC engine or steam engine.

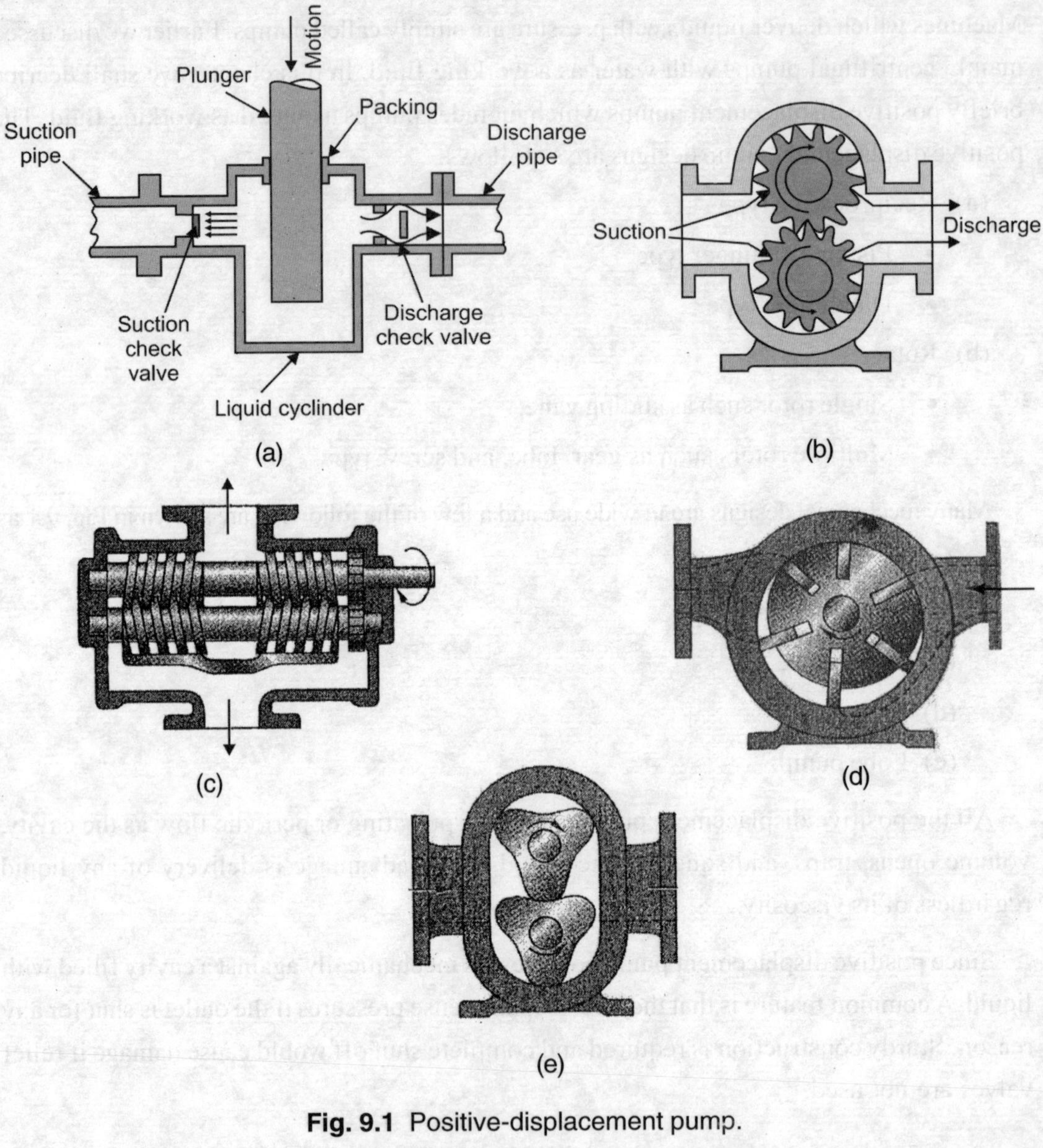

Fig. 9.1 Positive-displacement pump.

When the piston moves to the right as shown in Fig. 9.2 the pressure is reduced in the cylinder. This enables water in the lower reservoir to force the liquid up the suction pipe into the cylinder. The suction valve operates only during suction stroke. It is then followed by delivery stroke during which liquid in the cylinder is pushed out through the delivery valve and into the upper reservoir. During the delivery stroke suction valve is closed due to higher pressure. The whole cycle is repeated at a frequency depending upon the rotational speed of the crank. The rate at which the liquid is delivered by the pump clearly depends upon pump speed since volume delivered in one stroke = AS, where A = area of piston, S = stroke of the piston. Thus, if the pump speed is N(rev/s), then the volume delivered in SI units is

$$Q = ASN \text{ since } N = \omega/2\pi$$

$$Q = AS\,\omega/2\pi = \text{StrokeVolume} \times \omega/2\pi \qquad \text{..... (9.1)}$$

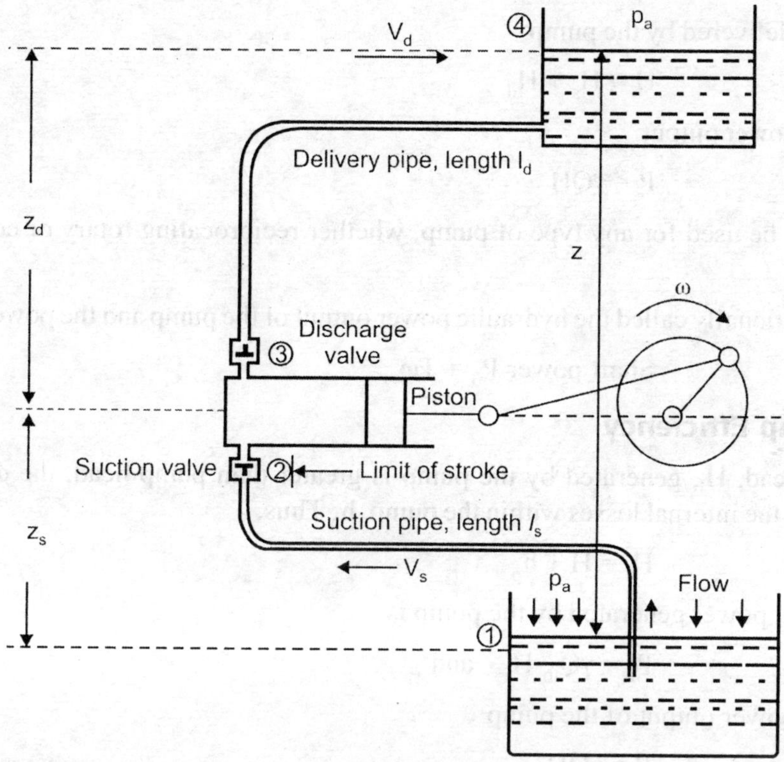

Fig. 9.2 Reciprocating pump installation.

Thus the pump discharge is directly proportional to rotational speed and is entirely independent of the pressure against which the pump is delivering.

9.3 Analysis

9.3.1 Power Output

The power output of any pump is the availabe power to force the liquid to move. The equation of power can be delivered from the following equations by applying Bernoullis equation, neglecting hydraulic losses.

Total suction head Hs

$$H_s = \left(\frac{P_s}{\gamma} + \frac{V^2 s}{2g} + z_s\right) \qquad ..... (9.2)$$

Total delivery head H_d

$$H_d = \left(\frac{P_d}{\gamma} + \frac{V_d^2}{2g} + z_d\right) \qquad ..... (9.3)$$

Total head delivered by the pump

$$H = H_s + H_d$$

Hydraulic power output

$$P = \gamma QH \qquad ..... (9.4)$$

Eq. 9.4 can be used for any type of pump, whether reciprocating rotary or centrifugal pump.

This is traditionally called the hydraulic power output of the pump and the power input is

$$\text{Shaft power } P_0 = T\omega \qquad ..... (9.5)$$

9.3.2 Pump Efficiency

The internal head, H_i, generated by the pump is greater than pump head, the difference accounting for the internal losses within the pump, h_p Thus,

$$H_i = H + h_p \qquad ..... (9.6)$$

The internal power generated by the pump is

$$P_i = \gamma Q_{th} H_i \quad \text{and} \qquad ..... (9.7)$$

the actual power output of the pump

$$P = \gamma QH \qquad ..... (9.8)$$

If the power input to the pump from the prime mover is P_o then overall efficiency set is calculated as follows

$$\eta_o = \frac{P}{P_o} = \frac{\gamma QH}{P_o} \qquad ..... (9.9)$$

The hydrualic efficiency is power output by internal power

$$\eta_h = \frac{\gamma QH}{\gamma QH_i} = \frac{H}{H_i} \qquad ..... (9.10)$$

Mechanical efficiency of the pump is

$$\eta_m = \frac{P_i}{P_0} = \frac{\gamma Q_{th} H_i}{T\omega} \qquad ..... (9.11)$$

The volumetric efficiency is

$$\eta_v = \frac{Q}{Q_{th}} = \frac{Q}{Q+Q_L}$$

Where Q_L hydraulic losses due to leakage in piston clearances

$$\therefore \quad \eta_0 = \frac{P}{P_0} = \frac{P_i}{P_o} \times \frac{P}{P_i} = \frac{P_i}{P_o} \times \frac{\gamma QH}{\gamma Q_{th} H_i} = \frac{P_i}{P_o} \times \frac{H}{H_i} \times \frac{Q}{Q_{th}}$$

$$\boxed{\eta_o = \eta_h \eta_m \eta_v} \qquad ..... (9.12)$$

The overall efficiency is the product of three parts.

9.4 Application of Piston Pumps

The pumps are extensively used for power transfer applications in the off shore, power transmissions, agriculture, aerospace and construction industries, to list just a few. They have also applications in chemical processing, car washing, as well as food dairy and beverage processing. Their versatility and popularity are due fact their relatively compact design, and high viscosity performance.

Piston pumps are more efficient compared to other types of pumps. Volumetric efficiency is around 90% are mechanical efficiency is also 90%. They provide very high power density, stiff, high response source of power, for demanding applications including servo systems.

Types of Piston Pumps

This general type of pump includes a number of variations some of which are described below.

1. Radial Piston Pump
2. Swashplate Piston Pump
3. Wobble Plate Pump
4. Bent Axis Piston Pump
5. Gear Pump

9.4.1 Radial Piston Pump

Radial piston pumps include a rotating cylinder containing equally spaced radial pistons arranged radially around the cylinder centre line. A spring pushes the pistons against the inner surface of an encircling stationary ring mounted eccentric to the cylinder. The pistons draw in fluid during half a revolution and drive fluid out during the other half. The greater the ring eccentricity is, the longer the pistons stroke and more fluid they transfer. The radial piston pump is shown in Fig.9.3.

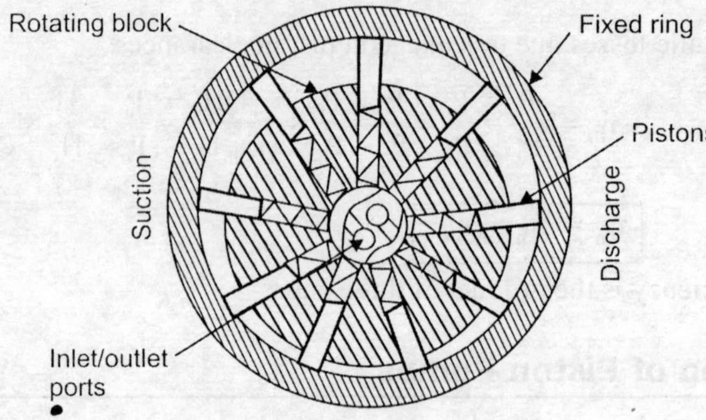

Fig. 9.3 Radial Piston Pump.

9.4.2 Swashplate Pump (Axial Piston Pump)

Swashplate pumps have a rotating cylinder containing parallel pistons arranged radially around the cylinder centre line. A spring pushes the pistons against a stationary swash plate located at one end of the cylinder, which slits at an angle to the cylinder. The pistons draw a fluid during half a revolution and drive fluid out during the other half. By adjusting the position of the swashplate the amount of displacement can be changed. The more the swashplate turns

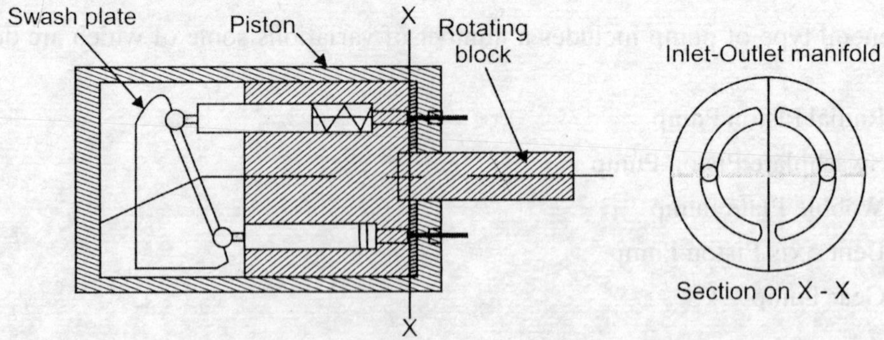

Fig. 9.4 Swashplate pump.

to the vertical position, the more the amount of displacement decreases. The greater the swashplate angle relative to the cylinder centre line, the longer the pistons stroke and the more fluid they transfer. In the vertical position the displacement is zero. In that case the pump may be driven but will not deliver any oil. Normally the swashplate is adjusted by a hydraulic cylinder built inside the pump housing. The pump is shown in Fig. 9.4.

9.4.3 Wobble Plate Pump (Axial Piston Pump)

This pump includes a stationary piston block containing a number parallel pistons arranged radially around the block centre (at least five). The end of each piston is forced against a rotating wobble plate by springs. The wobble plate is shaped with varying thickness around its centre line and thus as it rotates it causes the pistons to reciprocate at a fixed stroke. The pistons draw in fluid from the cavity during half a revolution and drive fluid out at the rear of the pump during the other half. The fluid flow is controlled using non-return valves for each piston. These pumps can generate pressures of up to 700 bar. The pump is shown in Fig. 9.5.

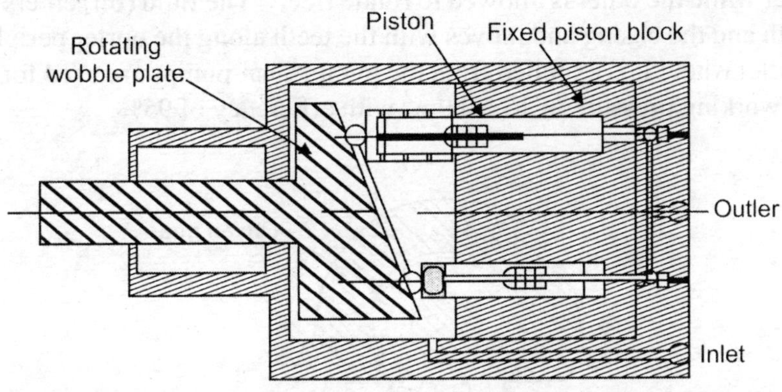

Fig. 9.5 Wobble plate piston pump.

9.4.4 Bent Axis Piston Pump (Axial Piston Pump)

Bent axis piston pumps have a rotating cylinder containing parallel pistons arranged radially around the cylinder centre line. The cylinder is driven by a shaft which is arranged at an angle to the cylinder axis. The shaft includes a flange with a mechanical connection to each piston. As the shaft rotates the pistons are made to reciprocate over a stroke based on the relative angle of the shaft and cylinder. The pump is shown in Fig. 9.6.

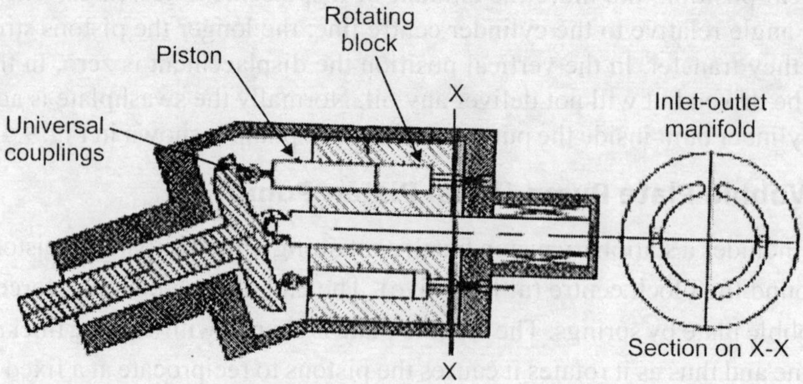

Fig. 9.6 Bent Axis Pump.

9.4.5 Gear Pump

A rotary gear pump consists essentially of two intersecting spur gears which are identical and which are fitted by a closely fitting casing as shown in Fig. 9.7. One of the gears is driven by a driver while the other is allowed to rotate freely. The fluid (oil) enters the space between the teeth and the casing and moves with the teeth along the ourter periphery until it reaches the outlet where it is expelled from the pump. Gear pumps are used for flow rate up to 400 m^3/h, working pressure of 15 MN/m^2 with efficiency of 95%.

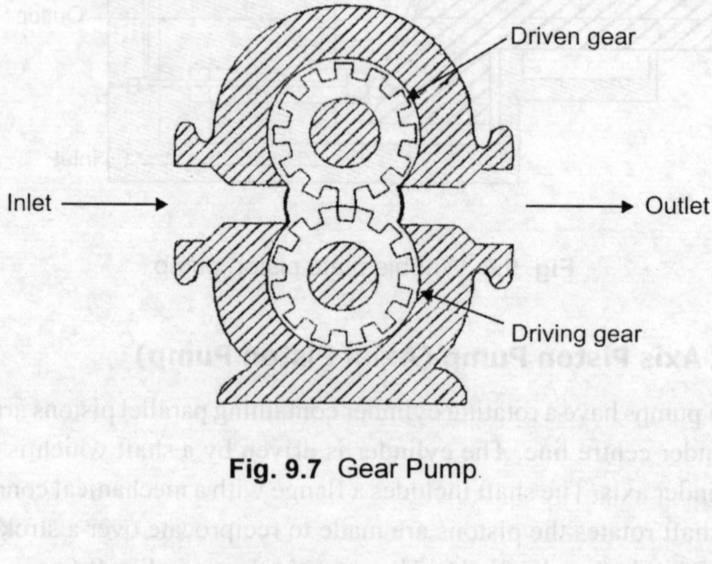

Fig. 9.7 Gear Pump.

Solved Examples

E.9.1 The reciprocating pump is used to increase the pressure 0.2 m^3/s of water from 200 kPa to 600 kPa. If the overall efficiency of the pump is 85% how much electrical power is required to pump the water ? The suction tank is 10 cm below centre line of the pump and delivery tank is 10 cm above the centre line of the pump. Assume inlet and exit cross-sectional areas are equal, and velocities suction and delivery neglected.

Solution

Total head across the pump is

$$H = H_s + H_d = \left(\frac{P_s}{\gamma} + \frac{V_s^2}{2g} + Z_s\right) + \left(\frac{P_d}{\gamma} + \frac{V_d^2}{2g} + Z_d\right)$$

$$H = \left(\frac{200 \times 10^3}{9800} + 0.1\right) + \left(\frac{600 \times 10^3}{9800} + 0.1\right) = 81.6 \text{ m}$$

Since the losses are neglected.

hydraulic power $= \gamma QH = 9800 \times 0.2 \times 81.2 = 159$ KW

$$\text{The overall efficiency } \eta_0 = \frac{\text{hydraulic power}}{\text{shaft power}}$$

$$\therefore \text{ Shaft power} = \frac{159}{0.85} = 187.2 \text{ kW}$$

Electrical power = 187.2 kW

E.9.2 The gauge is installed at both suction and delivery. side. The water flows at the rate of 37.5 l/s the gauge at the suction indicated a vacuum pressure of 54 kPa and at the discharge section the gauge shows 160 kPa. Assume the suction and discharge sections are at the same level with the diameter of 15 cm and 12.5 cm, respectively. Determine the total head of the pump.

Solution

- Velocity at the suction side $\frac{Q}{A_s} = \frac{37.5 \times 10^{-3} \times 4}{\pi \times 0.15^2} = 2.1$ m/s

- Velocity at the discharge side $\frac{Q}{A_d} = \frac{37.5 \times 10^{-3} \times 4}{\pi \times 0.125^2} = 3.0$ m/s

Total head across the pump

$$H = H_s + H_d = \left(\frac{P_s}{\gamma} + \frac{V_s^2}{2g} + Z_s\right) + \left(\frac{P_d}{\gamma} + \frac{V^2 d}{2g} + zd\right)$$

$$H = \left(\frac{54 \times 10^3}{9800} + \frac{2^2}{2 \times 9.8}\right) + \left(\frac{160 \times 10^3}{9800} + \frac{3^2}{2 \times 9.8}\right)$$

$$H = 5.5 + 0.2 + 16.32 + 0.459$$

$$H = 22.47 \text{ m}$$

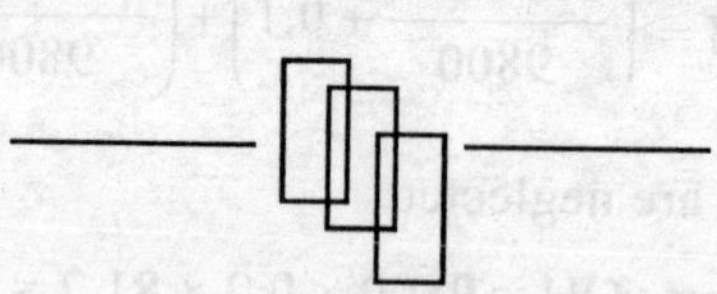

Multiple Choice Questions

1. The capillary rise in a tube is obtained by equating :
   (a) cohesive and adhesive forces
   (b) gravitational force to shear force
   (c) surface tension force to weight of liquid
   (d) pressure forces to gravitational forces.
2. The fluid property which contributes cavitation is :
   (a) atmospheric pressure
   (b) vapour pressure
   (c) cavitation number
   (d) suction head.
3. The unit of dynamic viscosity in SI system is :
   (a) $N.sm^{-2}$ (b) Nsm^{-1} (c) $N.s^{-2}m^{-2}$ (d) $Ns^{-1}m^2$
4. The shear stress is directly proportional to viscosity for liquids which are Newtonian such as :
   (a) water (b) milk (c) paint (d) honey
5. In a wind tunnel the velocity of air is 40 m/s and gas constant is 287 J/Kg/K, T = 288 K and k = 1.4. The Mach no is :
   (a) 0.01 (b) 0.001 (c) 1.01 (d) 0.11
6. Pascal law is applicable when :
   (a) fluid is at rest (b) fluid is in motion
   (c) fluid is compressible (d) fluid is incompressible
7. The cavitation number σ is for fluid flow given by,
   (a) $\frac{P-P_a}{\rho V^2/2}$ (b) $\frac{P_a-P_v}{\rho V^2/2}$ (c) $\frac{P-P_v}{\rho V^2/2}$ (d) $\frac{P_a-P_v}{V^2/2}$

   where P = absolute pressure, P_v = vapour pressure
   P_a = atmospheric pressure, V = velocity
8. A perfect gas is one which :
   (a) obeys characterestic equation
   (b) zero viscosity
   (c) zero specific heat
   (d) highly compressible

9. Euler's equation is based on the principle of :
   (a) conservation of mass
   (b) conservation of momentum
   (c) conservation of energy
   (d) all the above a, b and c.

10. A jet strikes a stationary plate perpendicular with a velocity of 10 m/s. If the plate suffers a force of 180 N for jet diameter of 50 mm, the power is :
    (a) 0.375 N (b) 0.75 N (c) 1.5 N (d) Zero

11. Cavitation cannot occur in :
    (a) Francis turbine (b) centrifugal pump
    (c) piston pump (d) Pelton wheel

12. A draft tube is a must in :
    (a) Francis turbine (b) Pelton turbine
    (c) axial pump (d) Centrifual pump

13. The pressure difference measured at the two ends of Pitot tube is :
    (a) static pressure (b) dynamic pressure
    (c) stagnation prèssure (d) total pressure

14. Piezometric head is equal to :
    (a) sum of elevation head and velocity head
    (b) sum of pressure head and velocity head
    (c) sum of pressure head and elevation
    (d) pressure head.

15. The coefficient of discharge of a venturimeter is approximately equal to :
    (a) 0.98 (b) 0.6 (c) 0.75 (d) 1

16. Euler's number can be expressed as ratio of pressure force to inertia force and is given by,
    (a) $\frac{2\,\Delta p}{\rho V^2}$ (b) $\frac{\Delta P}{\rho V^2}$ (c) $\frac{\Delta p}{\sqrt{\rho V}}$ (d) $\frac{\sqrt{\Delta p}}{\rho V^2}$

17. The dimensionless parameter relating to inertia force to viscous force is given by,
    (a) $\frac{\rho l V}{}$ (b) $\frac{\rho l V^2}{\mu}$ (c) $\frac{\sqrt{\rho l V}}{\mu}$ (d) $\frac{V^2}{\mu / \rho}$

18. The Strouhal number is given by ratio of centrifugal force to inertia force and is given by,

(a) $\frac{l\omega}{V}$ (b) $\frac{l\omega}{V^2}$ (c) $\frac{\sqrt{l\omega}}{V}$ (d) $\frac{l^2\omega^2}{V}$

19. The pressure force and tension force when balanced are related to radius (R) of soap bubble as :

(a) $p = \frac{2\sigma}{R}$ (b) $p = \frac{\sigma}{R}$ (c) $p = \frac{4\sigma}{R}$ (d) $p = \frac{8\sigma}{R}$

20. Indicate the correct statement relating to turbine?

(a) Kaplan turbine gives best performance at partial loads

(b) Pelton turbine gives fairly good results at low loads

(c) Francis turbine gives worst performance at part loads

(d) Propeller turbine gives best performance at low loads.

21. If a Pitot tube kept at centre line of orifice discharging under a head of 1 m indicates a head of 0.95, then coefficient of velocity is :

(a) 0.955 (b) 0.965 (c) 0.975 (d) 0.985

22. Bernoullis equation is derived based on the following assumptions :

(a) flow is incompressible, steady and irrotational

(b) flow is steady, compressible and irrotational

(c) flow is steady, incompressible and rotational

(d) flow is unsteady, incompressible and irrotational.

23. When two pumps are connected in parallel the following relation holds good :

(a) $Q = Q_1 + Q_2$ (b) $H = H_1 + H_2$ (c) $Q_1 = Q_2$ (d) $\frac{Q_1}{Q_2} = \frac{H_1}{H_2}$

24. A ship has a length of 150 m and speed is 36 km/h. The Froude number is :

(a) 0.025 (b) 0.25 (c) 2.5 (d) 3.0

25. The specific speed of a turbine is given by $N_s = \frac{N\sqrt{P}}{H^{5/4}}$. A turbine works under a head of 120 m and develops 22 MW. The specific speed is :

(a) 150 (b) 15 (c) 1.5 (d) 1500

26. A turbine generates 10 MW under a head of 100 m while working with a speed of 500 rpm. The turbine selected is :

(a) Francis (b) Kaplan (c) Pelton (d) Propeller

27. In a Francis turbine the maximum hydraulic efficiency is obtained when :

(a) absolute velocity at exit is radial

(b) relative velocity at exit is radial

(c) relative velocity at inlet is radial

(d) whirl velocity at exit is zero.

28. The effective head at the Pelton wheel is :

(a) $H = H_t - h_{fp}$ (b) $H = H_t - h_{fp} - h_n$

(c) $H = H_l - h_{fp} - h_n - h_b$ (d) $H = H_t - h_{fp} - h_n - h_b - h_e$

where H_t = total head ; h_{fp}, h_n, h_b, h_e are hydraulic losses in penstock, nozzle, buckets and eddies, respectively.

29. The highest overall efficiency is possible in :

(a) hydropower stations (b) steam power stations

(c) gas turbine power stations (d) combined cycle power stations

30. A hydro power station is constructed because of :

(a) head (b) flow

(c) head and flow (d) nearness to river

31. Euler's head is given by the following equation for the turbine as,

(a) $E = \frac{(u_1 V_{1w} - u_2 V_{2w})}{g}$ (b) $E = \frac{(u_2 V_{2w} - u_1 V_{1w})}{g}$

(c) $E = \frac{u(V_{1w} - V_{2w})}{g}$ (d) $E = \frac{u(V_{2w} - V_{1w})}{g}$

where u = peripherial velocity, v_w is whirl velocity.

32. The Kaplan turbine works at partial loads only :

(a) when guide vanes are adjusted (b) when runner vanes are adjusted

(c) both (a) and (b) are adjusted (d) when gate valve is adjusted

33. The specific speed of the turbine is given by

(a) $\frac{\omega\sqrt{P/\rho}}{(gH)^{5/4}}$ (b) $\frac{\omega\left(\frac{P}{\rho}\right)^{\frac{1}{2}}}{(gH)}$ (c) $\frac{\omega\, P/\rho}{(gH)^{\frac{1}{2}}}$ (d) $\frac{\omega(p/\rho)^{\frac{1}{2}}}{(gH)^{\frac{3}{4}}}$

34. The specific speed of a turbo pump is given by,

(a) $\frac{\omega(Q)^{\frac{1}{2}}}{(gH)^{3/4}}$ (b) $\frac{\omega(Q)^{\frac{1}{2}}}{(gH)^{5/4}}$ (c) $\frac{\omega(Q)^{\frac{1}{2}}}{(gH)^{1/2}}$ (d) $\frac{\omega(Q)^{\frac{1}{2}}}{(gH)^{2}}$

35. The overall efficiency η_o, hydraulic efficiency η_h and mechanical efficiency η_m are related by,

(a) $\eta_o = \eta_h \cdot \eta_m$ (b) $h_0 = \frac{\eta_m}{\eta_h}$ (c) $\eta_0 = \frac{\eta_h}{\eta_m}$ (d) $\eta_0 = \sqrt{\eta_h \cdot \eta_m}$

36. The pressure at a depth of 10 m in a liquid of specific gravity of o.8 is :

(a) 78400 Pa (b) 7.84 kPa (c) 784000 Pa (d) 7.84 Pa

37. Consider each of the following flows and state which one is one dimensional.

(a) flow around a rocket

(b) flow around an automobile

(c) flow through an artery

(d) flow through a vein

38. Indicate which one of the flows is unsteady

(a) flow through a irrigational channel

(b) flow near the entrance of a pipe

(c) flow around an automobile

(d) flow through human heart

39. Select the flow which has a stagnation point

(a) flow around an automobile

(b) flow through an artery

(c) flow in the waves of the ocean near the beach

(d) flow through vein

40. Select the pump with the following data ω = 146 rad/s; Q = 0.183 m^3/s; H = 60 m

(a) radial (b) axial (c) mixed flow (d) gear

41. Glycerine of Kinematic viscosity 0.9 $N.s/m^2$ and density 1260 kg/m^3 is pumped along a horizontal pipe of diameter 0.01 m at a flow rate of 1.8 l/min. Then Reynold's number is :

(a) 5.32 (b) 53.2 (c) 532 (d) 5320

42. In a Pelton turbine bucket angle is 165^0 and ratio of peripherial velocity to jet velocity is 0.46. The hydraulic efficiency is

(a) 97.6% (b) 97% (c) 98% (d) 97.2%

43. In a Pelton turbine installation H = 60 m, Q = 0.138 m^3/s. The hydraulic power is :

(a) 81.5 kW (b) 81144 Watt (c) 81.5 MW (d) 815 kW

44. In a Pelton turbine the jet diameter is 238 mm, head is 130 m, flow rate is 7.2 m^3/s. The number of jets required is :

(a) 1 (b) 2 (c) 3 (d) 4

45. When two pumps are connected in series the following relation holds good

(a) $H = H_1 + H_2$ (b) $H_1 = H_2$

(c) $Q = Q_1 + Q_2$ (d) $\frac{Q_1}{Q_2} = \frac{H_1}{H_2}$

46. Which of the following liquids is classified as Newtonian fluid ?

(a) honey (b) petrol (c) glycerine (d) paint

47. In a Pelton turbine installation effective head is 180 m and Euler's head is 168 m. The turbine develops 3750 kw shaft power and 4475 kw power developed by the runner. The overall efficiency is

(a) 75% (b) 78% (c) 72% (d) 68%

Answers

1.	(c)	**2.**	(b)	**3.**	(a)	**4.**	(a)	**5.**	(d)
6.	(a)	**7.**	(c)	**8.**	(a)	**9.**	(c)	**10.**	(d)
11.	(d)	**12.**	(a)	**13.**	(b)	**14.**	(c)	**15.**	(a)
16.	(b)	**17.**	(a)	**18.**	(a)	**19.**	(a)	**20.**	(a)
21.	(c)	**22.**	(a)	**23.**	(a)	**24.**	(b)	**25.**	(a)
26.	(c)	**27.**	(d)	**28.**	(b)	**29.**	(a)	**30.**	(c)
31.	(a)	**32.**	(c)	**33.**	(a)	**34.**	(a)	**35.**	(a)
36.	(a)	**37.**	(d)	**38.**	(d)	**39.**	(a)	**40.**	(a)
41.	(a)	**42.**	(a)	**43.**	(a)	**44.**	(c)	**45.**	(a)
46.	(b)	**47.**	(b)						

References

1. Munson B.R; Okiishi T.H. Fundamental of Fluid Mechanics 4th edition. John Wiley and sons, NY, 2002
2. Douglas J.F., Gasiorek J.M., Swaffield J.A., Fluid Mechanics, 3rd edition, Longman, Singapore. 1995
3. Arora K.R. Fluid Mechanics Hydraulics and Hydraulic Machines, Standard publishers, New Delhi, 2005
4. Jagdish Lal, Hydraulic Machines, 6th edition, Metrophliton Book Co, New Delhi, 2004.
5. Shames I.H. Solution Manual Mechanics of Fluids 3rd edition, Mc Graw Hill, New York, 1993.
6. Potter M.C., Wiggert D.C. Mechanics of Fluids, 2nd edition Prentice Hall, New Jersey, 1997
7. Potter M.C., Wiggert D.C. Solutions Manual Mechanics of Fluids, 2nd edition, Prentice Hall, New Jersey, 1997.
8. Shames I.H. Mechanics of Fluids, 3rd edition, Mc Graw-Hill International, New York, 1992.
9. Husain Z., Gas Dynamics through Problems, 1st edition, Wiley Eastern Limited, New Delhi, 1989
10. Rayner Joel, Basic Engineering Thermodynamics 4th edition, Longman Group England, 1989.
11. Husain Z. Steam Turbine Theory and Design, First edition. Tata Mc Graw-Hill India. New Delhi 1994.
12. Kirilov, E. E. Theory of Turbo Machine, Machine Construction, 1972.
13. White F.M. Fluid Mechanics, 3rd edition, Mc Graw-Hill Bork C, New York, 1994.
14. Stepanoff, A. J. Centrifugal and Axial Flow Pumps 2nd edition, John Wiley & Sons, New York. 1957.
15. Alan Bender, New Joy of Knowledge Encyclopedia, 6th edition Orioh publishing Co, London, 1989.
16. Bullough D.A. Cohin Cherry; Kirkaldy J.F. New Joy of Knowledge Encyclopedia, 7th edition, Oriole publishers London, 1990.
17. Holler H.K., Grein H. et.al. Utilization of Water Power by means of Hydraulic Machines Sulzer, Escher, Wyss, Zurich, 1994
18. Adam Sharef, Flying high, LIMA 97 Langkavi, 1997

19. Fanzi M., Temengor Hydroeletric Power Station, Project Report, 2003
20. Kraftwerk Union, Printed in Germany, 1984
21. International Conference on Wind Energy Trends and issues, Bhopal, 2006
22. Chang Kong Leong, Computer Software Development to Stimulate the Performance of Combined Cycle Power Plant, M.S. Thesis, Penang, 2001

Index